WINCHESTER
MODEL 94
A CENTURY OF CRAFTSMANSHIP

by
ROBERT C. RENNEBERG

COVER PHOTO

The fabulous example of a special order Model 1894 that is featured on the cover is one of only 157 recorded examples with a color-casehardened, sometimes referred to as color-finished, receiver.
It also has eleven additional special features as follows:
Oil finished stocks of "XXX" rated walnut (marked XXX on the lower left tang) in the shotgun style with a pistol grip, "H" style checkering and a hard rubber buttplate (actually six options). A Winchester Model 34, 3-leaf express rear sight, a Lyman ivory bead front sight and a Lyman tang sight. A matted round barrel (matted barrels are another of the rarest Model 1894 options with only 203 listed in the available records). To complete the package it was thoughtfully and aesthetically designed with a four cartridge (sometimes referred to as a half) magazine.
Serial number 22905 in caliber 30WCF was completed, sent to the warehouse and sent on the way to its original owner on June 5, 1897 – obviously it was a very special order item as it went from completion to delivery in a matter of hours. This specimen is the epitome of a well thought out and superbly executed example of an "upgraded" Model 1894. One can only contemplate why it was decided not to order it as a takedown model as well.
Another rare and fine piece of Americana that will likely be forever preserved in its present 112 year old, remarkably cared for, unmolested and unaltered condition.
(Rob Kassab collection).

©2009 Krause Publications, Inc.,
a subsidiary of F+W Media, Inc.

Published by

Gun Digest® Books

An imprint of F+W Media, Inc.

700 East State Street • Iola, WI 54990-0001
715-445-2214 • 888-457-2873
www.gundigestbooks.com

Our toll-free number to place an order or obtain a free catalog is (800) 258-0929.

Manuscripts, contributions and inquiries, including first class return postage, should be sent to the GUN DIGEST Editorial Offices, Gun Digest Books, 700 East State Street, Iola, WI 54990-0001. All materials received will receive reasonable care, but we will not be responsible for their safe return. Materials accepted is subject to our requirements for editing and revisions. Author payment covers all rights and title to the accepted material, including photos, drawings and other illustrations. Payment is at our current rates.

CAUTION: Technical data presented here, particularly technical data on handloading and on firearms adjustment and alteration, inevitably reflects individual experience with particular equipment and components under specific circumstances the reader cannot duplicate exactly. Such data presentations therefore should be used for guidance only and with caution. Gun Digest Books accepts no responsibility for results obtained using these data.

Library of Congress Control Number: 2009923234

ISBN 13: 978-1-4402-0391-6
ISBN 10: 1-4402-0391-1

Designed by Dave Hauser

Edited by Dan Shideler

Printed in China

Dedication

This book is dedicated to the "collector."

A breed unto themselves, collectors have become the main reason for the gathering of highly detailed/technical data on a vast, seemingly endless array of subjects. A collector wants and needs an accurate, handy reference containing all the information currently available for his particular specialty; not only does it make him more knowledgeable, it makes him more confident and comfortable with his decisions and less likely to be led astray.

Without "collectors" this book need not have been written.

It is with my most humble esteem and considerable trepidation that I dare come forth and present you with a sensibly devised "Second Edition" of my earlier work on the Winchester Model 1894/94. The first edition, both the original and the revised, have met with such a generous out-pouring of compliments, not only in the U.S.A. but worldwide, that to try to successfully enhance the reader's experience and provide substantial and worthwhile additions to the previously published information is extremely daunting. Honestly, very little in the way of new and reliably factual information has come forth from any of myriad sources in the eighteen years since the first edition was published (much to my relief and delight). There is much, however, in the way of "fine tuning" that I have done with the original manuscript, as well as the addition of many previously unpublished and likely unseen photographs and interesting factual "tidbits." And fear not, no part of the new information found herein will in any way effect acquisitions you may have made based on the information found in the previous editions.

You will immediately notice that I have in addition to the upgrading of the original composition and information, taken the book into a four-part mode. It now includes as much information that I could accurately find and present on the "siblings" of the Model 1894/94, the Model 55 and the Model 64; this to complete the entire saga of the series. The lightly researched, Post-64 versions, with little (at this time) collector interest, have also been upgraded –

as has the "Fun Facts" section.

… To all my contributors – I have done the best that I can with any submissions solicited/received and greatly appreciate all your efforts in this regard. Please understand that any quality issues with any of the new photographs herein are solely due to enormous scope and variations of acquisition of the subjects.

The reworking of the original copy and the addition of the new material will hopefully enhance the reader's knowledge and appreciation of all facets of this iconic family of fine and still "Totally American" firearms.

Again, I dedicate this book and my efforts to you, "the collectors."

RCR 2009

Acknowledgments

To ensure there are not any inadvertent omissions, particularly on this page, I wish to jointly thank everyone involved; especially my wife Jane (who pushed me really hard for this second edition), my family, my friends, and of course my many collector acquaintances (these are all certifiable "Winchester nuts"). I thank you one and all for everything you've done to help me realize the completion of this project – AGAIN!

I thank you for the love, the support, the technical information, the suggestions, the criticisms – all those absolutely essential and invaluable things without which there could be no book and certainly no "sequel."

You know who you are – I hope you know and understand how much I appreciate you.

I'm not going to name names here, again for fear of omission, but I must give my very special thanks to the late George Madis, who gave me the initial inspiration and support for edition one and of course, to all those wonderful people from the "Buffalo Bill Historical Center" and the "Winchester Arms Collector's Association" whose invaluable help was so unselfishly given and greatly appreciated.

For the rest of you – as I said, "You know who you are."

Photography (except where otherwise noted)
William T. Higgins, Babylon, N.Y. (First and First Revised Edition)
Michael G. Klein, Commack, N.Y. (Second Edition)
Rob Kassab, 1st VP-W.A.C.A., Boca Raton, Fl. (Second Edition)

Various and many other contributors.

With great sincerity, again I thank you,
Bob

In Memoriam

An additional acknowledgement and dedication must be made to my friend George Madis. One of the foremost "founding fathers" of Winchester reference books and my inspiration for this chronicle. I'll always remember his famous quote, "Bob, you can never pay too much for a quality Winchester – you can only buy it a little early." Few are those that know that George was also an accomplished firearms engraver. He is sorely missed by so many. – RCR

TABLE OF CONTENTS

PART III – The Model 64
Chapter 13 – The Model 64

Part IV – MISCELLANY
Chapter 14 – Fun Facts

Here we have an unbelievable multi-barreled Model 1894 set serial number 403436. Several Model 1894s with extra barrels are known and recorded but this is the only known five barreled combination seen so far. It appears in every way to have been factory assembled and every barrel is in exactly the same configuration except for the caliber. It is a takedown version of course, with a 26-inch barrel in each of the available Model 1894 calibers of the era (38-55, 32-40, 25-35, 30 WCF and 32 Special). All barrels have the half round, half octagon feature; the same, rather rare 3-leaf express rear sights; and the same German silver front sights.

All five barrels have full-length magazine tubes and individual forends (many multi-barreled sets came with only one magazine tube and one forend – by this method manufacturing was less expensive but the tube and the forend had to be changed with each barrel to make a complete assembly). It also has the extremely rare double set trigger, a Lyman tang mounted rear sight and matching highly figured walnut stock and forends of undetermined grade, but most likely XX or XXX. The original casecoloring on the hammer, lever and buttplate is still bright. Another remarkable feature is that in spite of the other multitude of options it does NOT have checkering and is of the straight stock configuration. Almost all high-grade guns have checkering and a pistol-gripped stock. It was built in 1907 and except for the 38-55 barrel appears to be unfired and essentially unassembled since who-knows-when.

Perhaps the best and most interesting part of its history is that it spent 90 percent of its existence in a little town called Port Lions on Kodiak Island, Alaska and it survives in 99% condition. It still remains in Alaska, on the mainland now, but is still in as-new condition despite more than 100+ years in one of the harshest-to-firearms environments imaginable.

Reputedly ordered and purchased new by a now un-known but obviously aesthetically astute gentleman, it was subsequently relinquished to a crusty and caustic old Viet Nam-surviving, helicopter-flying, 101st Airborne Green Beret Lieutenant Colonel named Riley Morton, who, incidentally, is still surviving and is somewhat of a legend on Kodiak Island. After years of surviving ol' Morton's less-than-careful possession (that's why the condition is so remarkable) it was again relinquished (and I understand it took some begging on the new owner's part), this time to its present and proud owner(s) on the famous Kanai Peninsula, south of Anchorage – but STILL in Alaska! It's only a three owner beauty!

This set has never been "on-the-market" per se, and was only recently presented for viewing at the famous Win-chester Arms Collector's show in Cody, Wyoming, prob-ably the only time it has been out of Alaska since it was purchased. It is assuredly one of the ultimate specimens of a Model 1894 rarity and there couldn't be a more fit-ting addition to this book. "It makes me smile". (Clinton and Dolores Coligan collection – photography by Magic Moment Photography, Soldotna, Alaska)

~Foreword~

Authoring a work about something so deeply ingrained in me has truly been one of the highlights of my life. The Winchester Model 94 – and its family of siblings, the Models 55 and 64 – have provided me with endless hours of entertainment, either through the studies of the guns themselves or through the many wonderful people I've had the privilege to meet while indulging in the hobby. I hope you find this book thoroughly enjoyable, and I hope it entertains you, educates you and further enhances your appreciation of the marvelous Model 94.

While I do realize the possibility of omissions, and I certainly realize the possibility of error, I hope these will prove to be few. Please try to understand the immense scope of the research that went into these chapters. Consider, if you will, the staggering number of variables, the complete loss of all records spanning many years, and the general irregularities that occur in mass production: all these combine to sow the seeds of inaccuracy.

Note the abbreviated bibliography. Only during my earliest research in which available books provided me with basic guidance, and in a later reference to a very interesting magazine article, did I refer to someone else's work. There were no other books to refer to, and no factory records exist for serials after number 353999. A full 90 percent of the information in this book comes directly from the hands-on examination of a thousand or more Model 94s. These guns speak for themselves.

All of the photographs, except where noted, are taken from fully authenticated specimens in my personal collection. Be sure to read the captions carefully. They contain a wealth of interesting information, some of which may not appear in the text proper.

The remaining 10 percent of my data was obtained by years of speaking with the experts: those countless phone conversations with the wonderful (and extremely patient) researchers at the Buffalo Bill Historical Center Museum in Cody, Wyoming; the dozens of collector-to-collector conferences to authenticate or disprove the merits of many fine but questionable pieces; and the countless hours of brain-picking and "gun talk" at scores of gun shows.

I may often say "approximately" or use a term such as "found near serial such-and-such," but it must be said like that. It is certainly not due to a lack of research. It is merely an important and very necessary measure to preserve accuracy and maintain credibility in the face of inevitable mass production variables.

I've been as comprehensive and accurate as I possibly could be, but to further this aim, you can help. Feel free to call me. Cite examples or facts I may have omitted, refute facts, discuss anything in the book you like or don't like. I'm constantly seeking new information, and I'm always trying to narrow the gap on those frustrating but unavoidable variables. (The preceding invitation, which appeared in previous editions of this book, has proved to be very important; moreso than I expected, in fact. Responses to it have provided much of the new information in this edition.)

Thanks – and enjoy!

Bob Renneberg

A nicely posed photograph of a WWI "doughboy" with his trusty Model 1894. (Photo courtesy of Rob Kassab)

Introduction

The grandson and heir apparent of the Volcanic-New Haven Arms Company. Son of the "Load on Sunday – shoot all week" Henry Repeater. Proudly hailed and loudly proclaimed as "The gun that won the west." This is the legend – this is the Winchester.

This book will not be, nor is it meant to be, a history of the Winchester Repeating Arms Company. It is merely a chronicle of and a tribute to one of that company's greatest and most enduring efforts. It will be an accurate chronicle, as accurate as I can possibly make it. Hopefully, it will prove to be a valuable and often consulted asset to those of us who may design to acquire even a modest collection of these fine guns. At the minimum, it should impress even the casual student of firearms with the tremendous amount of statistical and observational data that can be obtained by the careful study of just one single model.

To achieve the greatest effectiveness in this presentation and to provide the reader with a bit of insight into just how incredibly vast the scope of research can become, I will begin with a brief but moderately detailed outline of events and developments leading to the introduction of the subject model. After I acquired a pristine 1950 variant of this model, it very quickly became one of the passions of my life.

There were scores of arms manufacturers busily producing all manner of weaponry through America's developing years. Some were obscure, some quite well-known and well thought of, and some – through luck, perserverance and the reaping of enormous profits generated by the demands of renewing post-Civil War America – endure to this day. Even of these, how many from just the mention of their name can evoke the images, the reverie and the wonderment of a time and place that have long been gone? One and only one: Winchester – the "old west" – synonymous.

Winchester was born precisely at the beginning of the "Great Westward Expansion." The timing was extraordinary. A reliable, powerful repeating rifle would soon become one of man's most precious tools. Even in this modern age, it's not very difficult envisioning how it must have been. Indians, buffalo, outlaws, all manner of wild and hungry beasts. Endless vistas of pristine and scenic countryside that would someday become "sea to shining sea" America. Freedom in its original, most primal form – the law of the land. Man on his own, fending for himself; living as he could and going wherever life led him. A good horse and his Winchester: always there and always ready. It fed him, it clothed him, it protected and comforted him. It was a veritable part of him. Who could have asked for anything more?

Admittedly, the earlier designs of these guns soon proved to be of marginal utility. With the dulling of the gloss of the repeating feature, the realization came that the "Volcanics," with their unique cartridges, were really quite unreliable, and even the big and brassy "Henry" was overly prone to stoppages due to dust and dirt or damage to its vulnerable open magazine tube. The Model '66, being a logical development of the Henry, was better but was technically no more than an "improved" Henry; it was even chambered for the same laughably underpowered 44 Henry rimfire cartridge. Problems? Yes! While it's true that these old guns made their marks, "sowed their seed" so to speak, the times were rapidly changing. The need for more powerful arms was becoming apparent. The evolution of cartridge development and metallurgy continued, and exciting new designs of both guns and cartridges soon appeared.

The new 1873 model, deemed well able to withstand the punishment of the equally new centerfire cartridges, was a beautifully designed, well made and very accurate rifle that quickly became a Winchester success story. It was the first truly successful centerfire repeating rifle, and it proved to be exceedingly popular, with production ending as late as 1923. With the introduction of Col. Colt's latest revelation, a handgun known as the "Frontier Six Shooter" or the "Single Action Army Model of 1873," you could have your rifle and your sidearm in the same caliber, using the very same cartridge. The Model 1873 eventually became known as "the gun that won the west" and was even featured in the 1950 movie, *Winchester 1873*, starring James Stewart.

Before long however the power issue reared its head again. It seemed that these "pistol" cartridges weren't up to the task; they just weren't as effective as originally expected. Winchester wasn't caught napping, though; it soon unveiled the monstrous Model of 1876. This model was also known as the Centennial Model, commemorating and celebrating 100 years of American independence. In actuality the '76 was but a big brother to the 1873. It was built with the same patent data inscribed on its barrel, and was equally as handsome. It was also equally as well made and accurate – but it was bigger, much bigger. If it was power they wanted, it was power they got. In calibers such as 45-60, 45-75, 45-90, or 50-95 Express, this was a powerful weapon for sure. In its heavy, long-barreled version it was "the buffalo gun". It was as powerful as a big bore Sharps but it was a repeater. The '76 could be a truly massive piece. Some examples, ordered with 32-inch, 34-inch, and even 36-inch extra heavy octagonal barrels could weigh well over 15 pounds, even before they were loaded.

Unfortunately this upsizing technique to beget the necessary action and receiver strength was an exercise in futility; the design weaknesses, now being stressed to the limit, quickly became apparent. The old toggle and link system was really sweating under the abuse of these immensely more powerful loads, and when they tried to adapt the popular 45-70 cartridge that was being used so successfully in the single-shot Sharps and failed, the '76 was doomed.

Only about 64,000 of these behemoths were produced through 1898, making it one of Winchester's lowest production models. To cite examples, the Model 1866 was produced to about serial number 175,000 before its demise, and the Model 1873 saw production numbers closely approaching 721,000. Consequently the big '76 is quite scarce today, especially with options and/ or "condition," and has amassed a formidable collector following.

It is at this point we find John Moses Brown-

ing entering the repeating rifle scene. Browning and his brothers were no strangers to Winchester. By 1879 they had already designed and patented their lovely single shot model, and after producing some 600-odd pieces mostly made by hand in their own Ogden, Utah, shop, they sold the patent to Winchester. Although the patent date reads 1879, the gun was marketed as the Model 1885 to coincide with its year of introduction by Winchester. Many variations of this rifle, from the plainest utility grade to magnificently appointed "Schuetzen" models, were steadily produced over a 28-year span. Production numbers were reaching past the 115,000 range when it was finally discontinued in 1913 and continued with "parts on hand" specimens being assembled into the 1920s. It is a popular model and a prime collectible today.

While Winchester was in the process of purchasing the rights to the 1885, Browning decided to show the factory representatives his "tooling model" of an exciting new design. Though it was only made of wood (yes, wood), they quickly realized that Browning's design genius would soon provide them with a big bore repeater of previously unthinkable capabilities. It was an arm of reasonable size and weight, especially when compared to the monstrous '76, yet it had excellent power handling capability; it was very smooth in operation, and would prove to be ruggedly reliable to a fault. An aesthetic masterpiece, it was the fabulous Model 1886.

This model remained in production for almost 50 years, and was produced in many different calibers and every conceivable configuration. Although it was not produced in overwhelming numbers (production only reached about 160,000), it set a goal for Winchester: to remain on the top, to continue to be innovative. To continue to develop, refine, and thoroughly test each product so they would always be regarded as the best. With John Browning's able assistance, they would do just that.

The Model 1886 was discontinued in 1932, but with some minor design refinements and the latest advancements in metalurgy, it was reintroduced in 1936 as a "continuation" model, and was designated the Model 71. The Model 71 was one of Winchester's "standardized" issues, produced with its own serial sequence and a very limited option list. It was cataloged in only one caliber (348 Winchester), and only two variations; standard and deluxe. Options on either variation included only a choice of sighting equipment and a choice of a 20-inch or 24-inch barrel.

If you ordered the deluxe version, you also got a nicely checkered stock and forend, a sling with quick disconnect swivels, and inletted swivel mounts. The Model 71, even with its extremely limited option list and a rather limited following, amazingly managed to survive a lengthy production run of 23 years and about 47,000 copies. It has a strong collector following, and perfect examples are commanding premium prices.

Note: At least one Model 71 exists in factory 33 WCF and 45-70 and many have been converted to the enormously amibitious 450 and 50 Alaskan calibers.

So pleased was Winchester with the 1886 design that in a very short while a decision was made to try and capitalize further on the model's success. The idea was to scale the entire gun down, refine the loading gate, retain that wonderfully smooth short throw action in a smaller package, and introduce this new model to replace the much more complicated and fragile Model 1873. Originally introduced in all three of the '73's calibers, the rifle was released as the beautiful, delicate-appearing, and immensely popular Model 1892. Once again we see a new model wearing the very same patent markings of its predecessor.

Note: This downsizing technique was exactly the opposite of the 1873/1876 model development.

Obviously the quest for more power was no longer an issue. The big '86 could comfortably handle 50-caliber, 450-grain bullets, boosted briskly along by 100 grains of black powder. (Note that I say comfortably, but this was only comfortable to the rifle, certainly not to the shooter.) This cartridge, even when used in the heaviest versions of the '86, produced a very hefty recoil, and the prospect of a long day of shooting would have been decidedly unpleasant.

A cartridge of this size and power was deemed more than sufficient for the needs of the day, so the company now focused its attention on its new little gem, stressing the proven reliability of the design and the compact, neat and handy package they had the brilliance to put it into. As

hoped, the '92's small size, aesthetically pleasing lines, and pistol-matching cartridge line made this little gun one of Winchester's most popular, most copied, and most passionately collected models.

The Model 92, like its big brother, had a production run of just under 50 years. In 1923 a sister model was introduced. Cataloged as the "new" Model 53, it was actually a 92, but the first of Winchester's "limited option" or "standardized" models. (The 86/71 didn't appear until 1936.)

The 53 was offered in all three of the 92's original calibers, and was given its own serial range. The reassigning or new-assigning of serial numbers was a first for Winchester with the introduction of this model. We may presume it was an attempt to further separate the 53 from the 92, and enhance the idea that it was indeed a "new" model.

Although it was supposed to be a somewhat limited option series, the Model 53 is found in many variations. Most versions will be seen as solid frame, 25-20 or 32-20 rifles with 22-inch barrels. However, takedowns, deluxes and most Winchester options were available. The 44 caliber is especially prized. Optioned-out 53s are very rare and desirable and are highly prized collectibles. Transitional variants are also seen. Some will be found carrying serials in the Model 92 sequence and some will have identifiable Model 92 parts and/or Model 92 barrel markings. Even with its limited popularity, the Model 53 remained in production for about 10 years and production figures closely approached 25,000.

In 1933 the Model 53 was discontinued. A new model was introduced. This, the Model 65, I will define as a continuation model.

Note: The following are the author's definitions – a "brother" or "sister" or "big brother" model is a similar or essentially identical arm produced concurrently with the original model, having the same patent markings and usually carrying its own serial sequence. A "continuation" model is a similar or essentially identical arm produced after the discontinuation of the original model but having the same patent markings and usually serialed into the original sequence. The Model 65 was made available to replace both the newly discontinued Model 53 and the previously discontinued Model 92 rifle.

The Model 92 in the rifle version was discontinued in 1931. The carbine version was available until discontinued in 1941, with some guns being assembled from parts on hand into 1942 or slightly beyond. The Model 65, unlike the Model 53, was serialed directly into the Model 92 series (some exceptions exist) and thus we call it a "continuation" model.

The Model 65 had a much more strictly regulated option list than the Model 53 but still could be nicely "personalized." For example, there were no take-downs and the only available calibers were 25-20, 32-20, and the 218 Bee. Standard versions predominate, but deluxes may be seen in all calibers. Barrels were round and 22 inches or 24 inches only, with 24 inches being standard for the 218 Bee. You had the usual full choice of sighting equipment, and there have been some variations in buttstock configuration authenticated on several examples.

Despite these limitations, the Model 65 still managed to maintain a 14-year production run of about 5,700 pieces. It was discontinued in 1947. This should be considered an extremely low production figure, and the Model 65 in any configuration is a collector's prize. A deluxe or "optioned" specimen with "condition" is very nearly priceless.

Objectively, a 56-year, three-model production run of essentially the same gun, reaching a total number of approximately 1,035,000 copies, was quite remarkable. Only during the later production years of the Model 92 were there impending signals of a possibly more popular, more enduring and more remarkable model.

Sometime near the introduction of the Model 1892, the need was perceived for yet another model. A piece that could chamber a true rifle cartridge while not being burdensome to carry. Winchester was alert to this need, may even have had some concern, but its concern was unfounded. A certain Mr. Browning was once again doing his homework. A completely new and revolutionary design was soon to commence its journey into history.

When U.S. patent number 524702 was granted to John M. Browning on Aug. 21, 1894, he probably had no idea of the impact this design would have on the already historic and legendary Winchester Repeating Arms Company. Winchester, however, recognized its value immediately — it filled the void — it was perfect. Just how perfect it was was at this time inconceivable. But just how impressed Winchester was, and how convinced they were of the merits of Browning's latest show of wizardry, is reflected by their unprecedented haste in transposing the design from patent model, to tooling, through testing, and into final production. This was much faster than the patent process — the patent being applied for on 1/19/94.

With an initial offering of only two calibers*, production began on what was to be "the rifle", the ultimate. It featured a newly and ingeniously designed lever action tube-fed repeating system, complete with a slim but sturdy new frame, all of which Mr. Browning integrated perfectly with the graceful and delicate two-piece walnut stocks of the beautiful little Model 92. It was handsome to be sure, but it was much more than just another gun. It was a rifle in possession of such perfection of design vs. function, such elegance, and such overall aesthetic appeal, that it would quicken the heartbeats of riflemen the world over. Chambered for two thoroughly tested cartridges, either of which easily surpassed the capabilities of those used in the Model 92, and conspicuously absent of the considerable bulk of the powerhouse Model '86, it was perfection. It was the Model 1894.

The company hummed with life. The period between patent approval and initial production was only about seven weeks. In part, this incredible show of efficiency was due to the use of some "carryover" parts, meaning that some parts originally made for other models were incorporated into the new design as "interchangeable." But this was Browning's style, a show of his brilliance. There was also an unbelievable and inspiring show of support and confidence by the entire staff of Winchester to get this new model from blueprint "to market" in such a short period of time.

---

* The Model 1894 was originally designed for use with smokeless powder cartridges and was the first successful repeating gun so designed. Unrelated to the gun itself, however, there were problems encountered in the efficient and "quality-controlled" manufacture of the smokeless ammunition. Winchester decided to release the gun in two of its previously developed black powder calibers and chamber it for the new cartridges when the production problems were solved.

The earliest recorded date of production on the Model 1894 is Oct. 20, 1894. This date, according to files at the Buffalo Bill Historical Center Museum in Cody, Wyoming, corresponds with production records of some guns bearing serial numbers in the low twenties. There are no records for any of the guns with serials from 1 to 17 except for serial number 8, and that gun wasn't received in the warehouse until 1895.

The lowest serialed guns that I can personally verify are numbers 3, 5, 8, and 22. Numbers 3 and 5 have no recorded history, number 8 was warehoused only in 1895, and number 22 is in existence and is on record as being produced and warehoused on Oct. 20, 1894.

Because there are no records for numbers 1 through 7 or 9 through 17, one can only assume that these guns would have been produced or at least were supposed to have been produced on Oct. 20, along with many others. Logically, yes, but without actual records we can never be sure.

There were immense problems of record keeping for all the models and their options; there were many models in production concurrently, and all recording was hand-written and hand-filed. Combining this with the inherent problems of archaic storage methods and the devastation of a major fire makes the exact dating of many early Winchesters a questionable exercise indeed. Though we may be close, the exact date of production of serial number 1, and the exact date of public introduction of those few early, unrecorded guns will probably never be known. The first recorded *release* of any Model 94s from the factory was to order number 173, and began with a caliber 38-55 rifle bearing serial number 24; this was on Oct. 26, 1894.

The Model 94 was out, and it was here to stay.

Production proceeded at an amazing rate; there were over 60,000 copies produced by the turn of the century. In 1927, President Calvin Coolidge was presented the Model 94 with serial number 1,000,000. By the mid-twenties, production had surpassed that of the Model 92, a very strong indicator of continuing success.

The Model 1894, like some of its ancestors, would also develop "siblings." Somewhere in the "think tank" of the company, a decision was be-ing made, and to facilitate that decision, a familiar course would be taken. A "sister" model was being born. As before, it would be introduced as a limited option model, with its own serial number sequence, and its reason for being would be to replace the soon to be discontinued Model 94 in the rifle configuration.

Thus appeared the Model 55. Introduced in 1924 as a caliber 30 WCF takedown rifle with a 24-inch barrel only, it rapidly developed into a full-blown, name-your-option series and started with its own serial number range. This model, its developments and its variations will be fully explained and deciphered in Part II of this book. Production ceased in the mid-1930s after about 21,000 examples were produced.

After serials near 1,110,000, only Model 94s in the carbine version will be encountered. Model 94 rifles were discontinued somewhere near that number. Also, at or about that number the seemingly inevitable brother model makes its appearance (the Model 64), and for a short time there were three differently designated, but basically the same, models in production at the same time. With all using the same receiver, mostly the same parts and all using the same serial range, it's no wonder that many examples from this era can be found with "crossed" parts and features.

The Model 64, yet another "continuation" model (continuing both the Model 94 rifle and the Model 55) was a markedly handsome piece. It was also a limited production item with no takedown feature offered. This model and its variations, including a Post-64 remake, will also be fully explained and deciphered in Part III of this book. Despite being inherently quite attractive, it was only moderately successful with only about 100,000 units produced in the Pre-64 version (to serial 2,200,000) and about 4500 in the Post-64 (Model 64A) versions.

After serials around 1,085,000, only Model 94s in the carbine version will be encountered. Model 94 rifles were discontinued somewhere near that number.

"POST-1964"

The often berated and usually scoffed at "Post-64" varieties of the Model 94 will be included in this book. True enough, they started as an abomination, and true also, they will never measure up to their earlier "brethen" in any comparison of quality or aesthetics, but this is only a reflection of the modern, more economically efficient workforce. This efficiency, as it were, is why most products manufactured today rarely reflect careful workmanship and personal pride as those of the past. The most important thing, however, is that these guns are still Model 94s. I feel that a complete documentation is definitely in order. A book called The Winchester Model 94 could not be definitive if I stopped my research at serial 2,600,298, reportedly the last "Pre-64" Model 94. The "Post-64" versions, however, will be only loosely addressed.

Factually, there have been many more "Posts" than "Pre's" produced, and factually also, there are more Post-64 engineering variants than "Pre's" by far. As of this writing, somewhere around 7,000,000 of these Post-64 models have left the factory. In and of themselves they could constitute a very large, very complex and quite interesting collection of variants. Keeping pace with the engineering changes – the experimentation with finishes – the caliber introductions and re-introductions – the commemoratives (don't forget, there are foreign and domestic commemoratives) – the special issues – the 1981 company change (U.S.R.A.C. July 1,1981) – the Angle Ejects – the new "Trapper" models – the "rifle" versions – the "Ranger" model, the Shotgun, etc. – one can easily perceive that any such endeavor would be quite formidable.

Don't be close-minded monetarily about these models either. A wise speculator might do well to build a relatively complete collection of these "undesirables" while they are affordable. Remember when the 94 was a "lesser" model? Or when a "stone mint," "pre-war" carbine could be had for less than $100? How about a new-in-the-box," "Pre-64" for $64.50? Buy yourself a 30-year-old copy of the Shotgun News at a gunshow. Check out those prices. WEEP!!

For the purpose of accuracy and comprehensiveness in this presentation, a Model 94 is a Model 94. From Oct. 20,1894 to March 31, 2006, they are all family and are all deserving of mention.

There is only one variation that will be purposely avoided, and that will be the commemoratives. I feel they have already been masterfully represented in Tom Trolard's fine book *Winchester Commemoratives* and I recommend it highly to those whose interest leans that way.

Please read on, and enjoy this book. Enjoy the history, the mystery, the research – but most of all enjoy the Model 94. In all its seemingly infinite array of variations it can certainly be considered one of the great collectibles of the firearms world. It has no copies, and as of the demise of the company in March of 2006, it still has no prospects for copies. It's still the original, and its lineage is pure. "The Model 94".

Discover it – study it – enjoy it.

The lowest serial numbered Model 1894 known to exist, which can be fully documented by factory records as being produced on the first day of production, Oct. 20, 1894, is serial number 22. It was released from the factory on Oct. 27 and returned for repair (for undisclosed reasons) in November of 1895.

PART I:
The Model 1894/94

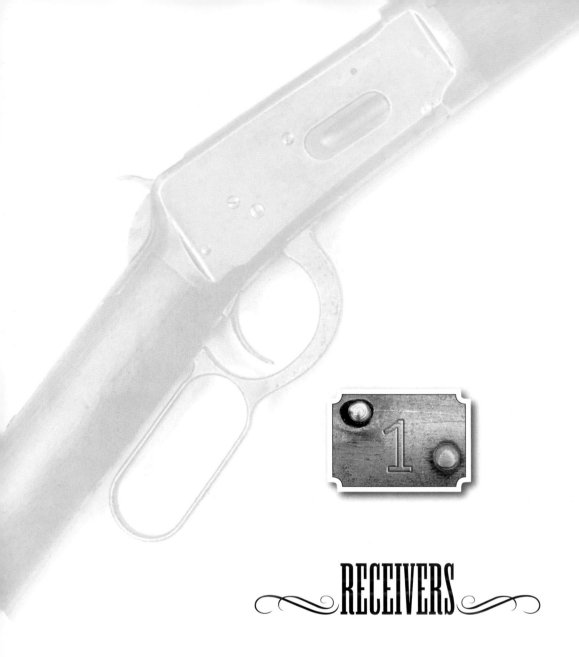

RECEIVERS

INTRODUCTION

The receiver is the part of the gun that houses most of the moving parts relating to the actual chambering, firing, ejecting, and rechambering of the cartridges. This group of parts is called the "action." The Model 1894 incorporated a newly designed action in a light, thin-walled frame (receiver) that was quite revolutionary.

Consisting of a simple, vertically moving breech block that rises to cover the entire rear of the breech bolt when the action is closed, the system is integrated and connected by an un-usual (by previous lever action standards) link/pivot system. This arrangement at once provides the necessary length of throw for a true rifle cartridge, and the strength to withstand the increase in chamber pressure and heavier bolt set-back.

Also incorporated in the action is a newly designed safety system. Utilizing a lever actu-ated plunger and "safety catch," this new sys-tem physically blocks the trigger and disallows hammer fall/cartridge discharge, until the ac-tion is fully closed and locked.

A simple, light, strong, smooth and reliable masterpiece – the Model 1894/94.

Throughout the evolution of the Model 1894/94, there were many changes in receiver design. Most of them were subtle – virtually in-visible on a casual inspection – but glaringly apparent upon a serious study. In this chapter I will provide in-depth detail on all the inter-nal/external changes, and will include a com-prehensive study of the takedown model.

REPEATING RIFLE
Models 94 and 55

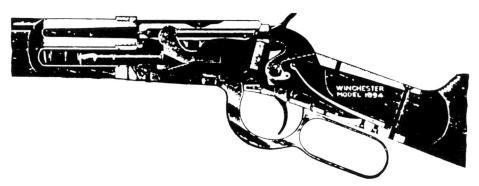

To dismount, take out tang screw and remove butt stock. Take out finger lever pinstop screw and finger lever pin. Take out link pin screw and link pin. Take out the finger lever and link. Take out the finger lever link screw, and separate the link from the finger lever. Take out the carrier screw from each side of the gun, and remove the carrier. Take out mainspring screw and mainspring. Take out the hammer screw and hammer holding up safety catch pin while doing so. Take out lower tang. Take out locking block. Take out the breech bolt. Take out the cover spring screw and cover spring. Take out the carrier spring screw and carrier spring.

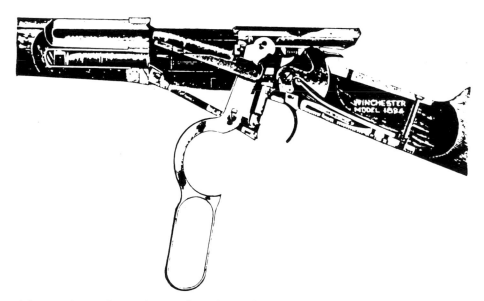

To assemble, put in carrier spring and carrier spring screw. Put in cover spring and screw. Slip in the breech bolt. Slip in the locking block from below. Put the hammer in place, and slide the tang into place. Put in the hammer screw, remembering that the sear cannot be moved without pressing up the safety catch pin. Catch the mainspring on to the stirrup, and put in the mainspring screw. Put in the carrier and replace the carrier screws, one on each side. Assemble the link to the finger lever.

Taken from an early 1930s Winchester sales catalog.

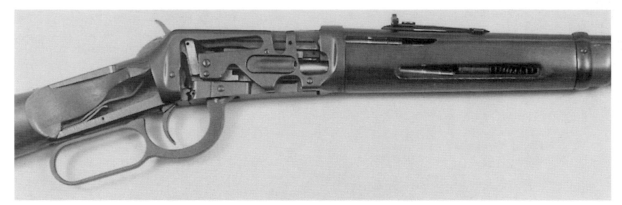

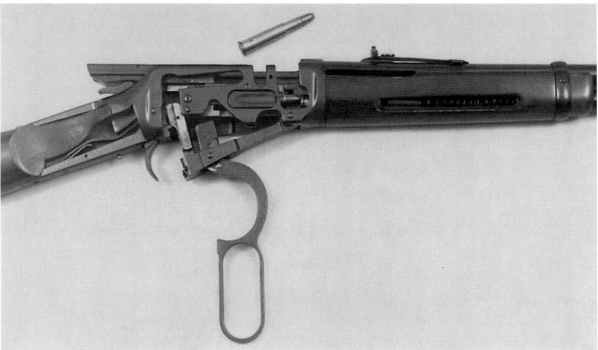

These two views, shown by example of an extremely rare Model 94 factory cutaway (mid-1970s version) clearly illustrate the internal parts relationship with the action closed (top) and the action open (bottom.) The key to the success of this design lies in the much longer action "throw" afforded by the lever/link system and the solid breechblock that rises into place behind the bolt when the action is closed and locked. The longer throw allows a full length rifle cartridge to feed through the action, and the breechblock design provides the strength to withstand the much greater chamber pressure and subsequent bolt setback forces during recoil.

Note how the cartridge seen through the cut-out in the forend on the upper photo has been fed toward the action by the magazine tube spring and follower.

Here we will also explore various manufacturing methods. We'll examine various types of material that were utilized, and there will be a well-detailed explanation on the types and methods of finishing.

As you will notice, there is little mention of markings. In as much as a thorough study of markings on both the receivers and the barrels can be tedious and quite involved, and that a conscientious study of all Model 1894 markings is very important for the accurate evaluation and/or authentication of any given specimen, I've decided to detail and illustrate them in a separate chapter (Chapter 7).

Receivers were originally manufactured from a solid, high carbon ordnance steel forging. The "blank" forging was only a roughly shaped piece of steel, and required hundreds

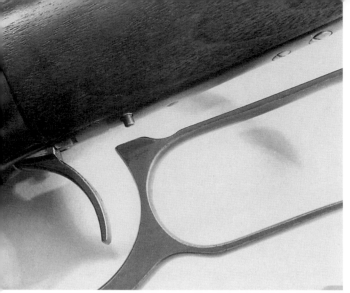

A clear view of the trigger block safety plunger and catch that was simply but cleverly designed to disallow the trigger from releasing the hammer unless the lever is completely closed and the action is locked.

Without the lever being firmly closed upon the plunger (this fault being illustrated), a small piece of steel called the "safety catch" protrudes through an opening just behind the trigger. The trigger is thus physically blocked. The action of the lever pressing upwards on the plunger raises the safety catch from this blocking position and allows normal trigger function.

Note also that without the lever being fully closed, part of the link (seen just forward of the trigger) is still not completely seated. Inasmuch as the link and breechblock are connected, this would indicate that the breechblock is not fully elevated and locked in position behind the bolt.

Firing the gun with the action thus unlocked could have some rather disastrous results. Never remove the safety catch system from the gun. Set trigger systems do not have a safety catch and may fire while in the unlocked position.

of separate machining operations and dozens of inspections before being inventoried as a usable part.

The previous and highly acclaimed Winchester manufacturing methods, with all the usual high standards of quality and attention to details, prevailed for the Model 94.

The only changes of consequence on any of the first model/second model (through Pre-'64) versions of the receiver was the very early first/ second model cartridge guide screw change, a change to the "extra steel" and "nickel steel" alloy also fairly early in the production cycle, and another and final change to "proof steel," during the 1933-34 era.

The screw change is easily noticed and is detailed later in this chapter. The change to different alloys is also quite apparent. One can

readily note the resistance to the bluing process and ultimate "flaking" problem encountered with the nickel steel frames, and the subsequent vast improvement in finish quality and durability after the introduction of the proof steel models.

As previously mentioned, the Post-64 receivers, until the introduction of the angle eject models, were "mystery metal" castings. The cutback in manufacturing steps, details, quality of finish, etc., is readily apparent in these models.

With the introduction of the angle eject series, we are pleasantly re-introduced to the 100 percent forged steel receiver, and with most of the old-time quality of workmanship returning as well. This receiver design is the latest in the series and was still in production to the end.

PRICING

The introductory pricing for the Model 1894 was about $18.00 for the carbine; $19.00 for the round-barreled rifle; $21.00 for the octagon-barreled rifle; $25.00 for a takedown round-barreled rifle; and $27.50 for a takedown octagon-barreled rifle. These prices are approximate and for standard specimens only.

METAL FINISHING

It is interesting to note that the bluing process used by Winchester was originally called "browning," and the area of the factory where this process was accomplished was called the "Browning Shop." While there is a method of metal finishing called browning, and in actuality it is exactly that (the metal acquires a distinct brown color), this was not a standard method employed at Winchester. True "browning" was a special order extra-cost option, and is extremely rare on any Winchester.

The bluing process was one of the many steps in manufacturing that in the early years of Model 94 production was accomplished by outside contractors.

These contractors employed many craftsmen, and most of these came with their own secret formulas and application methods. These different formulas, while being basically the same and deemed acceptable in meeting Winchester's high standards, did produce some slight variations.

As with the variations noted in stock finishing, bluing variations will be all but undetectable on any gun that is not absolutely pristine, and then only if you have several pristine examples from different periods of manufacture to compare with each other.

Also frequently occurring in the metal finishing areas, as in the stock-maker/finisher's department, was the "pride factor." Parts known to be going on the higher grade guns, often received a little "extra." Men of this era were proud craftsmen; a little more time and effort to achieve a finer polish, or an extra coat or two of bluing solution to produce a richer, deeper color, was certainly not too much to expect – it was usually done as a matter of course.

Special guns were as special to these fine gunmakers as they were to the customer.

There were three types of bluing processes employed, and each was accomplished in its own special area. Each method had its own virtues and final result, and accordingly, each was applied to specifically different parts.

One method, called rust bluing, was precisely as implied. A part was swabbed with a solution of water, ferrous chloride, mercury chloride, alcohol, copper sulphate and nitric acid (the chemical mixture could vary slightly depending on the craftsman) and was left hanging in a damp, warm room called a "humidity area." A fine coat of rust appeared in a few hours. This "controlled oxidation" was then removed by carefully rubbing the part by hand with a very fine grade of steel wool.

To develop the richest and deepest blue-black color, it took several cycles of swabbing with the solution, allowing the part to rust, and careful rubbing with the steel wool. The final step in the process was to rinse the part in very hot water, quickly blow it dry, and while still warm, carefully coat it with a good grade of oil.

Very time consuming but very beautiful, this method was used only on barrels and some receivers. It was usually reserved for "high grade" guns but was the method of choice for all shotgun barrels.

Note: The browning process was essentially identical to rust bluing, including the chemicals used, but there was no rubbing of the parts with steel wool between the coats of solution. The rusting was allowed to slowly and evenly build up. When a nice, even dark brown color was achieved, the part was dipped in scalding water to halt the chemical reaction/oxidation process. After quickly drying from the heat of the water bath and while still warm, a good grade of oil was carefully rubbed in with a cloth. The rubbing of the cloth during the oiling removed any remaining loose rust and the part was left with a fine, smooth, dark brown finish.

A second method was variously known as machine bluing, charcoal bluing, carbon bluing, or heat bluing. Parts were placed on racks and put into an oven containing bone meal, charcoal, and either pine tar or sperm oil. The parts were heated to a temperature of between 1,200 and 1,400 degrees and left for several hours. The combination of heat and the resulting smoke produced by the various ingredients gave the

This is an example of one of the more well-known problems in metal finishing that Winchester encountered, beginning during the early 1900s and continuing through the pre-World War II years.

This is a receiver with the serial range between about 500,000 and 1,200,000. These receivers have a very high nickel content, and this one is showing a classic case of the often-seen condition called "flaking." Note the difference in finish condition at the barrel/receiver junction and the fine quality of bluing that remains on the hammer and lever.

There are many specimens in these serial ranges that are near mint in every way, but the receivers have completely reverted to "the white." New-in-the-box specimens are not immune to this phenomenon either. Disturbingly, many completely unused and unhandled examples of the pre-war Model 94 have been found showing serious amounts of flaking.

parts a deep blue color. When the proper color was achieved, the parts were removed from the oven, quenched in oil, and left to dry.

Not without drawbacks, this method left the parts with an unacceptably brittle nature. To remove this brittleness, the cooled parts were returned to the oven, reheated to a moderate 500 to 700 degrees and this time left to cool naturally.

The part was now designated as heat treated or tempered, and was extremely durable. Small parts such as hammers, levers, screws, and sometimes even receivers were blued with this process.

The third process, of which there are three variations, was the immersion method. The earliest and most dangerous variation was called nitre bluing. A solution of refined nitre and 10 percent peroxide of manganese was heated to 700 to 800 degrees. The parts were immersed in this solution for about 30 minutes.

The second method, called the "DuLite" process (the solution itself was named DuLite and was developed in the late 1930s) required a solution temperature of only about 300 degrees, but required several separate immersions to achieve an acceptable color.

The third method was a "black oxide" process using a solution of large amounts of caustic soda, sodium nitrate and sodium dichromate. This was the later method employed with marginal success on the "mystery metal" receivers of the late 1970s to early 1980s.

With all three methods, when the color was acceptably dark, the parts were rinsed thoroughly in boiling water, quickly blown dry, and dipped in a bath of oil.

All parts post-World War II to present are blued with the immersion method.

Winchester, to the end, was constantly re-evaluating and experimenting with finishes. Many late model factory experimental specimens (and so marked) that are found in private collections are examples of different polishing and coloring techniques that may or may not have proven acceptable.

Various types of plating, such as nickel, silver, or gold, may occasionally be found on a Model 94 receiver, as well as casehardening or "color finishing." Any of these finishes must be considered extremely rare and unusual. Guns found with these features must be reliably documented/authenticated as original before acquiring any collectible status or value.

Casehardening/color finishing is accomplished by surrounding the selected part/parts with a mixture of bone meal, charcoal, and small bits of scrap leather or even leather dust, and packing it all into a tightly sealed container. The container is then heated red-hot for several hours. After a formulated period of time, the part is removed from the mixture and quenched immediately in water. Hardening takes place only on the very surface of the part due to carbon absorption from the superheated mixture, but the original properties of the metal below the surface are left intact. The part is wear- and rust-resistant, but not brittle.

The combination of the ingredient mixture, the heat, and the quenching procedure produces the beautifully mottled and colorful finish so prized and admired by Winchester collectors.

THE TAKEDOWN RECEIVER

Until the demise of the rifle version (in the early 1930s), Model 94s were offered in both the solid frame and the extra cost takedown style. The solid frame predominates by far.

The solid frame version is rather self-explanatory. The barrel is screwed tightly to the face of the receiver and must be disassembled using a wrench and vise. Assembly requires the same wrench and vise technique, and further testing for alignment and headspacing must be done to assure safety of operation.

The takedown version is a marvelous design – very simple and very effective. The face of the receiver is machined flat, and a matching flange is semi-permanently attached to what becomes known as the "barrel assembly." The barrel threads are of the interrupted type and require no more than about 90 degrees of travel to engage the flange portion of the barrel assembly tightly to the face of the receiver. The flange and the receiver are factory-adjusted to provide perfect alignment and perfect headspacing every time the gun is disassembled/reassembled.

Adjustments for wear are provided by the use of three adjustment screws that can be seen by removing the forend wood and looking at the forward edge of the flange. These screws, when tightened carefully, would dimple out the receiver side of the flange just enough to provide some additional metal to the worn area, thus effectively restoring the tightness of the receiver/flange junction.

Carefully used and well maintained specimens may never need this adjustment.

The magazine tube is utilized as a key part of the takedown system. After the barrel unit and the receiver are properly assembled, the threaded magazine tube is inserted into the receiver and screwed down tightly. (Only takedown model magazine tubes are threaded.) By passing through the forend and the correspondingly threaded flange and finally into the receiver, it effectively prevents the misalignment or loosening of the two units.

On some variations (the full-length magazine models), the small takedown lever on the front end of the magazine tube that acts as a kind of "crank" has a small extension that fits into a crescent-shaped recess in the underside of the barrel; on others (guns with shorter than standard magazine tubes), this feature may not be present.

Simple, ingenious, and quick to disassemble/assemble, the system was quite successful.

Earlier problems with the units were traced to a general lack of understanding of the system by the public – revised, simplified versions of the instructions were quickly made available and problems with the takedown units diminished dramatically.

On some models it may be possible for the magazine tube to be completely removed from the barrel assembly while on others it may not. There seems to be no definitive pattern.

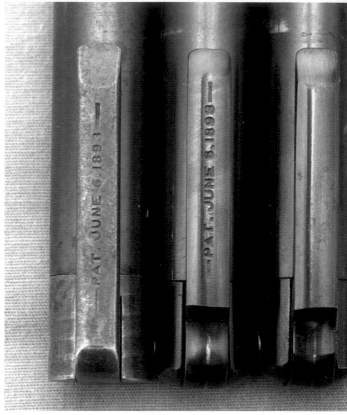

The forward end of the magazine tube on takedown models has an additional piece used as a "crank" to unscrew the tube for disassembly of the gun. There are two main styles. There is a "scalloped" version (the two right side illustrations) that is used when the magazine tube is shorter than full barrel length. The scallop provides clearance to be able to turn the tube and unscrew it without the crank interfering with the barrel itself. The "unscalloped" version on the left is used on full barrel length tubes where clearance is not an issue. As seen in the photo, some takedown levers have no patent date inscription.

(left) This is the flange end of the barrel assembly of a takedown Model 94. Clearly illustrated are the interrupted threads that allow assembly/disassembly of the gun with only a 90 degree turn of the barrel. Also clearly illustrated is the damage to the extractor cut that will occur if the takedown procedure is improperly attempted. In this case, the action was not opened prior to attempting to unscrew the barrel assembly and the extractor was forcibly jammed into the cut; severe damage to the extractor and noticeable marring of the extractor cut are the result.

(right) The machined face of the receiver on the takedown model. The magazine tube passes through the forend and screws into the lower opening after the barrel assembly is installed, locking the barrel assembly and receiver in position.

This is a view of the forward side of the barrel flange with the forend wood removed. Illustrated are the three adjustment screws used to restore the tightness of fit between the barrel assembly and the receiver of a "worn" gun.

The screws are carefully tightened, just enough to make a set of dimples on the face of the flange. This effectively provides extra metal to this area and restores the correct barrel to receiver fit.

It would be unusual for properly cared-for guns ever to need this adjustment. Interestingly, and unexplained, some takedown flanges have been noted without adjustment screws or provisions for them.

This photo illustrates the threaded portion of the takedown tube that mates with the takedown flanges on the barrel. Only magazine tubes for takedown models are threaded. Standard tubes are retained by a retainer with pin, barrel band screws (carbine) or the button magazine arrangement outlined in the Model 55 section (Part II).

WINCHESTER TAKE DOWN RIFLE

Rifle Taken Apart

Models 53, 55, 94,92, and 86 Take-Down rifles can be taken apart as shown in illustration. This is easily done in a few seconds without tools, and the gun can be packed in a small space for traveling, as in a trunk or suit case, or carried in a Victoria case like a shotgun, or rolled in camp bedding.

Takedown instructions from an early 1930s Winchester sales catalog.

To Take Rifles Apart

Lift up the magazine lever found at the front end of the magazine and unscrew the magazine about one inch. Throw down the finger lever, and unscrew the barrel one quarter of a turn to the left. Draw out the barrel from the frame.

In a new gun the barrel may unscrew with difficulty. If so, hold the gun by the fore-arm in the left hand, and strike the lower part of the stock with the right, so as to drive it to the right.

To Put Together

Draw out the magazine about one quarter of an inch. Throw down the finger lever. Slip the shank of the barrel into its place in the frame, in such a position that one quarter of a turn to the right will lock the barrel to the frame, screw the magazine into place, and lock.

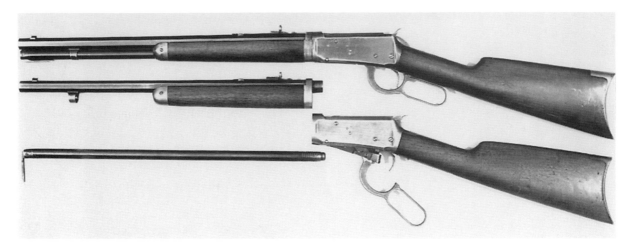

Two identical Model 94 takedown short rifles, pictured together to illustrate the relationship of the major parts when assembled/disassembled.

FIRST MODEL

From serial number 1 through numbers somewhere in the mid-7,000 range is the original John Browning design of the Model 1894. The serial range is consecutive but not totally inclusive, and after serials near 3,000, second model receivers noticeably predominate. As usual in mass production, if a part with a superseding design change is in production before the stock of earlier style parts has been deplet-

ed, both styles will be mixed in the parts bins. Subsequently, they tend to also be mixed on the assembly line. This phasing in and out of various design and engineering changes is what makes the study of a model and the compulsion to collect all its variants such an intriguing and often frustrating enterprise.

It is at this point that I feel an important item of clarification should be introduced. There has always been much ado about the

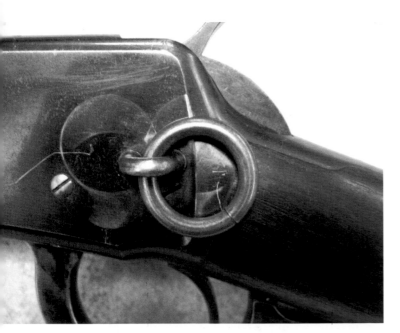

The lowest serial numbered Model 1894 carbine known to exist. Serial number 46. Note the unusual use of the Model 1892 style saddle ring staple. This is the only Model 1894 known to have this feature. It was released from the warehouse in 1895. (Wes Adams collection)

An illustration of the serial number of the lowest serial numbered Model 1894 carbine in existence. It is <u>not</u>, however, the first carbine to leave the factory – that was serial number 471. Serial number 46 was sent to the warehouse on March 26, 1895 and delivered on Sept. 4, 1895. Serial number 471 was sent to the warehouse on Nov. 1, 1894 and delivered on Nov. 3, 1894.

"first year of production" in all phases of arms collecting. What exactly is or what exactly do we mean by first year of production? Does it designate something made only during the introductory year or during the first twelve consecutive months after introduction? This certainly seems to bear importance enough for more than just a passing interest as the term is so frequently used, and when it is, it usually carries an air of reverence reserved for only those things deemed most precious.

Surely it could be argued either way; and probably we would never arrive at a universally acceptable agreement, but I do feel compelled to make a logical attempt at an answer.

My personal feeling leans toward the classification of only those pieces that are completely assembled and ready for shipment during the first calendar year of introduction as true first year of production models. If a model is introduced in January, you'll realize a twelve-month production run of first year guns, but if it's introduced in December, there will only be one month of production. Logical? Since "first year of production" implies the introductory or first calendar year, I'm continuing with my deductions and calculations accordingly.

As we know, the Model 1894 was patented on Aug. 21, 1894, and the earliest recorded date of production was Oct. 20. This date, according to available records, corresponds to guns

with serials beginning in the low twenties, and of these, number 22 is known to exist. As also mentioned previously, at least three guns with serial numbers lower than number 22 also exist, but of these, number 3 and 5 have no available record, and number 8 wasn't completed and delivered to the warehouse until 1895.

At this time, this allows serial number 22 the honorable distinction of being *authenticated* as the earliest Model 1894 known to exist.

Assuredly, there were not produced, and certainly are not remaining now, a great many first year Model 1894s. My research has found serial number 1,368 to be the last Model 1894 delivered to the warehouse in the calendar year of 1894. It was received there on Dec. 29. I also know, through research, that many of the guns displaying serial numbers between 1 and number 1368 may have been delivered in 1894. Actually, some of the lowest-numbered examples are on record as being delivered in 1895 or even 1896 (serial number 8, 1895; number 18,1896; number 19, 1895). Correspondingly, some guns with serials higher than 1,368 were delivered to the warehouse before Dec. 29, but not shipped.

How many of these early gems do you think could still be out there? Keep looking. You may be in the right place at the right time and find the next one.

First model receivers have several notable characteristics that are quite readily visible. The key anomaly is that the screws holding the cartridge guides in the receiver enter from the outside. They are clearly visible on both sides of the gun: on the right approximately 3/16 inch from the upper rear corner of the loading port in the so-called "10 o'clock" position, and on the left in the corresponding location.

Additionally visible on the left cartridge guide itself (inside the receiver, looking down through the breech opening with the muzzle facing away) will be a small spring-loaded plunger. Also noticeable will be a matching detent or relief cut in the side of the cartridge carrier. The mating of the two can be easily observed when the lever is all the way down, the bolt is back, and the carrier is fully elevated.

Ostensibly this was designed to give the carrier some additional lateral support at its uppermost position.

The presence of the externally installed cartridge guide screws can be considered the only

Muzzle detail of serial number 22 (upper) and number 401 (lower). Note how the magazine tube fits nearly flush with the muzzle on the earliest example. This feature is not noted on any guns with serials higher than number 22.

fail-safe method of identifying a first model receiver, as the plunger and detent system on the cartridge guide and carrier will occasionally be found on some guns with second model receivers.

There is finally a *verifiable* first Model 1894 in a caliber other than 38-55. It is a standard 30 WCF *takedown* with a *round* barrel – a rarity in the extreme. It carries serial number 5056 and was assembled and shipped on September 4, 1895, which is extremely early in the issuance of specimens in this caliber. Therefore it can, as of this writing, be accurately declared the only *documented* First Model 1894 in the designed-for caliber of 30 WCF. It is so far the only positively identified First Model (takedown or solid frame) in any caliber other than 38-55. Several other First Model specimens have been seen in caliber 30 WCF but cannot be validated as originally factory produced. Any existing 30 WCF specimens have been each examined, and each is rumored to have been factory re-barreled from 38-55 guns already assembled as 38-55s when the caliber 30 WCF was finally approved for production. However, as is common with hand-entered ledgers, there are no recorded entries to corroborate this.

I am convinced that this is likely *not* a rumor but the truth. The Model 1894 was designed to use the modern smokeless powder 30 WCF cartridge, but that cartridge was found to be

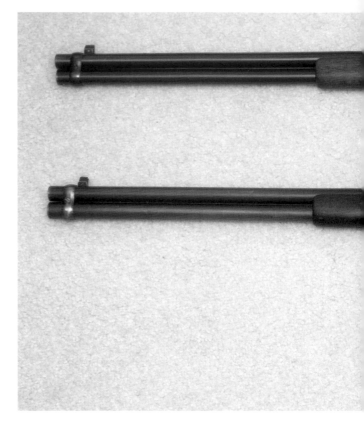

troublesome to manufacture using the then-current manufacturing techniques (reportedly due to the consistency of the smokeless powder). In somewhat of a rush to introduce the long-awaited caliber when it finally became

An illustration of Model 1894 first model carbine consecutive serial numbers. (Klein photo)

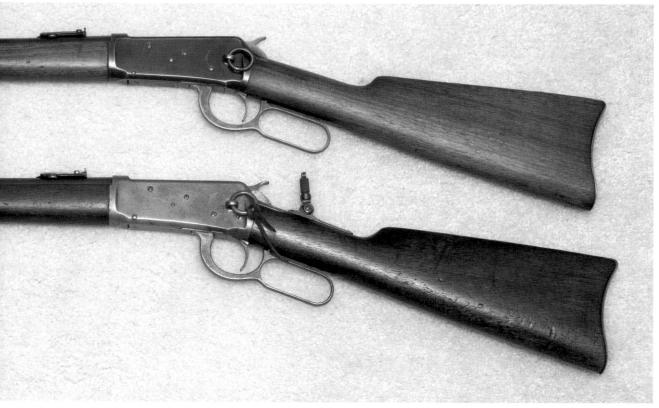

An extreme rarity is this pair of consecutively numbered first model Model 1894 carbines. This is the only consecutive pair of carbines known to exist and two of about only seven known first model carbines. Serial number 1296 was sent to the warehouse on Dec. 26, 1894 and shipped the same day – serial 1297 was sent to the warehouse on Dec. 26, 1894 and also shipped the same day. (Wes Adams collection)

available, it would not be unreasonable to assume that a barrel swap or two (or perhaps more) would be accomplished to fill existing orders more efficiently. There is also the very real possibility of early returns by customers for a change to the "hot" new cartridge or guns with damaged barrels being returned for repair and a caliber change. Returning to the ledgers for updating the new information would have easily been overlooked during such a hectic time.

Calibers other than 38-55 and 30 WCF have not in my experience been factory produced or seen as a later caliber change on a first model receiver. There have been many theories regarding this omission and the most viable is that the first model cartridge guide design for calibers other than 38-55 would require the placement of the "outside-in" retaining screws to be located in an area of the guide deemed too fragile or even geometrically incorrect for the screws to support them and would become unstable after minimal use (perhaps discovered

on the few that were hurriedly assembled or changed to the more powerful (in terms of pressure, 30 WCF). The screws were then relocated closer to the center of the guides and installed in the familiar "inside-out" method used on the second design receivers. *The preceding is all theory; no official records or any other evidence of this having actually happened exists.*

This group of receivers will most often be found blued as are the majority of Model 1894s. Casehardened or "color finished" receivers were reportedly available as an extra cost option (I have yet to see a verifiable color finished first model receiver). This was an option that, when ordered for either a Model 1892 or 1894, was heartily discouraged by the factory. There were many additional manufacturing steps involved, with a corresponding increase in labor and labor costs, and there was also a marked increase in material losses because these lighter and thinner receivers often cracked and/or warped during the application of the process.

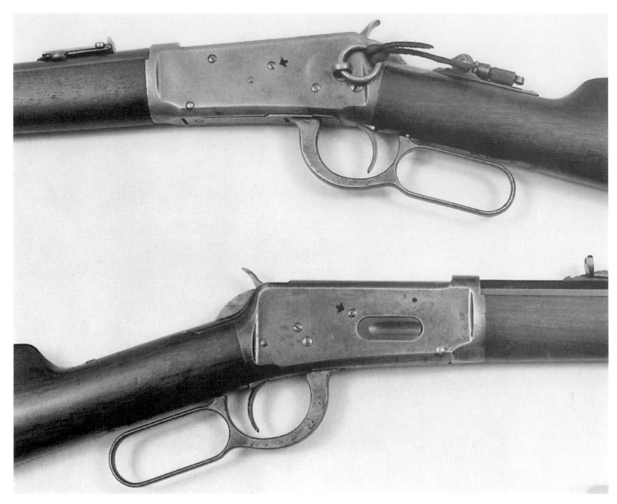

This illustration shows the two sides of a first model receiver. Notable is the head of a screw showing just above and aft of the loading port (arrow, lower illustration) and in the corresponding location on the opposite side (arrow, upper rifle).

These are the screws that hold the cartridge guides in place, and their appearance in this location is the only positive indication of a first model receiver.

With the use of high heat and rapid quenching on the relatively thin-walled Model 94 receivers, it's easy to see why problems with cracking and warping occurred. These problems made this option less than cost effective.

Model 1894s documented to have color finished receivers are among the rarest and most sought after of all variants.

SECOND MODEL

Serial numbers as early as the 500s are known, and quite a few guns will be found in the pre-2,000-3,000 serial range, but second model receivers will definitely not predominate until production numbers are well into the 3,000s. This style of receiver with some noticeable but mainly cosmetic changes from the first model accounts for the longest production period of the Model 1894 with no actual "re-engineering" being done. The period of manufacture runs from mid-1895 to late 1963, and corresponds at that point to serials somewhere above 2,600,000. Only two specimens in the 2,600,000 range have been seen as of this writing.

The second model receiver or second "design" is readily distinguishable. Noticeably absent from each side are the visible heads of the cartridge guide screws. In this model the guides are attached from the inside, with the ends of the attaching screws showing much like a pin on each side of the receiver. They are also found in a slightly altered location, approximately

11/16 inch forward of the screw location used on the first model. Internally, quite early in the second model production range, the spring-loaded plunger and detent arrangement with the carrier was phased out.

As first and second models were for a time produced concurrently, this feature may or may not be seen in some examples of the first model. It would be surprising to see it at all after serials near 8,000, but as usual there are no hard and fast rules in mass production. Serial number 8,001 may have the plunger and detent or even just the carrier with the detent and no plunger, and serial number 8,000 may have neither; it matters little. As a matter of policy, Winchester never wasted parts of an earlier design; they were used until the supply was depleted.

Variations of this nature are not to be considered "finds." Production of the Model 1894 continued at a steady rate, and we may note infinite variations of the guns as entities – but there were no changes to the receiver itself other than markings for a great many years.

At serials near 500,000, the spring in the lower tang under the mainspring that is used to actuate the hammer/trigger safety plunger was changed from a flat style to a bent wire style.

In the early 1920s the tang marking had the "18" omitted from the "1894," and the Model 1894 was now re-designated as the Model 94.

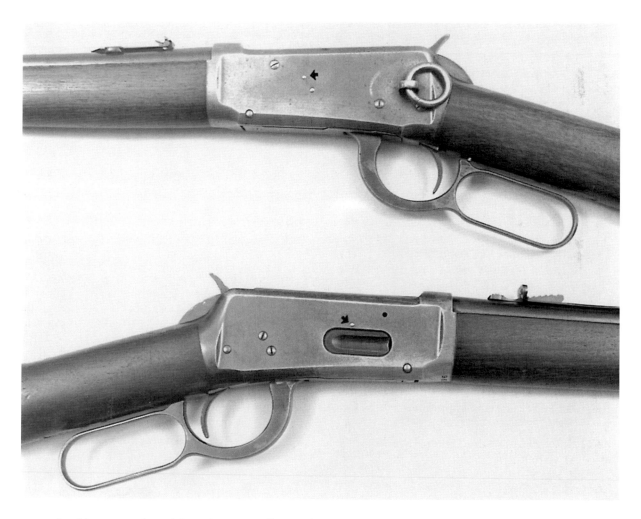

On this, a second model receiver, we will note that the guide screws appear to have been omitted. Slightly forward of the previous location we notice what appears to be a pin just above the loading port, and another in a corresponding location on the left side of the gun (arrows). These "pins" are actually the ends of the guide screws that are now installed from the inside of the receiver. Also nicely illustrated on the upper specimen is the very rare two-leaf express sight.

This photograph illustrates the upper tang change appearing to the 1,500,000 serial range. Note the rounded shoulder behind the hammer of the left example, and the change to the much sharper shoulder on the right side example. This change prevails to date.

This serial number is from a postwar "flat-band" model, and has an "X" suffix. Interestingly, this particular gun also carries an "X" stamping inside the lower tang and happens to be one of the lowest serial numbered examples of the new upper tang design I have personally seen.

Factory experimental? Possibly, but an "X" suffix was also used to change an inadvertent "repeat" or double-struck serial number. Since no substantiating records exist for this serial range, we must allow experience to guide our conclusions. (Author's collection)

Receiver changes that are admittedly slight but definitely noticeable begin appearing during the period of "pre-war"/"post-war" (World War II) transition.

In serial ranges near 1,350,000, the upper tang becomes devoid of all markings and no longer has a tapped hole for the upper screw of a tang mounted rear sight. Presumably this was a wartime production shortcut, but a "Winchester" marked tang or a tapped sight screw hole would never been seen in normal production again. (Serial 1,341,268 has marking but no hole??)

It will take careful observation to notice the next modification. Somewhere near serials in the 1,520,000 range, the upper tang is widened slightly on each side of the hammer notch. Where earlier it had a gradual, rounded, tapering look as it narrowed toward the stock screw, it now had a more sharply defined and angular shoulder.

This seemingly minor change is considerably more complicated than one would initially imagine. The machinery used in the manufacture of both the receivers and the stocks had to undergo some rather extensive modifications.

Why this change was made is somewhat of a mystery. It certainly can't be considered the starting point of a third model because it appears to be no more than cosmetic. It serves no apparent purpose other than perhaps a strengthening of that area behind and around the hammer, but there were no problems in

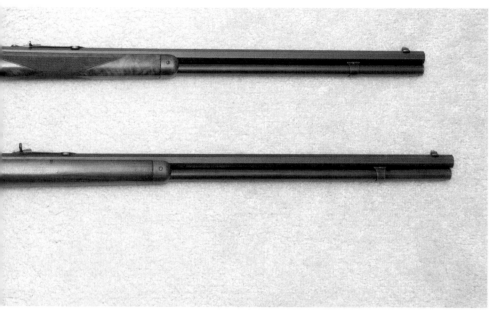

A full-size illustration of the consecutive pair of first and second models. Serial number 5860 is a magniicently pre-served deluxe edition that is described in detail elsewhere in Part I. Serial number 5861 is a standard second model octagon barreled specimen that was sent to the warehouse on August 31, 1895 and shipped on September 9, 1895. Both are in caliber 38-55. They are unfortunately not together at this time.

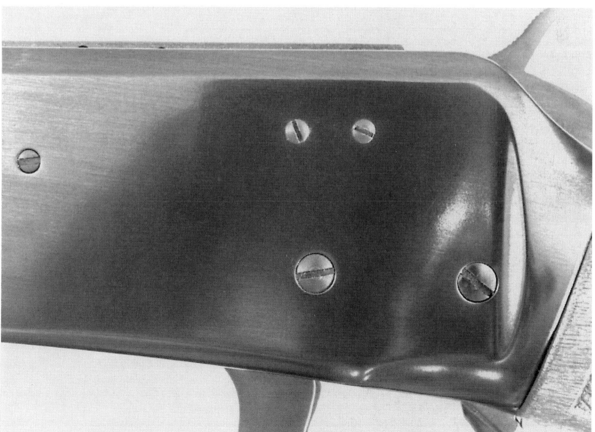

A clear illustration of the two factory tapped holes that appeared in the 1,790,000 serial range and prevailed until the introduction of the angle eject model. These holes were provided so the customer could easily mount a receiver type rear sight without having to go to a gunsmith.

Many highly collectible Model 94s (as well as many other models) have lost considerable value from having these holes drilled and tapped by an outside gunsmith in the years before the factory thoughtfully included them as standard.

this area before. Unfortunately, there is no definitive answer.

Note: This happens to be the point where a Post-64 style buttstock can be rather successfully fitted to a Pre-64 gun, requiring only some relatively minor inletting work.

The final significant change to this design was the inclusion of a pair of tapped holes on the left upper rear portion of the receiver near the hammer. Finally a receiver-mounted sight

An unbelievably rare consecutive pair of first and second model Model 1894s.

could be utilized without the need for gun-smithing. This welcome change occurred near serials in the 1,790,000 range and continued until the introduction of the angle eject models, on which it was again deleted.

THIRD MODEL

This is the design change that illustrates the historic and infamous "Pre-64"/"Post-64" changeover. The third model receiver is the first to carry the designation of Post-64, and while not being in production for a particularly long duration (only about 19 years) was produced in quantities equalling about half the production of all Model 94s to date. It accounts for all guns (commemoratives included) made from 1964 to 1983! The corresponding serial range is from about 2,700,000 to 5,250,000.

There is an ongoing dispute over the exact serial number of both the last production second model receiver (Pre-64) and the first third model receiver (Post-64), but second models most assuredly end near or at the very early 2,600,298 range and the third models were introduced somewhere near 2,700,000. The rumored last Pre-64 Model 94 assembled is number 2,600,298. The gap between this number and the very earliest known Post-64s is so far unexplained.

The problem is not in distinguishing a Pre-64 from a Post-64. The difference is glaringly apparent. The problem is finding very high

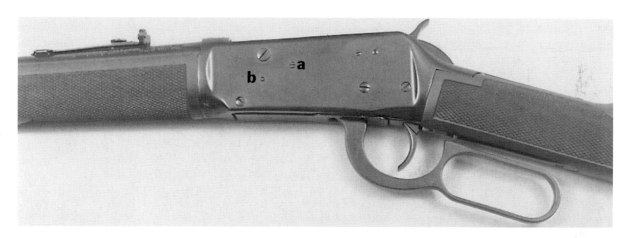

Third, 3a, and fourth model external receiver detail. On the upper example (left side) we see that the left cartridge guide screw (a) is installed from the outside (note the slot). The end of the carrier spring screw (b) is now visible between the bolt/lever pin stop screw and thelink screw.

On the lower (right side) example, we can see the end of the now "through" design carriers crew (c) just below the loading gate retaining screw. The right cartridge guide screw (d), visible above the loading port, is also installed from the outside.

numbered (near 2.6 million) Pre-64 receivers to examine. I personally have yet to uncover Model 94s in the serial range between the very high 2,590,000s and the very low 2,700,000s. If any reader has such an example or can show me some reliable documentation on specimens with numbers between these, I'd deeply appreciate it. A gap of about100,000 pieces in a sequential serial system is certainly mysterious and quite worthy of further investigation.

Overall quality throughout the Winchester line had noticeably been declining in a progression that could be traced back to World War II. Barrel markings became less and less sharp as serials progressed, and unsightly machine marks began to show during early postwar production. Even the fit and finish of the wood was falling way below previous standards.

The sharpness and attention to detail that so typified a Winchester had been steadily degenerating while labor costs in the postwar boom were rising at an alarming rate. Even the most casual observer could see the changes. Predictably, the lower quality product and the necessary increases in price affected sales.

Also negatively impacting Winchester's economic structure was the loss of all the easy revenue from lucrative government contracts and an uncharacteristically slow civilian market. There were lots of surplus military guns to be had, and at bargain prices too. Most Americans were too busy getting their post-war world back in order to be interested in spending hard-earned cash on expensive new guns.

The Korean conflict provided another short economic boost but soon the same post-war cycle began again. Economically, the company was still in trouble.

Management had to make a decision. Production costs had to be reduced to keep the product marketable. New methods had to be devised.

Introduced after a few years of development was the new "cost effective" third model.

This new model was such a blow to Winchester fanciers, such a departure from the quality of even the worst example of the previous design, so disappointing in appearance and feel, that sales plummeted dramatically.

It rattled when you shook it. The action was an abomination with a flimsy sheet steel stamping serving as the carrier, and the receiver itself didn't take kindly to the bluing process. Even

the fit and finish of the wood was terrible – on a par with the rest of the gun.

Equating this degree of quality with that of other products coming from certain areas of the Orient, the Model 94 became derisively known as the "Japanese" Winchester. Not altogether surprising, many people were convinced that the gun really was being made in Japan. It was NOT.

The receiver itself was now a casting, an investment casting. The material from which it was cast was an alloy of some kind of "mystery metal" that not only resisted polishing, but also refused to adequately react to the bluing solution. This alloy proved to be so inhospitable to finishing that it finally had to be plated with iron just to provide a consistent medium upon which the bluing solution could react.

Field use soon drew customer complaints pertaining to lack of finish durability, and it was back to the drawing board for more research.

The final solution was to use a black oxide finish, that while in reality was hardly more durable, but at least had a smoother, higher quality appearance.

The machining of this receiver could only be called adequate. Visible machine marks on the interior surfaces show little or no attempt at elimination, and this condition was unfortunately carried over externally to the sides of the lever and hammer as well.

Cosmetically and internally there are many obvious and some not-so-obvious differences from a second model. The relief cut on the upper tang behind the hammer on some examples is so rough and variable that it almost appears to have been done by hand – and an unskilled hand at that! The area around the serial number is now wider and has a very angular contour. The lip on the face of the receiver that originally provided a "nesting" place for the receiver end of the forend wood is eliminated, as is the corresponding inletting cut on the forend wood itself.

The cartridge guide screws once again enter from the outside as on first model receivers, but in the same position as the inside-to-out screws of the second model. This could only have been changed for ease of assembly/disassembly.

The lifter/carrier assembly became a simple stamping of blued steel and had a particularly loose and sloppy fit (hence the rattle). The lift-

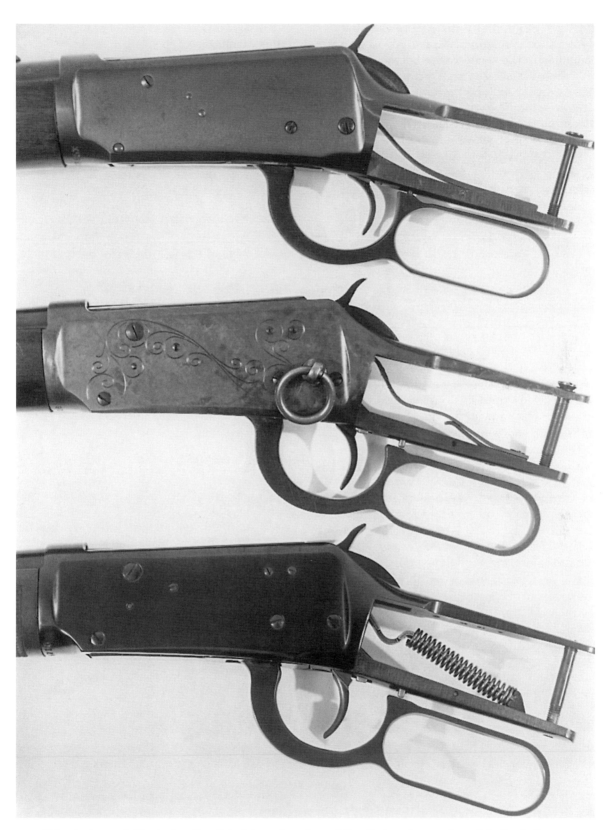

This photograph illustrates the flat style mainspring of the first and second models (top) ,the re-worked but still flat mainspring of the third and 3a models (middle); and the radical new coil type mainspring introduced on the fourth model (bottom).

er/carrier retaining screw(s) were changed to a single "through screw" design, installed from the left with the end visible on the right side of the receiver. The carrier spring screw "end" (this screw is installed from inside the receiver) can be seen in a forward position on the left side of the receiver between the bolt/lever pin stop screw and the link screw.

The hammer/trigger safety plunger spring reverts back to the original flat style.

The shape of the mainspring, while still a flat type, is altered slightly and is no longer hooked on the hammer "stirrup" (this part is eliminated). Now it merely presses against the contoured rear surface of the hammer, held in position only by its new shape.

The link pin and its locking screw are also replaced by the much simpler "through-screw" arrangement.

Most of the internals now varied quite widely as to manufacturing methods and tolerances.

In concert, these changes in design and lapses in quality were publicly criticized, harshly denigrated, and deemed far less than satisfactory for an arm that carried the name Winchester.

This style of receiver also marked the beginning of the "commemorative" series of the Model 94. Technically, the first commemorative was really the "Antique" model with production starting in the low 2,700,000 range, but true commemoratives (those which celebrate a special event or place) originated with the "Wyoming Jubilee" model.

This pretty little piece featured the casecolored receiver of the Antique variation, a medallion inletted into the buttstock and a gold-filled inscription on the barrel. Production of commemoratives has steadily continued through many different models from 1965 to present. Some Antique models (only very few have been noted) and all commemoratives will be found with their own serial number series.

By the late '60s, due to lagging sales and "unkind" references, Winchester was forced to rethink its product. The changes begin to be noticed around the 3,400,000 serial range and these "improved" models are characterized by a phenolic instead of steel buttplate. Let's call this receiver style, 3a. These guns, while not up to the Pre-64 standards, were nevertheless vast improvements over the immediately previous design.

No stamped parts are found in this version. Newly machined internals were designed and properly fitted, and consequently the action became considerably smoother and tighter. Even the wood fit better, and the overall finish of the gun was at least acceptable. Salesmen now carried "cutaways" to herald all the improvements, and indeed, it was a much better gun.

The "Japanese" model was as close to total and unredeemable disaster that Winchester's Model 94 would ever come, but now the company was again forging ahead, instilling the old confidence, tweaking the public's awareness.

Boldly, with their own confidence showing, they designed and introduced a new version of the old Model 64 – serialed into the Model 94's number sequence, it was designated the Model 64A. This attractive piece was nicely appointed and really wasn't a bad gun at all, but for some reason, just as with the original Model 64, sales figures were disappointing. It never acquired much of a following and after about a year of production was discontinued.

Now only the Model 94 carbine remained as "the" Winchester lever gun – the ultimate just kept on selling!

FOURTH MODEL

Introduced in 1978 at serials around 4,600,000, this style of receiver is essentially the same as its predecessor but definitely displays enough re-engineering to qualify as a new model.

The hammer/trigger/lever relationship is slightly redesigned for a noticeably smoother and better overall action feel, and the previous flat mainspring with its separate screw for tensioning gives way to an entirely new design incorporating a coil spring system. The forward part of the coil spring "assembly" rides in a slot machined across the rear surface of the hammer and the rear part of the assembly fits into a saddle arrangement mounted on the lower tang. This saddle is incorporated as part of a redesigned (again) hammer/trigger safety plunger spring system.

The lower tang no longer rides in locating grooves milled into the lower part of the receiver and now can move quite freely around the hammer screw. This is especially noticeable when the buttstock is removed and the action is opened and closed.

These changes working in concert modern-

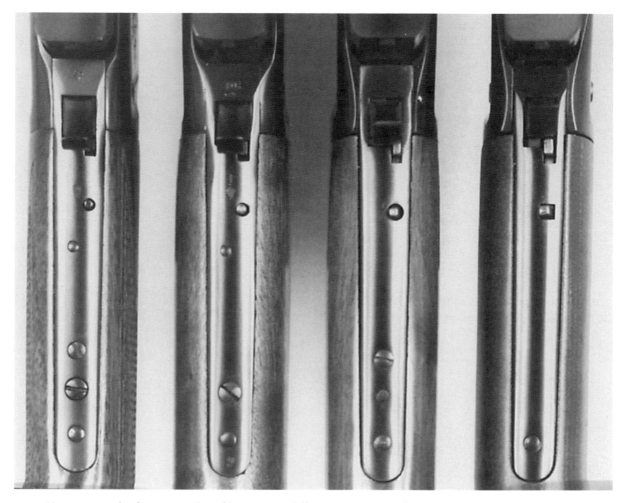

Here we see the four examples of lower tang differences. On the left is the earliest and typical "flat" mainstream type lower tang, with the end of the stock screw, the head of the mainspring screw, the head of the strain screw, the end of the spring retaining screw for the trigger block safety and the trigger block plunger all evident (bottom to top).

Second from the left is the version found intermittently throughout the early part of the "flatband" series – without a strain screw. These examples are typically found from serials of 1,350,000 to 1,460,000. The author has no explanation for this omission; the strain screw reappeared later in the flatband series and remained in use until the introduction of the coil spring system.

Second from the right is the Post-64 style. This is still a flat mainspring system, but note how the main-stream screw is installed from inside the tang with the end of the screw evident, instead of the head and now the spring retaining screw for the trigger block safety has been omitted; the spring is now pinned in place from the side.

On the right is the typical smooth lower tang of the coil type mainstream design showing only the end of the stock screw and the trigger block plunger. This style prevailed through the end of production.

ized the Post-64 Model 94 considerably and, in general consensus, were well-thought-out changes for the better.

This model is quickly and easily distinguished by observing the smooth screw-less lower tang and the continuation of the "top eject" configuration.

FIFTH MODEL (or 5A-Angle Eject BigBore)

Also introduced in 1978 was a new gun in a new caliber with a slightly reworked receiver. It was designated the "BigBore" model. This receiver, while identical in basic design to the fourth model, displays several interesting engineering modifications essentially incorporated

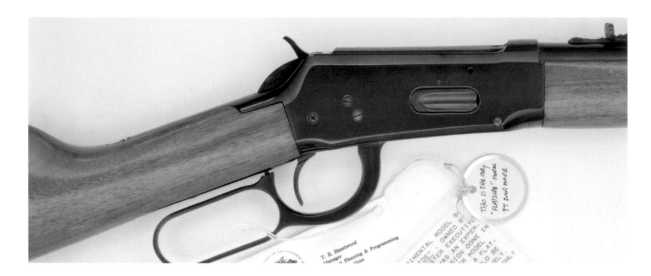

A very rare prototype Model 94 in 30-30 caliber, made in the mid-seventies. As you will immediately notice, the receiver is "flatsided" in configuration as compared to a production Model 94. It is this author's opinion that this specimen was developed as a research gun when the idea of introducing a larger and more powerful cartridge (Winchester 375) to the model's lineup was in the developmental stage. The reasoning for the change was that the extra thickness in the receiver would give the greater strength needed for the caliber. It was apparently deemed too unattractive for production but paved the way for the much more aesthetic BigBore model (5th model) with only the rear portion of the receiver enlarged. The BigBore was introduced in 1978. (Photos courtesy of Leroy Merz)

A full-size illustration of the rare prototype "flatside" carbine. Once owned by a company executive, it remains new and with all original packaging. (Photo courtesy of Leroy Merz)

This is the pre-angle eject BigBore (fifth model) receiver. Note the radical widening of the area surrounding the hammer, trigger, and breechblock for the new .375 Winchester cartridge.

This receiver was also continued in the angle eject configuration (model 5a).

to accommodate a newly developed cartridge – the .375 Win.

Externally, and immediately noticeable, is the widening and thickening of the rear of the receiver in the breechblock and hammer area. The additional metal provided a significant increase in rigidity and strength in this location, and was deemed necessary to withstand the much heavier bolt setback experienced from this unusually powerful (for a Model 94) new cartridge. This area of a Model 94 receiver must remain within specifications to provide the shooter with a gun of acceptable and consistent accuracy and be robust enough to assure the maintenance of proper headspacing.

Slight modifications to some of the internal parts for additional "punishment resistance" will also be noted.

This model will also be found with the first "standard" red rubber buttplate. While not being really a recoil pad as such, this cushion does provide the shooter with a much softer medium between himself and the gun than would a steel or composition buttplate.

BigBore models in the top eject configuration will always be found in their own serial number series – prefixed by "BB."

SIXTH MODEL (6A – Angle Eject, 6B - Angle Eject with Button Safety, 6C – Angle Eject with Tang Safety)

In 1983 at serials around 5,300,000 (serial numbers are now found on the left side of the receiver, on the bottom rail next to the link), we note the latest engineering revelation. We now find an entirely new and rather clever ejection-system, called "Angle Eject."

Not just a design exercise and certainly not without merit, this new system allows a telescope to be mounted directly on the receiver of a standard Model 94. The bolt and extractor are modified, and a machine cut is made along the upper right rail of the receiver to allow the ejection of the spent cartridge case off to the right side of the gun. Tapped mounting holes for telescope rings are also provided on the top of the receiver and there are no drilled and tapped holes on the side of the receiver for a receiver-mounted sight. This is a very neat solution to a very old problem.

Gone is the necessity of drilling extra and unsightly holes in the side of the receiver to install the ungainly and difficult to use offset scope mount system.

Gone also is the alternate necessity of using a long eye relief scope with the front part of its mount screwed into a hole drilled in the forend band and the rear portion wedged into the rear sight dovetail.

Standard mounts and rings can now be used, and a much wider selection of scopes becomes available.

Another welcome feature is the use of one hundred percent steel forgings in all angle eject models. This new model, while being perhaps the most radical departure from the original Browning design, is at least a serious attempt at product improvement and shows a real desire to return to that old-time Winchester quality.

In some of the later non-BigBore issues (in calibers 44 Magnum and 45 Colt) there will be some slight internal modifications noted. These are slight and consist mainly of clearance cuts and/or minor parts modifications, designed to allow these short, fat cartridges to feed reliably.

The BigBore model is also redesigned to the angle eject configuration (model 5a). All Big-Bores are now numbered directly into the standard 94 serial sequence but very early, angle eject models have an individual serial sequence with an "AE" prefix (serials from AE100001 to AE19000).

The "Angle Eject" model prevailed through the end of production.

The angle eject (sixth model, 6A) receiver detail. While the left side of the receiver is identical to that of the fifth model, except for the lack of receiver sight mounting holes, clearly visible on the right side (lower illustration) is the machine cut along the top rail that provides clearance for the sideways ejecting cartridge.

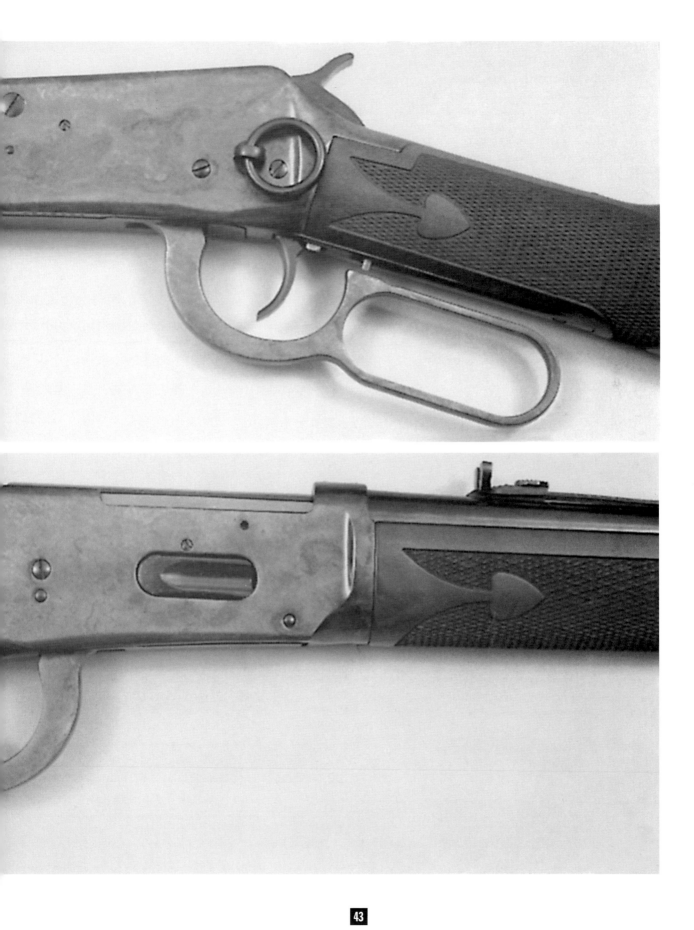

A rare and very unusual cut-away model made by the factory to illustrate the "button safety" system that was the next to last iteration of a technically unnecessary safety system. A lever action gun cannot be fired with the hammer in the down position. It must first be cocked, either by manipulating the lever, or if a round is already chambered, by manually pulling back the hammer by hand, thus knowingly making the gun ready to fire. This and the later version mounted on the tang became known as "lawyer buttons" due to the obvious concern for negative litigation toward the company in the event of a mishap. (Photos courtesy of Leroy Merz)

A second view of the angle eject receiver, showing the machine cut, the tapped and filled holes for installing telescope sight mounts, the revised position of the extractor in the bolt and the new pushbutton hammerblock safety system that was incorporated at serials near 6,000,000 (6B). This new safety system required slight modifications to the hammer, breechblock and receiver. It effectively blocks an unintended fall of the hammer from reaching the firing pin. Also nicely illustrated is the latest version of the third design hammer; note the hole for the hammer extension (see Chapter 4). (Author photo)

6C, the latest iteration of the Model 94 series safety system. It is called a "tang safety" by the manufacturer and colloquially called a "lawyer button" by the end user. It replaced the previous "button type" receiver-mounted safety at serials around 6,450,000. (Author photo)

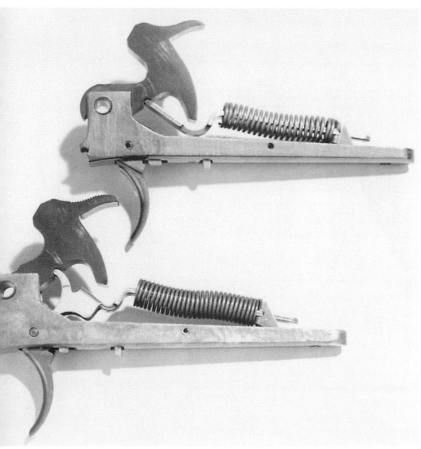

This photo illustrates the differences found in the third version of the third design hammer (see Chapter 4). These hammers are actually assembled units, including the hammer, the mainspring assembly and the lower tang with the trigger and trigger block assembly.

Also visible just below the coiled spring unit, on the tang itself, is the rollpin that now retains the triggerblock safety spring.

The upper specimen is of the earlier non-rebounding type and was standard issue on the fourth model (top eject) receiver (serials start at 4,580,000). It was supplanted by the newly designed rebounding type hammer (lower specimen) and top eject guns beginning with serials around 5,100,000 and continues to be present on all angle eject models.

Note the differences in the way the coil spring units are fitted to the rear of the hammers, the differences in overall hammer shape and the addition of the rebound spring mechanism at the front of the lower unit.

The rebound effect can be noted by holding back the trigger when the hammer is down and pushing the hammer forward toward the firing pin. It will spring back to approximately the old half-cock position. The hammer cannot be pushed forward if the trigger is not held to the rear. On these units there is also a pronounced reduction of trigger slackness when the hammer is down.

Differing safety systems in later production guns required slight differences in internal parts, but the basics remained the same through the end of production.

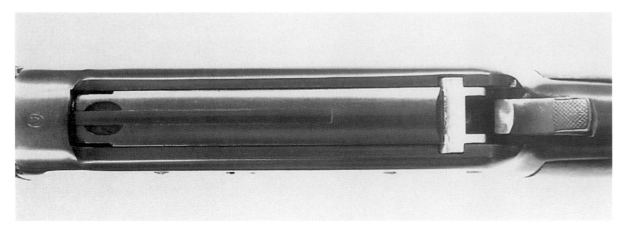

This illustration shows an original design bolt. Note the access cut for the extractor near the receiver (this may vary in size) and the very slight relief cut on either side, also near the receiver.

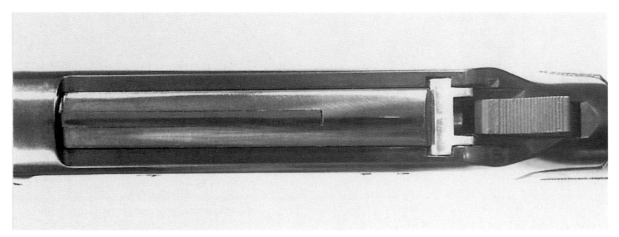

This is a second design (Post-64 to angle eject) bolt. The visible difference is the lack of the extractor access cut.

The small relief cuts seen on the sides of the original design bolt near the front portion of the receiver carry over onto the second design, but are ultimately eliminated at the introduction of the fourth model (illustrated) receiver.

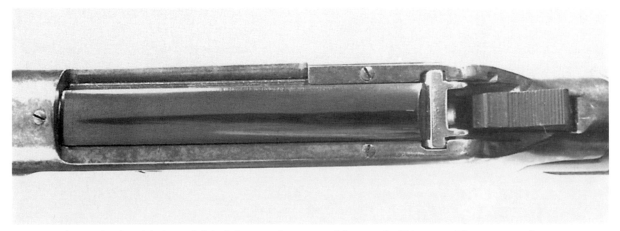

The angle eject (sixth model) bolt is smooth on top with no embellishments. The extractor is now redesigned to fit into the side of the bolt and is clearly visible in the new machine cut.

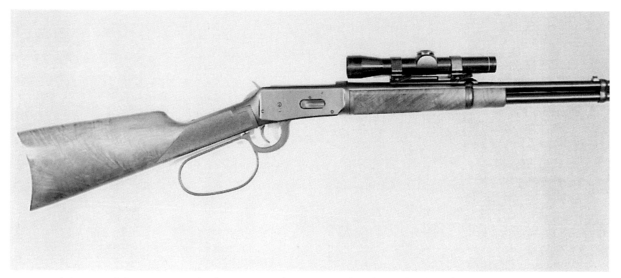

A late-model, custom stocked trapper with an original and very hard to find Leupold "DETA-CHO" scope mount. The scope is also a Leupold, the M8-2X, long-eye-relief model. This is a perfect magnification for the calibers offered in this short-barreled gun.

This system was devised to eliminate the need to drill and tap extra holes in the side of the receiver for an offset scope mount. Offset scopes were awkward to use, and many beautiful old Winchesters were severely devalued by putting extra holes in the receiver. Although unconventional in appearance, these 2X scopes mounted in the Leupold mounts are very "quick" on the target.

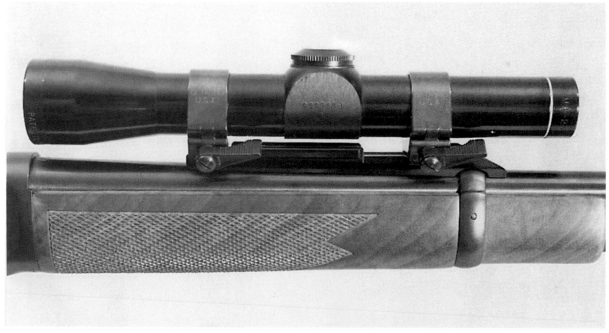

A close-up view of the "DETACHO" mount. When flipped toward rear of the gun, the two levers release the scope and rings from the mounts. The mount base remains screwed to an insert in the rear sight dovetail and a tapped hole in the forend band when the scope is removed. There is also an open type sight provided for close quarters use; it is an integral part of the mount base and is used in conjunction with the original front sight.

These mounts are precision made. When the scope is re-attached, it is automatically returned to a perfect zero. The mounts are now known as "scout rifle" mounts.

This is the earliest Model 94 that can be verified by Winchester Museum records: serial number 22. Serial numbers 3, 5 and 8 do exist, but numbers 3 and 5 have no existing records; number 8 was completed and shipped on Nov. 11, 1895.

Assembled as a standard rifle in caliber 38-55, this gun was completed and delivered to the warehouse on the first day of production, Oct. 20, 1894, and was shipped the following week on Oct. 27. (Author's collection)

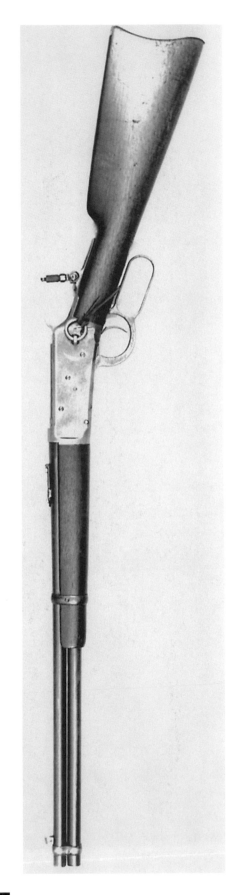

A rarity in the extreme is this first model carbine, serial number 1,296. A Winchester Museum letter states that this gun was manufactured as a standard carbine, in caliber 38-55. It was received in the warehouse on Dec. 26, 1894, and shipped on the same day, as part of a total shipment of 18 guns. There is no mention in the Winchester Museum records of the Lyman tang sight.

As of this writing, this is one of only seven first model carbines currently known to exist. (Wes Adams collection)

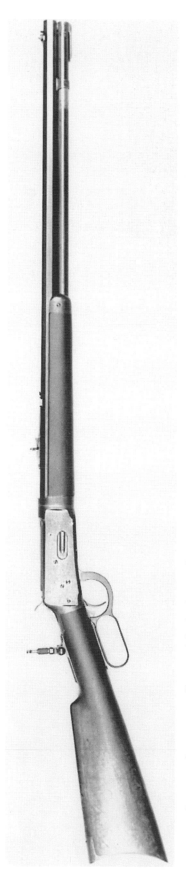

A very early, very rare first model takedown rifle. This specimen is serial number 139 and is the earliest Model 94 takedown rifle known to exist. Manufactured as an unoptioned or "standard" takedown rifle, in caliber 38-55, it was received at the warehouse on Nov. 14, 1894, and shipped on Nov. 17. There is no mention in the Winchester Museum records of either the Lyman tang sight or the Beach combination front sight.

Museum records also indicate that serial number 139 is the fourth takedown Model 94 by serial number but was the second or third assembled* and the second takedown shipped.** (Author's collection)

* Serial numbers 137 and 139 were both assembled on November 14, there is no way to tell which was completed first.

** Serial number 136 is noted in the Museum records as being the first Model 94 takedown to leave the factory. It passed final assembly and was delivered to the warehouse on Nov. 1, 1894; it was shipped on Nov. 3. Its present whereabouts is unknown.

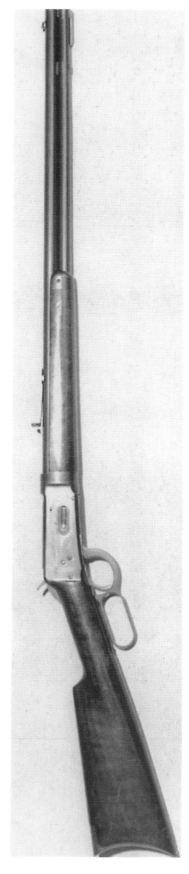

This is an example of how unpredictable collecting Winchesters can become. Here is an example of a seemingly standard and unremarkable takedown rifle in caliber 32-40. While it does have the rarer round barrel and "extra grain – extra finished" wood, it appears to be no more than a typical early takedown rifle. The inconsistency/rarity is that this specimen is serial number 734 and is a second model! Previous to the discovery of this example, second model receivers were thought to appear in serial ranges around 1700 but research has found them in the 500s. Assembled and delivered to the warehouse on Feb. 2, 1895, number 734 was shipped on March 2.

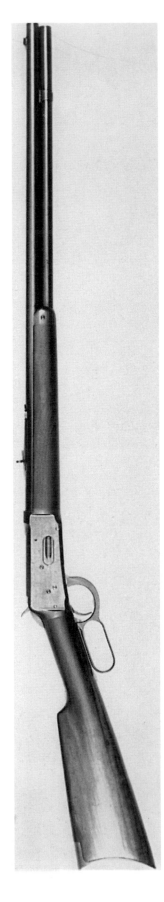

A very rare, round barreled, first model rifle. Round barreled guns trailed the octagon variety in popularity by about nine to one. This specimen, with the very early serial number 814, is a completely standard 38-55 rifle (round or octagon barrels were both considered standard). Of particular interest is the incredibly fine condition of this extremely early gun. Guns of this era were usually used as "tools," and very few have survived so many years in such an apparently unused condition. Number 814 was sent to the warehouse on Dec. 8, 1894, and was shipped on Jan. 24, 1895. (Wes Adams collection)

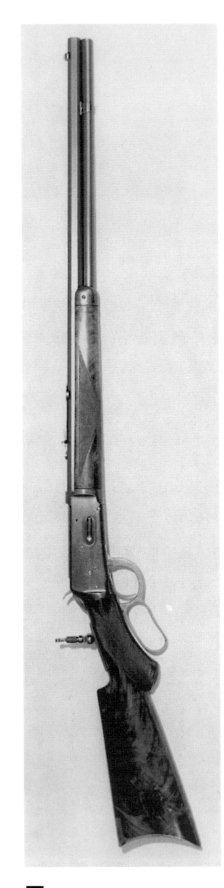

This is an extremely rare and beautifully preserved first model Deluxe short rifle, serial number 5860, in caliber 38-55. It features a fine set of "XXX" H-checkered stocks (with capped pistol grip and a half-inch shorter-than-standard buttstock measurement), a very rare 24-inch barrel, a flat-top sporting rear sight, and an unusually high serial number for a first model.

Factory records do not distinguish between first and second models, and since both were produced concurrently from serials in the 500s, we have no idea where the actual first model cut-off occurred. (Extensive research indicates the highest numbered first model so far verified is 7471). This fine specimen was delivered to the warehouse on Aug. 29, 1895, and shipped on Aug. 30. (Wes Adams collection)

BARRELS

INTRODUCTION

Barrels are perhaps the most widely differing, most changed, altered and controversial of all Model 1894/94 components. Read carefully all aspects regarding barrels in all relevant chapters of this book (e.g., Chapter 7, Markings) as many of the differences you may find are addressed in different areas of this book.

DIMENSIONS

Model 1894/94 barrels are considered "standard" when found in round or octagon styles and 26 inches in length on rifles and in a round 20-inch version on carbines. Any deviation from these specifications must be considered "special order."

Barrels with a half-round, half-octagon configuration were available on special order for rifles, and were offered in the same lengths and weights as the standard barrels. This option was discontinued in the very early 1930s, shortly before the rifle itself was discontinued. Octagon or half-round, half-octagon barrels were not available on carbines.

Available barrel lengths on rifles were from 15 inches to 36 inches and are most often found in "even" or two-inch increments. Odd numbered barrel lengths are rare when found on any Model 94, and on rifles, the extremely short (15 to 19 inch) or the extremely long (30-36 inch) lengths are also most unusual. Accordingly, any specimens authenticated as originally so fitted must be considered an extreme rarity and a collector's prize.

Barrel lengths beyond 28 inches were available in calibers 32-40 and 38-55 only, and only in regular, high carbon ordnance steel. Production of longer-than-standard-barrels was halted in or about 1908, but they were furnished on special order until the existing stock was depleted.

Barrels may show a 1/4 inch to 5/16 inch deviation in exact length, but any guns having such a discrepancy should be carefully inspected for originality. Damage to the muzzle quite often resulted in a "trimmed" barrel.

Barrels made for takedown rifles have been occasionally used on solid frame guns, and these specimens will measure 3/8 inch shorter than the norm (they were originally measured to include the takedown flange). If verifiable as correct, these examples are very rare.

Some "extra light" rifle barrels and carbine barrels are crowned; standard weight barrels are uncrowned.

This is a typical "uncrowned" muzzle. Note the relative flatness of the face of the muzzle, as if it had been cut with a saw, and note also the slight chamfering of the edge of the bore. The chamfering operation gave a smooth and finished ending to the rifling and provided a small measure of protection against outside damage.

This is a fine example of "crowning" on a lightweight rifle barrel. Note how the face of the muzzle has a rounded appearance and is polished. All carbines and all lightweight rifle barrels will be crowned.

Available barrel lengths on carbines were originally thought to be from 14 inches to 20 inches, inclusive, with the 15-inch trapper version being the most commonly seen of all Model 94s with an "odd numbered" length. Lately, however, unsubstantiated rumors of 10-inch and 12-inch models persist, and at least three carbines with 21-3/4-inch barrels were definitely factory produced and are in existence.

These 21-3/4-inch specimens have been extensively researched, and the barrels appear to have originally been designed/produced for the Model 95, 30-03/30-06 N.R.A. musket. Apparently modified by the factory after the muskets were discontinued (N.R.A. muskets were discontinued in 1926 and these barrels appear on Model 94s in 1927), they were cut down from the original 24-inch length to eliminate the 30-03/30-06 chamber, rechambered to 30 WCF, rollmarked with correct (for the serial range) Model 94 barrel markings, and rethreaded and fitted on Model 94 receivers. The 21-3/4-inch versions, and about 30 known 20-inch specimens, all have rifling with the 1-in-10-inch twist of the 30-03/30-06, instead of the 1-in-12 twist normally used for the 30 WCF; this further corroborates the Model 95 theory. Speculation is that these barrels were made up during the late 1920s when Winchester was in financial distress.

Standard dimensions of all Model 94 barrels, regardless of style or length, are a nominal 11/16 inch x 7/8 inch (muzzle and receiver) on the rifle, and 9/16 inch x 27/32 inch (muzzle and receiver) on the carbine. The Model 95 variant has nominal measurements of 5/8 inch x 15/16 inch (muzzle and receiver).

Special order "rapid taper" or "extra light" rifle barrels will have the 9/16 inch muzzle diameter of the carbine, and again this is regardless of the length. In actuality, however, there are many different muzzle diameters; these are largely dictated by the caliber. A very small muzzle diameter on a large caliber gun, for example, would result in the barrel material becoming far too thin as the barrel tapers from the receiver end to the muzzle. Safety and durability would be severely compromised. The so-called "pencil barrel" version will be noted to have a muzzle diameter of 1/2 inch or sometimes even less, but is only radically narrow in the smaller calibers.

All barrels with smaller-than standard muzzle diameters will be noted as lightweight or extra light in factory records – "rapid taper" and "pencil barrel" are colloquialisms.

There are conflicting theories on the muzzle diameters of shorter than standard barrels on both rifles and carbines. Some examples of short rifles with large-diameter muzzles that seem to be apparent "cut-offs" will often prove to be original.

A 16-inch short rifle with a standard 11/16 inch muzzle diameter would have a rather unaesthetic rapid taper. It is this author's opinion that although the factory definitely made barrels in shorter lengths as original, it also cut some down to satisfy special orders when no barrels of the proper length were available from existing stock. This may account for the differences found in forend length and sight positions on some short rifles. Once again we must use all our available resources and come to our own conclusions. Any non-factory work is quite easily detected if you pay close attention to the details.

The extralight variation was introduced in about 1896, initially in the standard 26-inch length only; but 24-inch and 22-inch versions were rapidly phased in. While the 26-inch and the 24-inch barrels were both considered standard on the extralight, the 22-inch barrel was a separate and extra cost option. All three barrel styles were available, with either the round or octagon style again considered standard, and the half-round, half-octagon type being optional. For example, a 22-inch half-round, half-octagon lightweight barrel is three options.

Rifles with the extralight features will average 4 ounces to 12 ounces lighter than the standard counterpart. Variations in weight have to do not only with the barrel diameter but the caliber, barrel length, other extra features and the style and density of wood.

All Model 94s have 6 groove rifling, with the twist rate varying from 1 in 12, to 1 in 22 according to the caliber.

Groove width varies throughout production with no hard standards being applied. Winchester was quite innovative and experimental with rifling (twist rate, groove width and depth, etc.), and was always striving to find the best combinations to suit the individual calibers.

As previously mentioned, the 9 known 21-3/4-inch barreled carbines and approximately 30 known 20-inch barreled carbines utilizing reworked Model 95, 30-03/30-06 caliber musket barrels have a 1-in-10-inch twist rate.

Takedown models were also made in all barrel styles, and once again the half-round, half-octagon style was an option; the extralight option was also available. While all barrel lengths shorter than standard were available on the takedown model, longer barrels were not offered but of course could conceivably exist.

There are rumors about the production of several takedown carbines, but these are unsubstantiated at the present time.

Winchester reportedly produced several Model 94s in the "musket" configuration. The facts are not widely available, but specimens are on record in 26-inch, 28-inch and 30-inch barrel lengths. They are full stocked in the traditional musket style, including the carbine style buttstock; they have saddle rings, a bayonet lug on the forend cap, and are found in the 300,000, 500,000 and 850,000 serial ranges. Current information reveals that there were five true musket examples: all were produced experimentally and all were originally in the Winchester Museum reference collection. Not all are thought to have survived. There were two bayonet designs used: the angular Model 1873 style and the typical blade type. All muskets were in caliber 30 WCF.

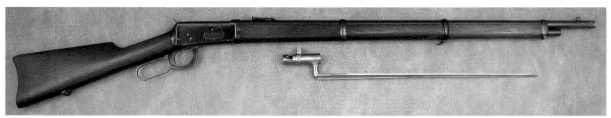

The extremely rare Model 1894 musket variation, serial number 503008, showing its original Model 1873 type bayonet. This is the only Model 1894 musket known to be in a private collection. (Rob Kassab collection)

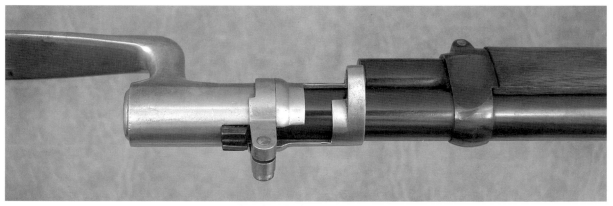

Bayonet lug detail of serial number 503008.

DIMENSION (Quick Reference)

1. 20-inch standard carbine - early (to about 950,000).
The center of the rear sight dovetail is 2-3/8 inches from the receiver.
The front sight is 1-1/16 inches + /-1/16 inch from the muzzle.

2. 20-inch standard carbine – with rifle sight option.
The center of the rear sight dovetail is 4 inches from the receiver.
The front sight is 1-1/16 inches + -1/16 inch from the muzzle.

3. 20-inch standard carbine – "pre-war" (about 950,000 to 1,300,000).
The center of the rear sight dovetail is 3-1/16 inches +/-1/16 inch from the receiver. This serial range includes the "transitionals," and many examples after serials of about 1,100,000 will be seen with the post-war 4-inch measurement.
"Ramp" style front sight.

4. 20-inch standard carbine – post-war to present (includes the modern 24-inch variants.)
   The center of the rear sight dovetail is 4 inches from the receiver.
   "Ramp" style front sight.
   On the '87 to '89 models with a dovetailed front sight, the center of the dovetail is 1
   inch from the muzzle. Very late-production variants may have either type front sight.

5. 20-inch standard carbine - M-95 barrel variant.
   The center of the rear sight dovetail is 2-3/4 inches from the receiver.
   The center of the front sight dovetail or front sight blade pin (two styles of front sights are
   used,) is 7/8 inch from the muzzle.

6. 21-3/4-inch carbine – M-95 barrel variant.
   The center of the rear sight dovetail is 3-1/16 inches +/- 1/16 inch from the receiver.
   The front sight blade pin is 7/8 inch from muzzle.

7. 14 - 15-inch trapper carbines.
   The center of the rear sight dovetail is 2-3/8 inches from the receiver.
   The late versions (1,000,000+) have the center of the rear sight dovetail 3-1/16 inches
   +/- 1/16 inch from the receiver.
   The front sight is 7/8 inch from the muzzle.

8. 16-18-inch trapper carbines.
   The center of the rear sight dovetail is 2-3/8 inches from the receiver.
   The late versions (1,000,000+) have the center of the rear sight dovetail 3-1/16 inches
   +/-1/16 inch from the receiver.
   The front sight is 1 inch from the muzzle.

9. Standard rifles and short rifles with the long forend.
   The center of the rear sight dovetail is 5 inches from the receiver .(Includes "extra
   light.") The center of the front sight dovetail is 1 inch from the muzzle.
   If the ramp style sight is used on an "extralight," the center of the ramp/dovetail is 1
   inch from the muzzle.

10. Short rifle with the short forend.
    The center of the rear sight dovetail is 4 inches from the receiver. (Includes "extra
    light.") The center of the front sight dovetail is 1 inch from the muzzle.

11. Standard takedown rifles and short takedown rifles with the long forend.
    The center of the rear sight dovetail is 5 inches from the receiver or 4-3/4 inches
    +/- 1/16 inch from the flange. (Some takedown rifles have the standard rear sight dovetail
    to receiver measurements corresponding with the front edge of the flange rather than the
    receiver itself. This may be seen with either forend length, follows no discernible pattern,
    and is quite unusual and is unexplained.) (Includes "extralight.") The center of the front
    sight dovetail is 1 inch from the muzzle.

12. Short takedown rifle with the short forend.
    The center of the rear sight dovetail is 4 inches from the receiver or 3-1/2 inches
    +/- 1/16 inch from the flange. (Some takedown rifles have the standard rear sight dove
    tail to receiver measurements corresponding with the front edge of the flange rather than
    the receiver itself. This may be seen with either forend length, follows no discernible pat-
    tern, is quite unusual and is unexplained.) (Includes "extralight.") The center of the front
    sight dovetail is 1 inch from the muzzle.

13. Musket. Twenty-six-, 28- and 30-inch barrels. There are many variables; limited
    specifications are available at this time.

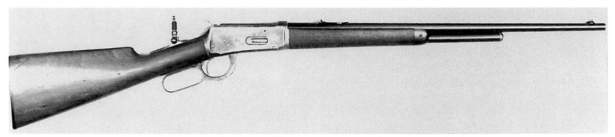

A fine antique Model 94 extra-light short rifle and in remarkable condition for its age, is serial number 28,202; it is chambered for the ever-popular caliber, 30 WCF. Received at the warehouse on Oct. 25,1897, it was shipped on Oct. 27.

Along with its six special order options, we also find two other very rare features. The options are a 22-inch extra lightweight barrel (this is actually two separate options); a 2/3 magazine; a flat-top sporting rear sight; a Lyman tang sight, and a shotgun style buttstock with checkered hard rubber buttplate. The first of the seldom encountered other (other meaning other than an actual option) rare features, is the lightweight barrel in the so-called "pencil barrel" style. This barrel has a muzzle diameter of only 7/16 inch (notice how much smaller the muzzle is than the end of the magazine tube).

The second "other rare" feature is that this is a very early extralight specimen and it was made with the front sight dovetailed into the barrel. The factory quickly realized how dangerously thin the barrel material could get under the dovetail cut (even more critical in the larger calibers) and consequently, almost all extra-light guns are found with ramp style front sights; the ramps are either made as part of the barrel itself or are silver soldered in place – they require no cutting into the barrel material.

There were many different barrel diameters and taper ratios in lightweight guns. Common sense tells us that they couldn't possibly make the muzzle diameter of a 38-55 barrel as small as they could a 25-35. While a dovetail cut into the barrel of a smaller caliber gun may have been perfectly safe, on the larger calibers (with radically tapered barrels) it was definitely not; the company chose not to take chances with any of them.

Six well chosen options and two other extremely rare features put number 28,202 solidly into the "super collectible" class. (G. Coty collection)

MATERIAL

The standard material for initial production Model 94 barrels was regular ordnance steel (a carbon steel alloy with a "black powder only") rating. Late in 1895 or early 1896, coinciding with the introduction of two new calibers (25-35 and 30 WCF), a new alloy was introduced. This alloy, called nickel steel (due to a five percent nickel content) was developed to withstand the much higher chamber pressures of these new smokeless powder cartridges.

All early Model 94s (until the proof steel introduction/designation) in caliber 30 WCF, 25-35 and 32 Special, have nickel steel barrels whether they are marked as such or not. Some early carbines, in particular, will be noted as chambered for the smokeless calibers but will not have the nickel steel markings. This is not unusual; this marking will not be seen consistently until serial numbers pass the 12,000 mark and the supply of earlier unmarked barrels is exhausted. Note, however, that any 32-40 or 38-55 caliber gun marked nickel steel is definitely a special order item.

For a time Winchester experimented with another alloy for the smokeless calibered barrels. Due to the difficulties encountered in the machining and finishing of the nickel steel, they began production of barrels made of an alloy of lower nickel content (1-2 percent instead of 5 percent). This alloy was designated and advertised as "extra steel." Extra steel barrels are usually seen on guns in the 45,000 to 75,000 range, corresponding with production in 1899, but don't forget those barrels that resided unnoticed in the parts bins and finally got installed on a later receiver. There are examples of extra steel barrels found in later serial ranges.

Due to complaints about rapid erosion in the chamber and throat area, extra steel was soon deemed unsatisfactory, and Winchester quickly and wisely returned to the good old nickel steel alloy. Any specimen found with a barrel marked extra steel may be considered quite rare (see "Marking" section).

In the mid-1920s, in an effort to solve the serious bore erosion problems encountered through the use of highly corrosive mercuric priming compounds, Winchester developed and experimented with a stainless steel alloy as a barrel medium. It was soon offered as an option on most models. Unfortunately, it quickly proved to be extremely cost-ineffective. It was hard to machine, resulting in far too many rejects, and it was impossible to finish satisfactorily. (These barrels were black enameled or "japanned," and this non-oil-resistant finish wore off almost immediately, even with normal use.)

Stainless steel was listed as an option for several years, but with the company discouraging orders and the public being less than overwhelmed by the added cost and questionable virtues, it was never a popular choice.

Model 94s seen with stainless steel barrels are quite often originally factory built and were made on special order. Many, however, are retrofits or re-barreled guns. All can be considered rare.

There are no available production records, but almost all stainless steel barreled lever guns except carbines will be found with barrels of the full octagon configuration. While most commonly found on the Models 53, 65 and the bolt action Model 70, stainless barrels were available at a modest extra cost for most models. Model 94s and 55s with these barrels, especially Model 94 carbines, are rarities in the extreme.

Stainless steel barrels were originally offered as an extra cost option ($8), but due to popularity problems they soon became a "no cost" option and were finally phased out of production in the mid-1930s. After this they were only available as "special order from existing stock." Some were scrapped during World War II, and some were reputedly installed as standard just to clear the remaining inventory as late as the early '50s.

After approximately 1933, a new alloy was developed. The official designation was "Winchester Proof Steel."

Much stronger and even more erosion-resistant than nickel steel, it was also easier to machine. This alloy included chrome molybdenum in the formula. Testing proved that, due

to the absence of the previously high percentage of nickel, it would better retain the depth of color and durability of its finish. One can readily note the improvement in finish quality and durability; the "flaking" condition so often seen on nickel steel guns all but disappears.

The use of this steel and the proof steel designation continues to end of production. (see "Marking" section).

DETAILS

Model 94 barrels have a very large and interesting assortment of engineering, design, and manufacturing variables. In this section of the barrel chapter we will examine the notable and noticeable variations, and also those not so noticeable.

Carbine barrels were originally produced with a slotted square post, integral not dovetailed to the barrel itself, to provide a mounting place for the "pinned blade" front sight. The forward edge of this post was one inch to 1-1/16 inches from the muzzle except for some 14- to 15-inch barreled trapper models having a 7/8-inch measurement.

At serials around the 1,100,000 range, the post front sight on all full magazine carbines was changed to the contemporary "ramp with hood" style. Some earlier ramp sight versions will be found without a slot for the hood. The post-type sight arrangement was only retained on carbines ordered with the short barreled trapper option, or those with shorter than standard magazine tubes. There were no carbines produced with a short magazine tube and ramp and hood style front sight, and there were no trapper carbines with ramp and hood front sights. Beware if you encounter one of these!

Note: The ramp and hood style as well as the dovetail-mounted type became the norm during the Angle Eject's production. Either may be found, with the dovetail type prevailing on most variants.

Also provided, unless a gun was specially ordered with the very rare "delete rear sight slot" option, was a 3/8-inch dovetail cut in the barrel for the rear sight. In the earlier versions this dovetail will be 2-3/8 inches from the forward edge of the receiver.

Customers electing to use a receiver sight or a tang-mounted rear sight exclusively could order the rear sight slot deleted. The resulting unbro-

A fine example of the earliest version of the change to a ramp front sight. As noted there is no provision (groove) for the sight hood. This very scarce example is in the 1,080,000 serial range, slightly before the majority of the ramp sighted specimens were in standard production and were issued with the machined-in slot and the hood.

A fine illustration of the very rare "delete sight slot" option on an early deluxe Model 1894. (Author photo)

Another example of the "delete rear sight" option. This time it's seen in combination with wavy style barrel matting and the ultra-rare, case-colored receiver on a fine deluxe rifle. Note the positioning of the caliber to avoid interference with the matting. (Author photo)

ken line along the barrel top to front sight made this an unusual appearing and aesthetically pleasing option. While this option incurred only a nominal charge – usually $1 – it was a seldom ordered feature. A rear sight slot "filler" was usually installed. Model 94s without a rear sight slot are extremely rare, especially carbines.

If an early carbine was special ordered with the rifle style rear sight, the dovetail would be machined forward of the standard location. This operation was necessary because the spacing between the standard dovetail position and the receiver was inadequate for the much longer rifle sight assembly. This option is quite rare

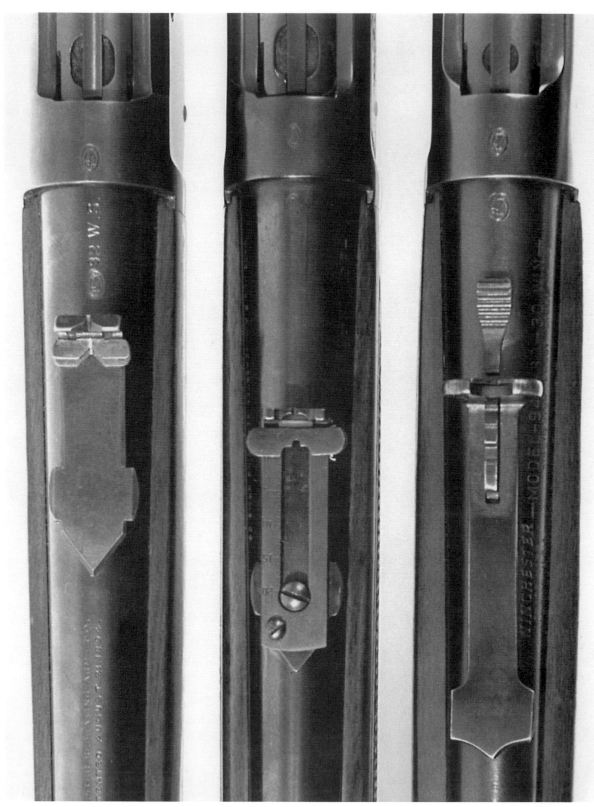

This photograph of three different-era carbines illustrates the difference in the position of the rear sight mounting cut relative to the receiver. From left to right: the 2-3/8-inch measurement (pre-serials of about 960,000), the 3-1/16-inch measurement (some serials between 960,000 and 1,300,000), and the final 4-inch measurement, beginning in the 1,100,000 serial range.

and is usually seen in combination with a rifle style buttstock.

At serials near 960,000, the standard position for the dovetail cut was relocated to 3-1/16 inches from the receiver. At serials around 1,100,000 it was moved again to the final and present location of four inches from the receiver.

Note: The final four-inch location was interspersed randomly with the 3-1/16-inch measurement until after serials of 1,300,000.

Many cuts, slots and holes can be found on the underside of Model 94 carbine barrels, as well as many markings. There is a relief cut for the passage of the front barrel band screw, a similar cut for the forend band screw, a small hole near the muzzle for the magazine tube cap retaining screw (after serials around 350,000 – see Chapter 3), and a slot for the flange on the magazine tube cap used with shorter than standard magazine tubes only if so optioned. Also noted will be a relief cut machined at the receiver end of the barrel to provide the required clearance for the magazine tube near the barrel/receiver junction.

This is a Model 94 carbine, serial number 1,028,178, with the collector's colloquial name of the 94/95 model. It also has a rather interesting and well documented history. Production figures and discovered details indicate several of these carbines showing up in four distinct variants, but so far have been found only in records pertaining to 1928. Research continues.

Carbine number 1,028,178 was obtained by a Mr. O. S. Wallace somewhere in south Texas in about 1928; he is known to have inhabited several southern Texas towns including Harlingen, San Benito and Brownsville, as well as the Mexican towns of Matamoros and Nuevo Progresso. Notable are his initials embossed in the stock, crudely stamped using a Q for the O and an inverted M for the W. Apparently, the correct stamps were unavailable at the time. It was housed in a very sturdy unmarked saddle scabbard.

Mr. Wallace had a reputation for being a hard drinker, scalawag and carouser who was not opposed to bending the law according to his needs. He was often wanted and often pursued by lawmen on both sides of the border depending on whose laws he was "bending" at the time. The subject carbine was reputed to have been used to dispatch at least one "bandito" who chose to relieve Mr. Wallace of his possessions while he was on the "south side." Evidently it was not a wise choice. That would account for Mr. Wallace's possession of the decedent's nickel-plated Mexican copy (in 3/4 size) of a Colt SAA in 38 S&W caliber and its attendant and quite decorative holster and belt; the belt has a very small waist size corresponding to the stature of many Mexicans of the day. The holster was slightly modified to properly house the revolver, making the rig somewhat questionable in its authenticity – it does, however, appear to have been with the carbine for a long time and seems to be period correct. The provenance of the revolver itself is not in question.

Another nice addition that came with the gun and aforementioned accoutrements is a picture of Mr. Wallace, obviously taken after a hunt and carrying the subject carbine in its original saddle scabbard. It is inscribed and dated, "O. S. Wallace, San Benito, Texas, and November 16, 1933." There is also a handwritten letter of authentication regarding the characteristics of the carbine and accoutrements written by noted Winchester authority, the late George Madis. (See additional photo on page 255).

The gun and the companion artifacts, as well as the story and picture, came from the estate and relatives of Mr. Wallace; they all swore to its authenticity at the time of acquisition. Historic Winchester Americana at its finest! (Author's collection)

It is in and near this relief cut that we find the various lower barrel markings (see "Marking" section).

If the ultra-rare carbine variation with the modified Model 95 barrel and rifle style magazine tube retainer is encountered, there will be a corresponding dovetail cut in the underside of the barrel for that retainer. This cut will be found 3-1/2 inches from the muzzle on the 20-inch version and 3-3/4 inches from the muzzle on the 21-3/4-inch version. The rear sight dovetail on this variety measures 2-3/4 inches from the receiver for the 20-inch version and 3-1/16 inches from the receiver for the 21-3/4-inch version.

These variants may or may not have a threaded and plugged hole in the barrel top. These holes are located just forward of the rear sight, between the sight and the receiver, or even under the sight itself. Only one hole will be usually found on a given specimen.

The front sight on these barrels is of a ramp style very closely resembling thatof the Model 55. This ramp has either a slot for a pinned

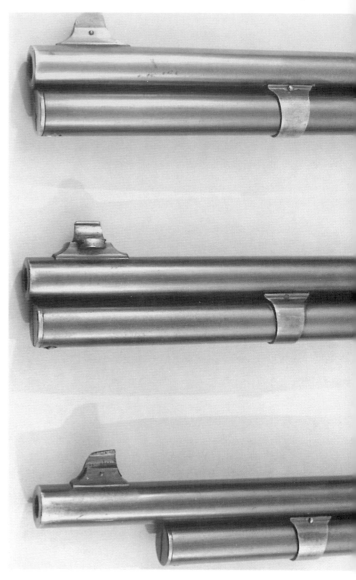

The muzzle ends of three different types of the Model 94/95 variants. From top to bottom we have a 20-inch variant with a short slotted ramp and a pinned blade type sight; a 20-inch variant with a slightly longer dovetailed ramp and a standard rifle type front sight; and the 21-3/4-inch variant, also having the short slotted ramp and a pinned blade type sight.

Be advised that the "short" magazine tube seen on the 21-3/4-inch version is not really short at all; it is the same standard length tube as used on the 20-inch versions.

Note: This is the only Model 94 variant with a shorter-than-barrel-length magazine tube installed by the factory without the rounded style end cap with flange (see Chapter 3). It is also the only Pre-64, Model 94 variant with a shorter-than-barrel-length magazine tube and a magazine tube retainer.

Illustrated on the barrels of two Model 94 carbine variants with the factory reworked Model 95 musket barrels are the positions of the threaded and plugged holes that will sometimes be found. These holes have been determined as originally used to mount the rear sight on the Model 95 musket. Some information on the Model 95 variants was excerpted from an article by the late Art Gogan of Salt Lake City, Utah titled "Hybrid Winchesters," found in the Spring, 1989 issue of "The Winchester Collector". This is a Winchester Arms Collector's Association publication. Gogan did extensive research on this intriguing variant. Also note the different positions of the rear sights. The upper example is the 21-3/4-inch variant and the lower example is a 20-inch version.

sight blade or a dovetail for a standard rifle front sight. The ratio of pinned to dovetail styles appears to be about 50:50.

Standard rifle barrels in either the round or octagon configuration have a 3/8-inch dovetail cut for the front sight, the center of which is 1 inch from the muzzle, and another 3/8-inch dovetail cut for the rear sight, the center of which is 5 inches from the receiver. The front sight dovetail center is consistent in its location for all barrel lengths at 1 inch from the muzzle, while the rear sight cut may vary in position.

Most notable is the different position of the rear sight cut on short rifles with the short forend. Observant collectors will note that with almost 100 percent consistency, the rear sight dovetail position on short barreled rifles follows the pattern of the forend wood. For example, if the gun has the shorter 8-3/8-inch forend, the dovetail will invariably be 1 inch closer to the receiver than if the standard 9-3/8-inch forend was used.

Inasmuch as the majority of short rifles but no standard rifles will have the short forend, we can presume that the relocation of the rear sight was to provide the longest possible sight radius on the shorter-barreled guns. Why this sight re-positioning wasn't done on short rifles with the longer forend as well is so far unexplained. Prevailing conjecture is that these are the "factory cut-downs" mentioned earlier in this chapter.

This pattern does not follow on short bar-reled (trapper) carbines.

As with the carbine, on the underside of rifle barrels we also find many different cuts, slots, holes and markings. There is a dovetail cut for the magazine retaining band (two on some longer than standard barrels); a hole for the magazine tube cap retaining screw (this first appears on rifles in the same serial range as it appears on the carbine); a slot for the flanged magazine tube cap that is used if a shorter than standard magazine tube is ordered; a dovetail for the forend cap tenon; and the magazine tube relief cut. As with the carbine, it is in and near this cut where the lower barrel markings will be found. On rifles, the size of this cut, in both depth and length, will vary according to individual barrel configurations. With standard weight octagonal rifle barrels, for example, there is sufficient clearance for the magazine tube, and no relief cut is necessary.

Very early "extralight" barrels have the same dovetail cut 1 inch from themuzzle as a standard rifle, but this cut in such a small diameter barrel – especially in the larger calibers – was quickly deemed "risky." It soon gave way to an integral ramp front sight arrangement. The 1/2 magazine "extralights" now looked amazingly similar to the later Model 55! These lightweight sporting rifles, as they were called, are the only Model 94s with an original ramp front sight and a shorter than standard magazine tube. Other cuts, slots and markings, etc., co-respond to those found on standard barrels.

This photograph illustrates clearly the relative positioning of the rear sight when installed on guns with the longer or shorter forend wood. The different in sight position relative to the receiver is exactly the same as the 1-inch difference in the length of the wood (the measurement for the 7-3/8-inch and the 8-3/8-inch style are the same). The sights on these two examples are both of the flat-top style, but note the 32B elevator on the upper specimen and the 1A type elevator on the bottom.

Barrels made specifically for takedown rifles are of necessity slightly different from standard barrels. On the full magazine versions, there is a crescent-shaped cut in the underside of the barrel to provide a nesting place for the takedown lever when the rifle is fully assembled. On guns with shorter than standard magazine tubes, this cut is omitted. The barrel is, for all intents and purposes, permanently attached to a "flange" that mates with the receiver when assembled. The barrel to receiver threads extending through this flange are of the interrupted type, thus providing quick and easy assembly/disassembly. Other details are the same as for the barrels on solid frame guns, but any measurements taken from the receiver end of a takedown barrel should take into account the thickness of the flange.

A clear illustration of the receiver end of a Model 94 takedown barrel. Shown is the flange that is semi-permanently attached to the barrel and mates firmly with the receiver upon assembly. Also visible are the interrupted style threads that allow assembly/disassembly of the barrel and receiver with only a 90-degree relative turn of the two assemblies (see Chapter 1).

The barrels of all Model 94s could be ordered with any number of options that required the muzzle to be threaded. Though rarely encoun-tered, silencers, flash suppressors and muzzle brakes were all available from the factory on special order. I have yet to see a factory-installed muzzle brake or flash suppressor.

Threading could be of the normal or the interrupted type, and all guns having factory threaded muzzles were provided with a nicely knurled or checkered cap. The cap was designed to cover and protect the threads when the "option" was not installed.

The position of the front sight and the length of the magazine tube on these varieties will usually differ from the norm.

Winchester discouraged this option, citing the nominal effectiveness of silencers on guns in Model 94 calibers, but production expense was actually the most likely contributing factor. Any Winchester with this feature is admittedly rare, but will also prove very difficult to authenticate. In serial ranges above approximately 1,100,000, or about the time when silencers became illegal without registration (1934), threaded muzzles will almost certainly be gun shop conversions.

Barrels were occasionally ordered with a non-glare upper surface. This treatment was known as "matting" and is seen in two distinct styles. The early version was a cross-checked pattern that was reputedly hand applied. The later version is a series of machine applied wavy lines running parallel to the axis of the bore. There was also a later version of the checkered style that was rolled on with a die.

All styles of matting could be ordered in full- or part-length, and in any width desired. The entire barrel could be done from end to end or perhaps only the upper flat of the octagon section of a half-round, half-octagon barrel. You could also order the matting on only the upper flat portion of an octagon barrel, or the upper three flats, or any width you specified on a round barrel.

Any type of matting is a very attractive and eye-catching accent. It is also extremely rare. Only 203 Model 1894s are on record as having matted barrels and only one with a matted receiver.

A beautiful example of the "straight checkered" style of barrel matting. This was reputedly hand-applied, but I have serious doubts due to the unbelievably intense labor that would be involved. (Author photo)

This is the machine-applied "wavy" pattern of barrel matting. Also note the unusual position of the proofmark and caliber marking. (Author photo)

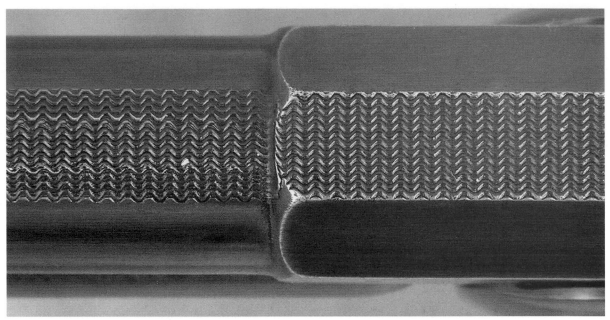

This is the wavy pattern aplied to a half round, half octagon barrel. An extreme rarity. (Author photo)

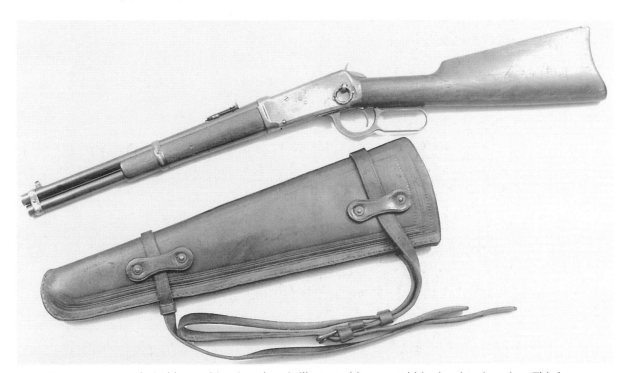

A rarer or most desirable combination than is illustrated here would be hard to imagine. This is an exceptionally rare 14-inch-barreled "trapper" model. Fourteen-inch Model 94s are among the scarcest of all barrel lengths. Only 15 Model 94s with 14-inch barrels have been certified and cleared by the BAFTE. (In comparison, more than 100 14-inch Model 92s have been cleared.)

Compounding the desirability of this outfit is the caliber – the very scarce 25-35 WCF, the rather high (for a trapper model) serial number of 865,268, and the hand-made and beautifully hand-tooled saddle scabbard that was included with the gun. The scabbard was undoubtedly custom-made for this particular gun.

This is a wonderfully colorful, authentic "cowboy type" rig from somewhere deep in South Texas; the scabbard is marked "Chon. Rivera, maker, Brownsville, Texas." (Author's collection)

This is a factory-ordered adaptation for a silencer or a muzzle brake. The cap is a protector for the threads.

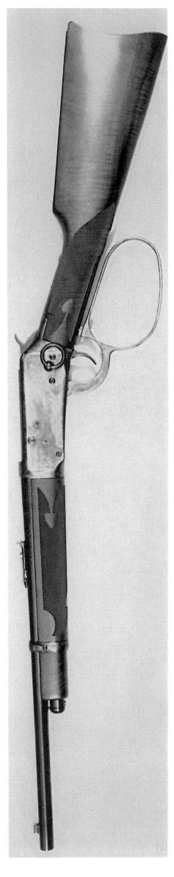

A very nicely appointed, custom-built trapper model from the USRAC custom shop. This is an angle eject model, serial number 5,522,300, and is chambered for the recently developed caliber, 7x30 Waters. This is the first of a set of three consecutively numbered 7x30 custom guns that were built in late 1989.

The features of this specimen include a 16-inch barrel with the early carbine style post front sight and gold blade insert; a "button" magazine with an original rounded, flange-type end cap; an original early carbine type rear sight; spade checkered, select parts with a high polish; and the receiver, forend band, buttplate, and lever all color-finished. (Author's collection)

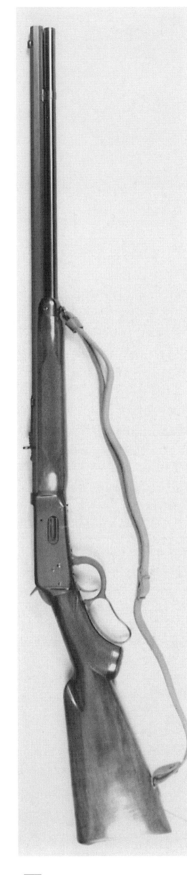

A striking example of "anything is possible from Winchester." This Deluxe rifle, serial number 2,137,xxx, is quite likely the last Pre-64 Model 94 rifle to be delivered from the Winchester factory. Clandestinely built in the mid-1950s with no fitter's or inspector's marks and having a very interesting history, this specimen is a very unusual, and very important, Winchester collectible. This could be the only existing example of a factory-built post-war/Pre-64 rifle, and it appears to be 100 percent original and genuine. It is unfired.

Allegedly assembled in the custom shop out of spare parts – using a period receiver, an early model 26-inch octagonal barrel in the classic 38-55 caliber (with markings corresponding to those found on the final production rifles of the mid-1930s [see Chapter 7]), an original full-length magazine tube, deluxe checkered Model 64 stocks with the wide style forend and inletted sling swivel mounts and sling – this fine example is reportedly one of the spoils of an internal thievery scheme, one that ended with no legal prosecution but several employment terminations. (Anonymous collection)

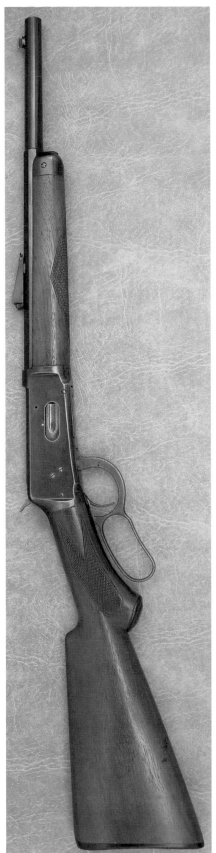
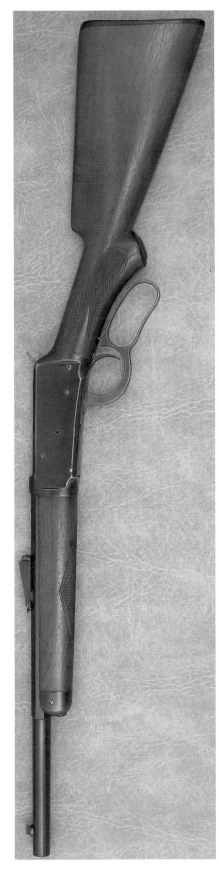

An unbelievably rare short rifle serial number 149228, caliber 32 Special. It is a deluxe version with "I" style checkering, pistol gripped shotgun style buttstock, with a hard rubber buttplate, a half round, half octagon 15-inch barrel and the typical 32 Special type 64A rear sight. It was manufactured and delivered in 1899. (Ron Kassab collection)

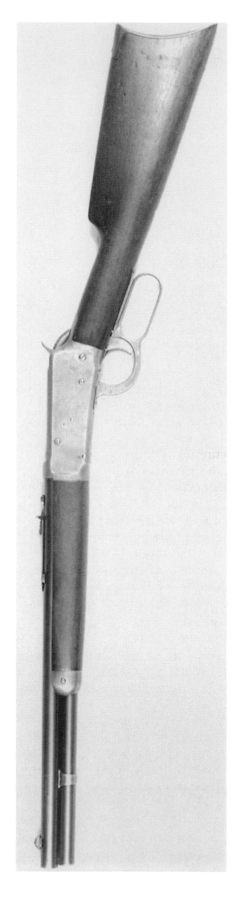

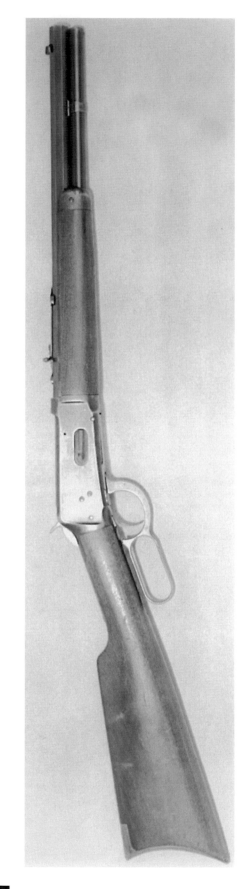

A fine example of an extreme rarity in the Model 1894 is serial number 576,398, a 16-inch-barreled short rifle. This is a round-barreled example, which makes this specimen all the more unusual; rifles with octagonal barrels were considerably more popular.

This caliber 30 WCF specimen has the seldom seen and very short 7-3/8-inch forend, an ivory bead blade front sight and a flat-top sporting rear sight. It is a scarce and rarely encountered variant.

This special order specimen, serial number 666,047, is a very rare short rifle with a 16-inch octagonal barrel. This example, in the very popular 30 WCF caliber, has the correct 7-3/8-inch forend and standard rifle sights. Other than the optional barrel length, this is a standard Model 1894 rifle. Very few 16-inch Model 1894 rifles are known to exist.

MAGAZINE TUBES

INTRODUCTION

The cartridge magazine on the Model 1894/94 is of the tubular type, containing a spring and plunger arrangement in which the compression of the spring provides the energy to force the ammunition out of the tube and back into the action when the lever is operated. The magazine tube is located directly under the barrel and on standard guns is approximately the same length as the barrel. Any magazine tube on the Model 1894/94 measuring other than full length is definitely special order. Loading the gun is accomplished by inserting the cartridges into the tube through an opening on the right side of the receiver, appropriately called the "loading port."

DETAILS

Standard carbines have both barrel and forend bands to hold the magazine tube in position. These bands are secured by screws that pass between the bottom of the barrel and the top of the magazine tube. Both the barrel and the tube are grooved slightly to just allow the passage of those screws. This arrangement and the clamping effect of the tightened bands themselves effectively retain the positioning of the tube.

On the earlier issues (to about serial 350,000), the magazine tube cap, which accesses the internal spring and plunger, is retained by a screw that does *not* protrude through the upper portion or "barrel side" of the cap. On the later issues, the retaining screw protrudes through the cap and the magazine tube and fits into a recess in the bottom side of the barrel. This design change provides an additional point of fore and aft support for the tube. One can easily observe the appearance or note the absence of that portion of the screw. Inconsistencies of this feature in guns that are not very near the transition point are certainly cause for further investigation as to authenticity.

On carbines with shorter than standard magazine tubes, the forward support function is altered slightly. The tube cap will have a rounded front contour and will also have a flange on the upper side that corresponds with a slot milled into the underside of the barrel. When this flange enters the slot and the forend band is tight, there is ample fore and aft support. The screw that retains the cap to the magazine tube does not protrude through the tube and into a barrel recess until after serials reach in the low to mid 300,000s.

Full-length magazines on carbines will be found to end very consistently within 1/16 inch of the muzzle; on some trapper carbines, however, they may appear to be almost flush.

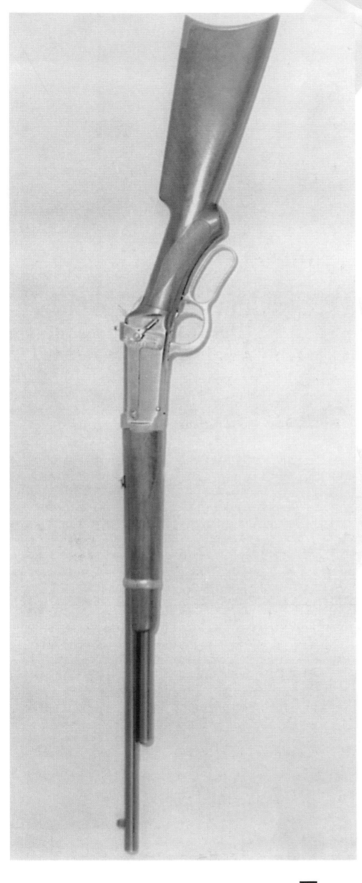

A wonderful Model 1894 collectible is this Deluxe carbine serial number 399,039. This fine example is in 32 Special caliber and features no fewer than eight special order options.

It has the very rare 15-inch (3/4 length) magazine tube, extra-grain I-checkered stocks including a capped pistol gripped rifle style buttstock (an extreme rarity on a carbine), an ivory bead front sight blade, a two-bladed folding rear sight with an ivory insert and the very scarce Lyman 21 ("Climbin' Lyman") receiver sight.

Number 399,039 was ordered and delivered on or near 1904 to an owner with an obvious penchant for aesthetics and is a worthy addition to any Winchester collection. (Author's collection)

This illustration is of a typical early style (pre-serials of approximately 1,500,000) magazine cap. These caps are notable by the slot cut into the front face. This practice had the unfortunate consequence of making the cap appear to be screwed into the tube, and indeed we find many of these caps severely marred by an inexperienced owner trying to remove them with a screwdriver. This particular cap (on a post-serial 350,000 specimen) illustrates quite clearly the way the cap retaining screw goes completely through the cap and into a recess on the underside of the barrel. As stated in the text, the caps on guns that are pre-serial 350,000 will not have the "through screw."

This illustration is of the later (post-serials of approximately 1,500,000) magazine cap. Note the absence of the slot. This design continued in use to end of production.

This illustration details the rounded style of magazine cap used on all shorter-than-standard magazine tubes. This "rounding" provided a much more aesthetically pleasing appearance on guns with this option.

This photo illustrates the "true button" type of magazine tube retainer. It is unusual to find this on a Model 1894/94. Although not to be considered a great rarity it is quite scarce on this model. It is fully explained in Part II of this book.

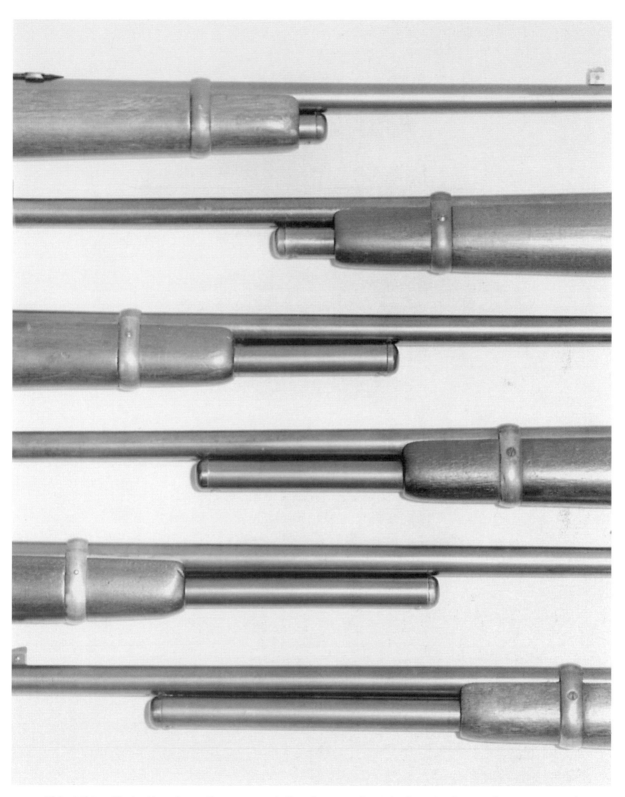

This striking illustration shows the many variations in magazine tube lengths that can be encountered in the earlier pre-war carbine variants. From top to bottom are the 11-inch and 12-inch or 1/2 magazine style; the the 13-inch and 14-inch or 2/3 magazine style; and the 15-inch and 16-inch or 3/4 magazine style. Note that these examples are all carbines; with the typically longer barrel lengths found on rifles, there are many more possibilities for magazine tube variations.

This illustration details the front barrel band and the forend band arrangement on a Model 94 carbine. On later issue carbines (after serials near the 1,100,000 range), the front sight is changed to a ramp and hood style; on these guns the front barrel band will be located behind the front sight. This photo also nicely illustrates the "through screw" of the magazine cap. The reintroduced trapper models from the early 1980s to 2006 will be found with the barrel band in front of the non-ramp (dovetailed) style front sight.

This illustration details the magazine tube retainer and the forend cap used on the Model 94 rifle. Note how the forend cap completely encloses the wood on the end of the forend, unlike the band arrangement of the carbine.

Standard rifles have a retainer and a forend cap to hold the magazine tube in position. The retainer is mounted in a dovetail on the bottom of the barrel and similar to the carbine's band/screw system, there is a pin through the retainer that fits into a corresponding groove on the upper side of the magazine tube to provide additional fore and aft support. The correct position for the retainer is 3-1/2 inches, plus or minus 1/16 inch, from the end of the magazine tube. This measurement should be taken from the forward edge of the cap to the forward edge of the retainer on the bottom side of the magazine tube. Another and even more useful measurement is from the muzzle to the retainer pin. This pin will always be 3-7/8 inches, plus or minus 1/16 inch, from the muzzle. Any deviation greater than this, especially on a shorter-than-standard gun, is definite cause for alarm. On takedown models the retainers are not pinned, and curiously, the cap-to-retainer measurement changes to 3-1/2 inches, plus or minus 1/16 inch, when measured to the rear edge of the retainer. As a rule, only guns with full length magazine tubes have retainers but some Post-64 special issues will be found with short magazines and a retainer. On rifles with much longer than standard barrels and full length magazine tubes (32-36 inches), we will usually find an additional magazine tube retainer. When used, this retainer is positioned exactly midway between the forward retainer and the forend cap.

The rifle type forend cap, which covers the entire end of the forend wood, supports and positions the magazine tube but does not really have a retaining function except on the "true"

button type magazines. (See Part II.)

The magazine tube cap and screw arrangement on rifles follows the same transitional pattern as the carbine, with a "through screw" into a barrel recess appearing at serials around 350,000. On rifles with shorter than standard magazine tubes (except takedown models), the same cap and flange retaining system as the carbine is used.

On takedown rifles with full length magazines, there is no through-pin in the retainer. The pin would have interfered with magazine tube removal during the takedown operataion. The threading of the tube into the corresponding threads in the takedown flange provides security for the tube. This security feature (the threading) is true of the shorter magazine tubes on takedown models as well. There are no threads on the magazine tubes of non-takedown models.

MISCELLANEOUS DATA

All magazine tube length designations – 1/2, 2/3, 3/4, etc. – are approximate. Actual tube length will vary slightly to accommodate the different cartridge lengths of the different calibers. Special length tubes to accommodate a specific number of cartridges or to provide clearance for a silencer were also available on special order and these tubes can be considered the rarest of any tube length if they can be reliably documented. All tube lengths can be found on both solid frame and takedown models.

FULL-LENGTH: Full-length tubes are those which end 1/8 inch from the muzzle on rifles and 1/16 inch from the muzzle on carbines. (See text for exceptions.)

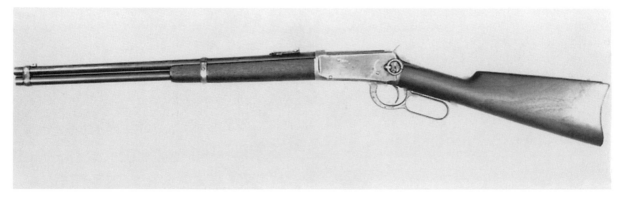

This is Model 1894 carbine serial number 8,949. This very early carbine is caliber 38-55 and is an example of a standard carbine with a full-length magazine tube.

3/4 LENGTH: Tubes that are approximately three-quarters of the length of the barrel on rifles or carbines. This length is quite rare, particularly on full-length rifles. It was unpopular because the long unsupported area between the tube cap and the forend was prone to damage and/or misalignment.

Model 94 carbine serial number 665,850. This specimen is in the rare caliber 32-40, has a three-leaf express rear sight and a rifle style buttstock. It is a fine example of a Model 94 with several unusual features, including the seldom encountered 3/4 length magazine tube.

2/3 LENGTH: Tubes that are approximately two-thirds of the length of the barrel on rifles or carbines. Quite popular in conjunction with all barrel lengths and quite aesthetically pleasing, it will be seen regularly.

Model 94 carbine serial number 944,518. This "eastern carbine" (no saddle ring), in caliber 30 WCF, features a rare shotgun style buttstock with a 4-1/2-inch hard rubber buttplate and the aesthetically pleasing 2/3 length magazine tube.

1/2 LENGTH: Tubes that are approximately half the length of the barrel on rifles or carbines. Popularly called or known as "button" magazines, these tubes can be seen with slightly different amounts of protrusion from the forend cap and two possible methods of retention:

If the magazine protrudes slightly past the forend cap to accommodate a specific cartridge's length, it will be retained by the cap with the flange method. If this slightly extra length is not needed, a special tube cap or button, will be retained by a specially-designed forend cap and is only seen on rifles (see Part II). This particular method is where the term "button mag" originated.

This magazine style is also quite popular on guns of all barrel lengths, although somewhat less so than the two-thirds variant.

Model 94 carbine serial number 1,050,831. This rare carbine in caliber 30 WCF is of the "eastern" (no saddle ring) style. It has the Col. Whelen-designed, fluted comb Model 55 type buttstock and buttplate, and a 1/2 length (sometimes inaccurately called "button") magazine on carbines. True button magazines are found only on solid-frame rifles. (For more information on the Whelen-designed buttstock and buttplate, see Chapter 5.)

HAMMERS

INTRODUCTION

Hammers for the Model 94 follow three basic designs.

Note that hammers used with set triggers have a slightly altered configuration to accommodate the additional parts inherent to the design. These hammers will be found as either a first or second design, and while externally appearing identical to a standard hammer, they are not interchangeable.

FIRST DESIGN

This is called the "split top" or "pointed top" design. It is characterized by having the upper line of the checkering pattern form a definite point, or "widow's peak," extending down into the pattern itself. The bottom line is doubled and slightly curved. This hammer is case colored. Production of this design ceased at serials near 110,000, but these hammers are seen quite regularly above that number. They become very scarce at about the 200,000 range and soon disappear completely. Hammers of this design used in conjunction with the double set trig-

ger system have been seen on guns in much higher serial ranges. Presumably this was due to a fairly large number on hand and a rather low demand factor. This hammer has by far the highest consistency of quality and design repetition of all models.

SECOND DESIGN

The single upper line on this hammer has no point and follows the curve of the hammer itself. The bottom line is also single with a slight curve. It is often noted as the "tombstone" design.

Case colored in the earlier versions, these hammers will be finished as blued starting with serials near 700,000, corresponding somewhat to the change to bluing on the levers. They were still casehardened, but rather than use the color process, they were blued.

Checkering, the border design, and the overall quality of these hammers will differ quite noticeably throughout their period of production. Production and installation of this design ceased rather abruptly with the introduction of the postwar "flatband" model at serials around 1,350,000.

THIRD DESIGN

This hammer design was a completely new concept. The spur had no checkering at all, but had a ribbed or grooved design applied crossways on its entire upper surface. These hammers are always found blued (except on later specially-designated angle eject models, where they are casecolored), and their appearance on the Model 94 corresponds very closely with the introduction of the post-war issues at serials beginning near 1,350,000.

Externally, on assembled guns from serials near 1,300,000 to present, these hammers appear identical; but there are three distinct engineering variants and one cosmetic exception.

TYPE 3A

This version, the earliest, has the same mainspring stirrup arrangement as the first and second design hammer. It is found in serial ranges from 1,350,000 to the end of the pre-64 production (the very early 2,600,000 range).

TYPE 3B

The second version has no stirrup. The mainspring fits into a curved recess in the rear surface of the hammer. It is found from serials beginning at 2,700,000 (post-64) and continues to about 4,580,000.

TYPES 3C, 3D, & 3E

The third version of the third design hammers is really an assembly consisting of the hammer, the trigger, the spring unit and the lower tang and trigger-block system. Within this version there are three variants.

The first style (3c) is a standard non-rebounding type hammer with the half-cock feature and the new coil spring system (approximate serials are 4, 580,000 to 5, 100,000).

The second style (3d) is a design upgrade with the rebound feature (no half-cock) and is used in all models from approximately 5,100,000 to present.

The third style (3e) is merely the addition of a threaded hole in the hammer spur for a screw-in thumb lever. This lever aids in cocking the gun when a telescope is mounted.

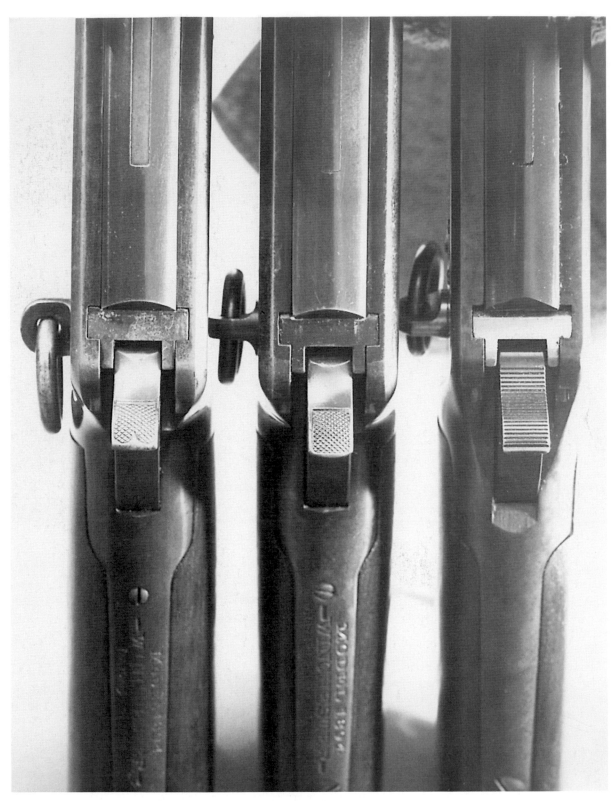

This illustration shows the differences between the first, second and third design hammer spurs (left to right). Note the change in border lines and the size of the checkering between the first and second design hammers, and the use of almost total upper spur coverage with the cross-ribbing of the third design. The upper line of the second design may be doubled on some guns.

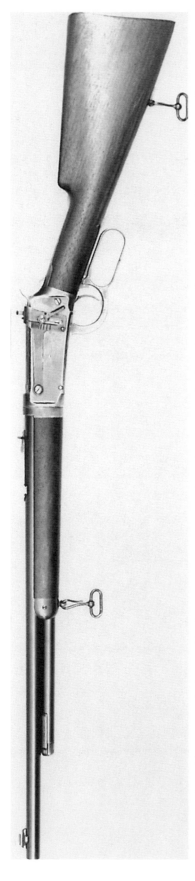

A fine old 30 WCF takedown rifle, this specimen carries serial number 97,869. This heavily optioned example was delivered to the warehouse on Nov. 2, 1900, and shipped the very next day, Nov. 3.

Showing a lot of class and having 9 very well-thought-out special features, this fine old rifle is by far one of my personal favorites. While it definitely shows a lot of normal wear, it shows absolutely no abuse; Winchesters like this, even though not in "mint" condition, are still very rare and important examples. They remain very collectible.

The options include a takedown frame; a 22-inch barrel; an extremely rare 3/4 magazine tube; a Lyman (King's Patent) hunting front sight; a flat-top sporting rear sight; a shotgun buttstock with a smooth steel buttplate, a Model 21 Lyman receiver sight and sling eyes with swivels (factory records indicate that the sling was also included, but unfortunately it has since been removed and lost.) (E. Curtis collection)

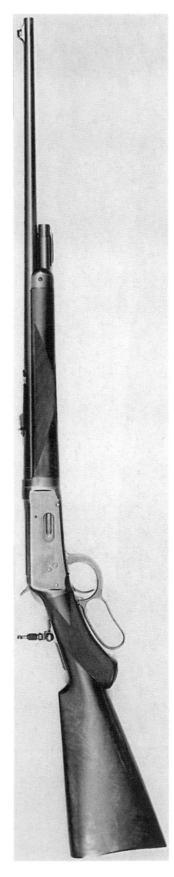

With no fewer than 11 special order features, serial number 49,796 in caliber 30 WCF, is a Model 94 worthy of the most advanced collection. The wood alone (a pistol gripped, XX grade, "H" checkered, shotgun style buttstock with hard rubber buttplate, and oil finish) is actually six separate options.

Remaining are the other special ordered features: the takedown frame; a 24-inch extra light round barrel (two options); a flat-top sporting rear sight, and a Lyman tang sight.

An aesthetic masterpiece, this wonderfully preserved specimen was obviously specially ordered by someone with an eye for beauty and function. This gun was received at the warehouse on Dec. 28, 1898, and shipped on Dec. 29. (W. Hoffman collection)

An illustration of "how it was." This is a faithfully restored standard grade octagon barreled first model caliber 38-55 rifle with serial number 1673. It was no more than a sadly-abused "gray ghost" before it was resurrected. The bore is still nearly non-rifled.

It now has a casecolored receiver, a Beach-style front sight, a rear sight slot filler and a Marble's "Gladstone" rear tang site. It is a fine example of the beauty and craftmanship that was taken for granted for an asking price of about $20 in the late 1800s. Originally assembled on Feb. 4, 1895, and shipped on June 18, it was restored by Doug Turnbull 97 years later in early 1992. (Author's collection)

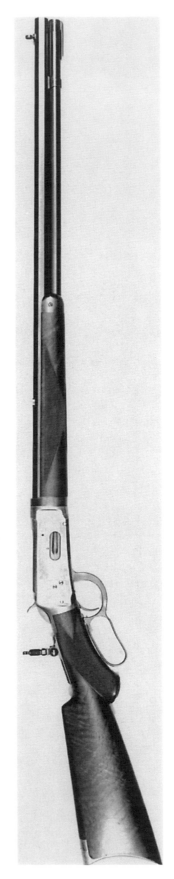

An extreme rarity is this fine Model 94 deluxe takedown rifle, serial number 16,400; it is chambered in the very popular caliber 38-55 and has a 26-inch full octagon barrel and a full length magazine tube. Among its nine special order features is one that is perhaps the most coveted of all Model 94 options: the casehardened (color finished) receiver. This option is about the ultimate rarity in the Model 94. Even with only about five percent of the original receiver finish remaining (you can see the mottled effect in the photograph), this gun is museum documented as originally being a factory casehardened example – therefore it immediately becomes firmly entrenched in the "super collectible" category.

The other optional features include the takedown frame; the pistol gripped, "H" checkered, XXX grade walnut stocks with oil finish (actually four separate options); a Lyman (Beach type) folding or combination front sight; a rear sight slot filler; and a Lyman tang sight.

A wonderful, well documented and ultra rare antique Winchester; it was sent to the warehouse on Oct. 26,1896, and shipped on the same day – the second anniversary of the very first Model 1894 shipped. (G. Coty collection)

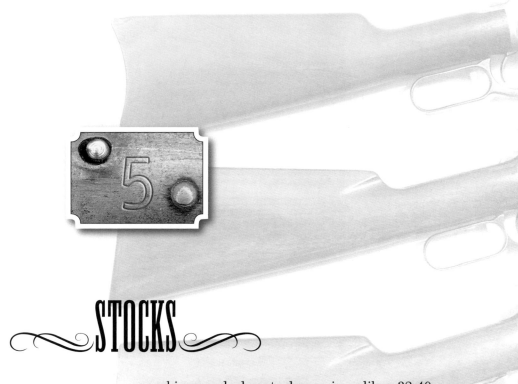

~STOCKS~

INTRODUCTION

Stocks and forends for Model 94 rifles and carbines consist of two separate pieces and will range from the completely standard or "utility" grade, featuring a plain but usually very good grade of walnut, to special order "deluxe" masterpieces that are absolute works of art that even a piano maker would admire – a concert that features the best efforts of man and mother nature. In the absence of the applied talents of a master engraver, nothing can more profoundly enhance the appearance of an otherwise ordinary firearm than a piece of the highest grade wood (the choices are many), carefully designed, flawlessly fitted and lovingly finished by a dedicated craftsman in the tradition usually reserved for a piece of fine furniture.

Walnut, as stated before, is the "usual" wood found on the Model 94, but birch, gumwood and a fairly wide variety of unspecified hardwoods will be encountered with considerable frequency. The appearance of standard stocks made of wood other than walnut has definitely been correlated by year/serial range research to known shortages thereof. Whatever other wood was plentiful at these times quickly became a substitute.

Some specimens found in the 800,000 to 1,000,000 serial range will be found with mismatched wood, the forend being gumwood and the buttstock being walnut. This can also be reversed but such examples are very unusual. This mismatching is almost always found on carbines and almost always in caliber 32-40. There is no definitive explanation for this.

DETAILS & SPECIFICATIONS

Model 94 stocks are based on the dimensions of 1-3/4-inch drop at the comb, 2-1/2 to 2-3/4-inch drop at the heel and a length of pull of 13 to 13-1/4 inches. These dimensions are to be considered nominal with slight variations noted within the different styles. Any dimension could be special-ordered, but any significant variation from the nominal should be verifiable as factory original before considering it collectible.

Stocks will sometimes be found with markings stamped into the inletted areas: EX.LT., 2X, 3X, etc., and many first models have the same number stamped into the buttstock inletting as is found on the right side of the upper tang (see "Receivers" and "Marking" sections). An 11/16-inch hole found behind the buttplate on an occasional Model 94 buttstock was for lightening purposes only and *not necessarily* for use with the rare trapdoor buttplate.

Standard rifles had forends measuring 9-3/8 inches held in place with a steel end cap and buttstocks with a steel crescent buttplate. Buttstocks originally had buttplates with a 1-9/16-inch upper tang, which was reduced to 1-1/2 inches very late in production (serials near 850,000). Short rifles usually had a one inch shorter or 8-3/8-inch forend but standard length forends on short rifles are not uncom-

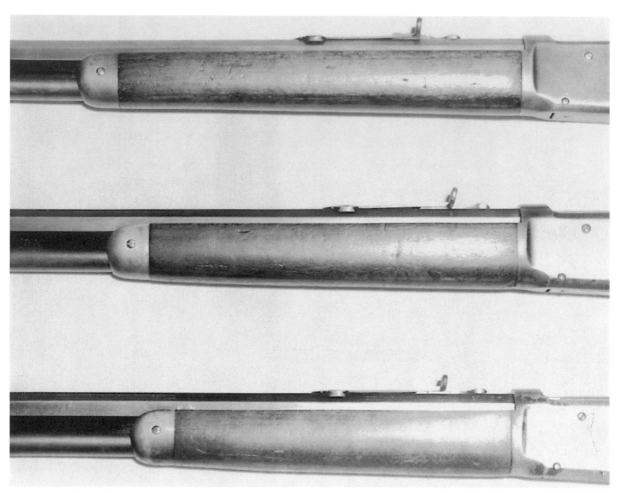

This photo illustrates the difference between the three different forends that can be found on rifles. From top to bottom: the standard length 9-3/8 inches; the 8-3/8 inch short rifle type; and the seldom-seen 7-3/8 inch specimen found only on ultra-short rifles (those with 16-inch or shorter barrels). Note the relative position of the rear sights.

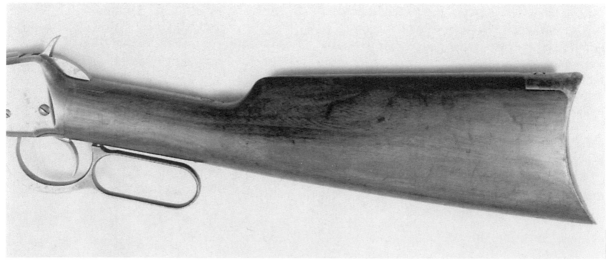

Typical example of a rifle style buttstock. Note the rather sharply contoured crescent buttplate. This type of stock was standard on a rifle and optional at no cost (but still very rare) on a carbine.

mon; those very rare short rifles with extremely short barrels (16 inches) may have forends measuring 7-3/8 inches. Standard buttstocks were of identical configuration and dimensions regardless of barrel length.

Specifications for the wood on standard carbines is somewhat more complicated. The forends of the earlier issues (to serials around 950,000) measure 9-1/8 inches. Beginning near that number and until *approximately* serial 1,790,000, the measurement became 9-1/16 inches. Admittedly, this is a minor difference and through mass production variances and perhaps years of hard use, that 1/16 inch will sometimes be unnoticeable. It is nonetheless a definite manufacturing change, even if only a byproduct of a stock making machinery upgrade.

Somewhere near serial 1,790,000, the forend also underwent a change. It became the "shortwood" forend, first seen on these later versions of the Pre-64 models, and measures 7-15/16 inches. This length remains consistent to present.

Original trapper carbines have forends one inch shorter than standard or 8-1/8 inches.

Note: Some perfectly legitimate 18-inch trapper carbines can have standard 9-1/16-inch or 9-1/8-inch forends, and this seems to follow no rule. It is, in fact, more common to see an 18-inch carbine with a standard length forend than with the shorter variation. Carbines with barrels of 16 inches or less should always have the 8-1/8-inch type.

Some Model 94s were produced in the "musket" configuration. These will be noted to have standard carbine style buttstocks and the long, full-barrel-length, traditional musket style forend. This forend is essentially identical in design to that found on the much more commonly

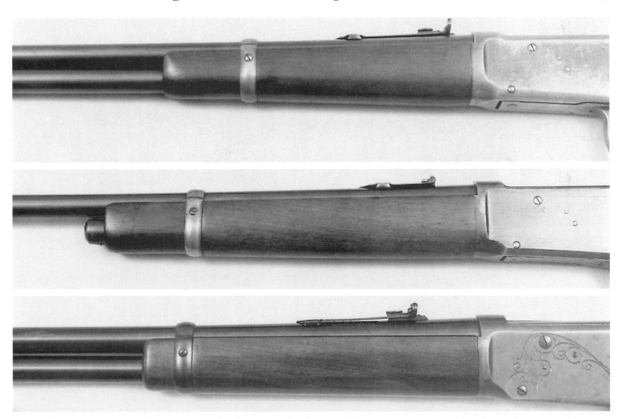

Three types of carbine forends. On the top is the typical 8-1/8-inch trapper carbine forend. As noted in the text, these forends are found on all trapper carbines, with the possible exception of some 18-inch variants. Note the installation and position of the rifle type rear sight on this example. This required the factory to change the position of the dovetail mounting cut to accommodate the extra length of the sight. In the middle is the standard 9-1/8-inch carbine forend. Notable on this example is the (rare on a carbine) 1/2, or "button," magazine and a three-leaf express rear sight. On the bottom is the typical late model (post serials 1,790,000), 7-5/16-inch forend. On this Post-64 example, the rifle type rear sight is standard; note the reversed thumbpiece, 3-C rear sight elevator, and the position of the rear sight.

encountered Model '73 or '92 musket and ends with a metal cap (sometimes including a bayonet lug), about three inches from the muzzle. Depending on the barrel length, the forend may have one or two forend bands. Model 94 muskets are believed to have only been produced "experimentally." There are few available records, and while several specimens have definitely been seen and examined, only one is known to exist in a private collection. Stocks of standard carbines through serials in the 1,100,000 range were of the well known "saddle gun" configuration utilizing the rollover, plain blued steel carbine type buttplate of the previous models.

At or about serial 1,100,000, the stock design was altered to utilize the shotgun style, serrated steel buttplate of the Model 55. Also found within this range (to about serial 1,300,000) will be some buttstocks with a fluted comb. This is the "Col. Whelen" design. Originally designed and designated for the Model 55, this buttstock is often found on the pre-war Model 94. At serials near 1,350,000 we note the appearance of buttstocks designed to utilize the flat steel buttplate with the diagonal checkering that prevailed through approximately 1972. At approximately serial number 1,790,000, the comb design becomes noticeably blunter; this modification closely coincides with the introduction of the 7-15/16-inch forend. After this change, the buttstocks remain essentially the same with only a change of buttplates that did not require a change of wood design to accomplish.

All standard carbine buttstocks, regardless of buttplate design changes, retain the *nominal* measurements of 1-3/4 x 2-1/2 x 13 inches.

Remember: All the above is considered standard.

An amazingly rare "Swiss style" buttstock with a cheekpiece. According to available records, only 37 stocks with cheekpieces and only 214 stocks with Swiss buttplates were produced up to serial 353,999, after which point the records are nonexistent. There is no record of how many were produced with both features. (Author photo)

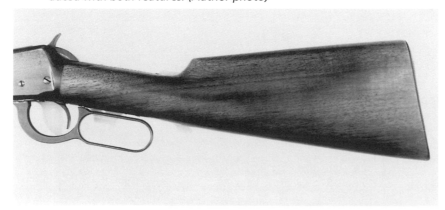

A stock of this design is found on guns in the same serial range as the bottom example in the following illustration. This is the much more commonly encountered non-fluted version and is also fitted with the Model 55 buttplate.

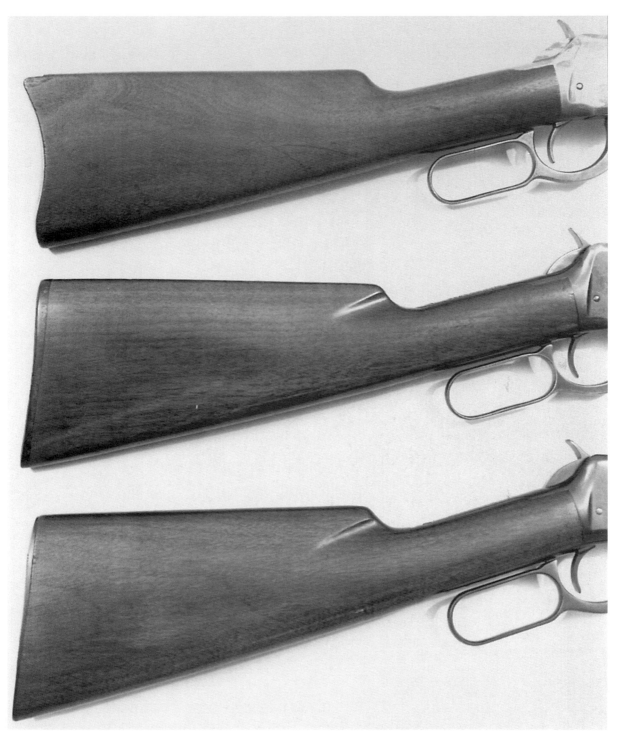

Three early types of carbine buttstocks. On top is the typical saddle ring carbine buttstock used until serials around 1,000,000. Note the rolled-over buttplate and the flatness of the upper edge or "comb" area of this stock. These stocks were a no-cost option on rifles, but are considered rare if verified as original. In the middle is the quite rare special-order semi-shotgun style buttstock, using the smaller, 4-1/2-inch hard rubber buttplate. Also noted on this example is the "fluted comb" design inspired by Col. Townsend Whelen. On the bottom is an example of the pre-war style buttstock (serials to approximately 1,300,000) using the Model 55 style buttplate. The Whelen flutes are evident on this example also. These fluted versions are rarely seen on a Model 94; they were designed by Whelen for the Model 55. Flutes were later incorporated on the pistol-gripped stocks of the Model 64.

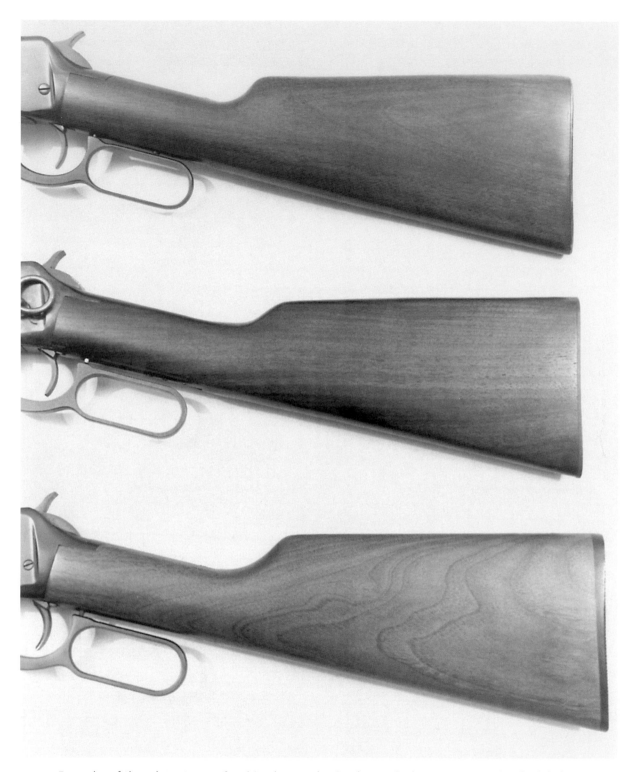

Examples of three later types of carbine buttstocks. On the top is the post-war version (serials from 1,350,000 to near 1,950,000). It has a flat steel, checkered buttplate and a sharply contoured front comb area. The center example is the blunt comb style of basically the same stock, also having the same type of buttplate. These stocks will appear near serials of 1,790,000 and will continue to approximately 3,500,000 but are largely seen as phenolic rather than steel after serial 3,000,000. The lower example is of the 2006-vintage model buttstock, with a noticeably sharpened comb and a plastic, "logo-style" buttplate.

OPTIONS

The option list for stocks on both rifles and carbines is very long. Available on special order were several grades of finishes, eight cataloged checkering and carving patterns, and one uncataloged pattern (the commonly encountered "I"checkering that was the least extensive and the least expensive). Customers could even submit a hand-drawn pattern specifying their own design, and the choice of wood was nearly limitless in either species or grade.

Walnut density is very inconsistent and is often dictated/affected by the original geographical location of the source trees. The walnut used pre-war came from different areas of the United States than did the post-war variety. Pre-war walnut, as noted on several Winchester models, is much denser and tighter grained than the post-war counterpart; this is easily noticed by comparing the weight of the pre-war/post-war stocks and observing the finer checkering applied to pre-war examples of deluxe guns.

Wood grading was achieved by a rather complicated system of comparing the density of the wood, the color/contrast of the grain, the flow of the grain, and the final fit and finish. Allowable tolerances in wood to metal fit were greatly reduced as the grade increased. Grading was designated in steps, from a high of 4X and 5X, which were considered presentation grades, through 3X, 2X, 1X, fancy grain, and standard. Designations may be a series of Xs rather than numbers.

Almost any kind of firearm-suitable wood could be special ordered.

WOOD FINISHING

The standard wood finishing method was a type of varnish. There was also an optional finish using varnish, called "extra finish." This consisted of some extra care in the grain filling and polishing of the wood, and an additional coat or two of varnish, hand-rubbed with steel wool between the coats.

Another option was the "oil finishing" method, with either a high gloss or a satiny glow as the end result. Very popular and very beautiful, the oil finish was used regularly on the higher grades of wood for deluxe or special order guns. Various combinations of tung and linseed oil and various driers and coloring agents were all part of the formulas, and a lot of extra care and labor was required to both prepare the wood and properly apply the finish.

Stocks were finely sanded and carefully scraped with a special tool, absolutely assuring smoothness. A coloring agent and grain filling mixture, usually an oil made from crushed walnut shells, was rubbed into the wood, allowed to dry, and rubbed smooth with fine steel wool. Several coats of the tung oil and linseed oil for-

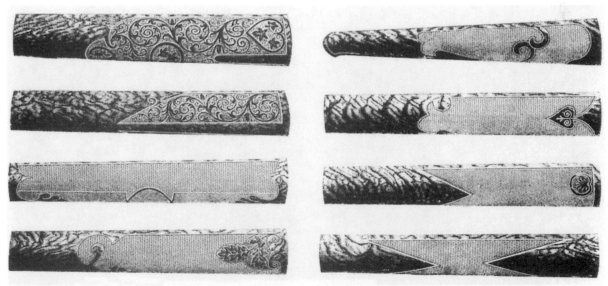

Styles of Carving and Checking Stocks and Forearms for Winchester World Standard Rifles and Shotguns. Prices: A -$160.00; B - $113.00; C - $80.50; D- $64.50; E - $39.00; F and G - $$34.00; H - $7.75.

This panel, taken from an early Winchester catalog, shows the eight cataloged checkering styles offered by the factory as extra cost options. The price, of course, varied according to the style.

This is an example of a typical straight grip shotgun-style buttstock. It has a smooth steel, five-inch shotgun buttplate; also noted is an original, factory installed, Winchester sling eye.

A finer example of a pistol gripped and capped, style "H" checkered shotgun buttstock would be hard to find. This example is of "XX" grade walnut (the lower tang is marked accordingly), and has the five-inch checkered hard rubber buttplate with Winchester logo. Note the Lyman tang mounted rear sight: a popular option, and very complementary to a fine "deluxe grade" gun.

mula were then applied, and rubbed with the hands between those applications until the desired result was achieved. If the high gloss type finish was specified, more driers would be added to the mixture, resulting in the somewhat harder and shinier finish.

The highest grades of wood usually got the most attention. Winchester had standards, but they were only minimum standards – there was no upper limit to achieving perfection. Judging from the unsurpassed quality of the fit and finish of the stocks on most high grade guns,

some "overachieving" must have resulted from the inspiration of working with such beautiful pieces of walnut.

These were the years of the truly dedicated craftsman, and deluxe guns are often seen with years of hard but careful use behind them, and with the stocks still showing the inherent beauty of the walnut and the uncompromising skill of the finisher.

Until just after World War I, Winchester employed the use of outside contractors to accomplish many of the more specialized manufactur-

A rare option indeed is this pistol gripped and capped style "H" checkered crescent type buttstock. This example is on an unbelievably rare, deluxe takedown rifle, with an authenticated case colored receiver. The lower tang is marked "XXX." Faint case coloring can be seen on the portions of the receiver and buttplate visible in this photo. Again we find a Lyman tang-mounted rear sight on a deluxe gun.

ing operations, and wood finishing was one of them. These contractors (there could be more than one at any given time) kept most of their formulas and methods a closely-guarded secret. While still adhering closely to Winchester's corporate standards, there was sufficient leeway for slight differences in color and final luster. Even the time of the year (temperature and humidity) played a role in promoting a need for the use of different formulas. Hot and humid weather, for example,would naturally require the use of different drying agents in the formulation than hot and dry weather, or cold and wet weather, etc. Admittedly, these differences were slight; so slight that over the years on all but the most pristine specimens, they will be virtually undetectable.

Shortly after World War I, Winchester began employing its own specialists in wood finishing. The formulas became uniform, and noticeable variations in either color or quality became essentially nonexistent throughout the line.

Non-standard buttstock configuration was also a very popular option. Available at the customer's request were carbine buttstocks on rifles, rifle buttstocks on carbines, pistol grip stocks, straight stocks, stocks with cheekpieces, and stocks with custom measurements. The combinations were almost infinite and were largely left to the imagination and the pocketbook of the customer.

POST-64

Post-64 buttstocks retained the standard blunt-combed semi-shotgun style that developed near serial number 1,790,000. Nominal measurements prevailed at 1-3/4 x 2-1/2 x 13 inches, and most were still made of a very nice grade of walnut. While there was again some experimentation with other hardwoods in the early to mid-'70s, this proved largely unsatisfactory and was soon discontinued in all but the Ranger line. Later issues with genuine walnut stocks were identified with a decal in most cases.

In the mid-1980s laminated stocks became available and are known as Win-tuff or Wincam, depending on the color. The Wintuff stock is of a more or less natural wood color, while the Wincam version is a greenish, camouflage-like shade.

Buttplates evolved as mentioned elsewhere, and checkering again became available with the introduction of the XTR model; actually, on the XTR model it was standard.

The forends for all models, including the lately resurrected rifle and trapper models, are of the carbine type; they retain the 7-15/16-inch measurement but are still not inletted into the face of the receiver.

Overall quality improved from an all-time low in the late '60s/early '70s, to a rather more than satisfactory look and feel at present.

Stocks, forends and buttplates of the commemorative models follow no rules as to patterns or styles of checkering, grades of wood, or shapes and dimensions, other than those designated within their respective series. See Trolard (*Winchester Commemoratives*).

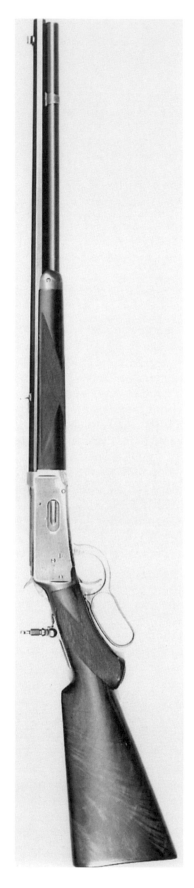

Deluxe short rifles are very rare. This beautiful example, serial number 85,816, in caliber 30 WCF, is perhaps one of the most aesthetically pleasing of all combinations. A highly optioned (nine options) specimen, the features include a 22-inch extra light (rapid taper) full octagon barrel (this is two separate options – note also the short forend wood); a pistol gripped, "H" checkered, XX grade, shotgun style buttstock with hard rubber buttplate and oil finish (five separate options), a folding rear sight with white insert and a Lyman tang sight.

Received at the warehouse on June 20, 1900, it was shipped on June 21. (W. Hoffman collection)

An odd Model 94 indeed. This is one of the 30 or so known to exist 20-inch barreled model 95 barreled variants, number 1,027,124 (note the rifle type magazine tube retainer). These are colloquially termed the "94/95" model. It also includes a very unusual set of sights. There's a Parker Hale "globe" sight complete with interchangeable apertures in the front dovetail, and a very rare Lyman combination sight on the tang. The rear sight slot has been filled.

Though obviously not a factory installation (there are elevator marks from the original rear sight on the barrel top), one must marvel at how such an unusual set of sights would somehow get installed on such an extremely rare gun. Did the installer/owner know what he was creating? Probably not. (W. Raymond collection)

BUTTPLATES AND GRIPCAPS

INTRODUCTION

Buttplates and gripcaps used on the Model 94 are basically similar and sometimes identical to those used on previous/other models – the few differences noted will usually be in the dimensions, materials used, and the logo changes.

ROLLOVER TYPE

This is the common carbine buttplate but can occasionally be found on rifles as a special order feature. Dimensionally identical to that ofthe Model 92, it is made of steel and will be blued on all but the earliest specimens where case coloring can be seen. Plating of different types was a possible alternative but this feature is very rare. Plated buttplates alone should be examined with the utmost skepticism; this option was usually combined with other parts being plated as well.

There also was a trap-door option avail-able with a drilled-out compartment to house a cleaning rod assembly. On all Model 94s (especially those with a carbine buttplate), this is no less than an extreme rarity and definitely special order. If reliably documented, this will add considerably to the value of the piece (especially if the cleaning rod is still inside).

CRESCENT TYPE

This is the common rifle buttplate of which there are two distinct versions:

Early version: To serials around 750,000; has a 1-9/16-inch upper tang.

Later version: Has a 1-1/2-inch upper tang.

All other features and options are the same as those on the rollover type.

Crescent buttplates are fairly common as a special order on carbines but only have value as a collectible if factory documented or otherwise reliably appraised as original to the gun.

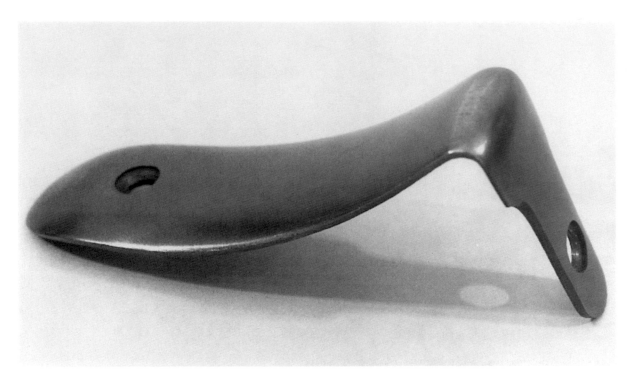

This is the style of buttplate typical to a carbine. Note the rounded contour where the wide, flattened upper flange or "rollover" portion begins. These buttplates are found in basically identical form on all models of Winchester carbines and muskets. They were also available as an option on rifles.

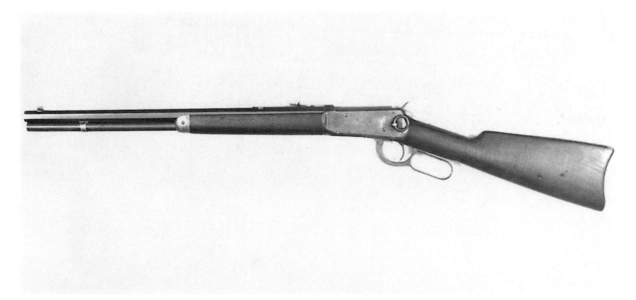

Model 94 rifle serial number 860,614, caliber 30 WCF. This very rare rifle has several interesting and unusual features. It has a six-inch shorter-than-standard, 20-inch full octagon barrel with the correspondingly shorter 8-3/8-inch forend. It was also ordered with a flat-top sporting rear sight, a saddle ring (very unusual on a rifle) and has a carbine style buttstock.

While essentially identical in length to a standard carbine, this rifle was apparently special ordered by someone who wanted all the features of a carbine, but also wanted the extra heft provided by the much heavier rifle barrel. Twenty-inch short rifles are seen fairly frequently, but this combination of features makes this specimen especially unique.

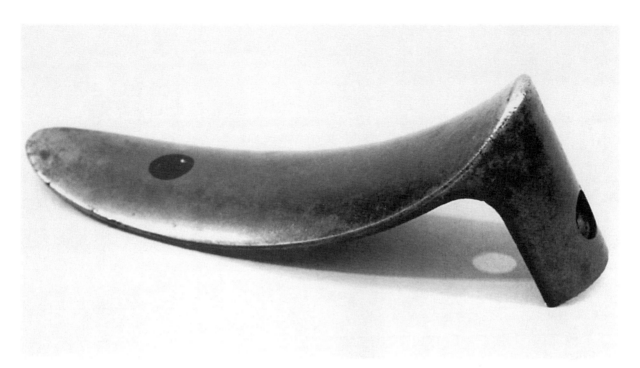

This is the typical rifle style buttplate. Note how the upper flange is more rounded than that of the carbine, and how the shape of the crescent is not interrupted by a rollover. This style of buttplate is common to all Winchester rifles and was available as an option on carbines.

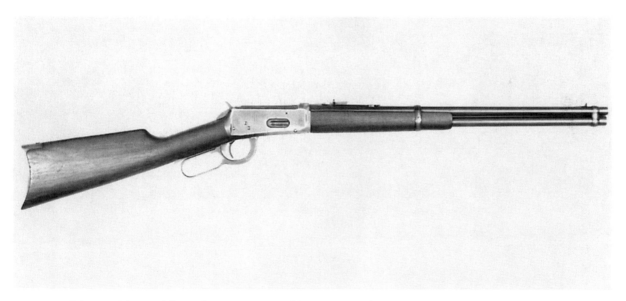

Model 94 carbine serial number 968,515 in caliber 30 WCF. This interesting specimen, while appearing to be nothing more than a standard carbine with a rifle style buttstock, displays several unusual features. The receiver is of the eastern (no saddle ring) style, it has a flat-top sporting rear sight, and was fitted with a higher than normal sight blade mounted in the original front sight post. Additionally, the factory found that the installation of the large sporting rear sight would result in the partial obliteration of the upper barrel markings. Consequently, these markings were moved to a position forward of the forend as seen on the earlier trapper models. Note how all these discrepancies (rifle buttstock/rifle sights/no saddlering/unusual barrel marking position), when seen in concert, point convincingly to a rare and unusual factory original.

SHOTGUN TYPE

This style of buttplate is found on both rifles and carbines in concert with the special order shotgun style buttstock. It is not the most common of the varieties, but it has by far the most variations within its own designation. Let's examine this most interesting option. Here are the variations:

A) Smooth steel, checkered steel or checkered hard rubber, with a slight pointed rollover portion onto the heel of the buttstock, the rubber version usually having a Winchester logo in the center. The trapdoor feature was available in the steel versions but is extremely rare.

B) Serrated steel, five inches, Model 55 style.

C) Serrated steel, 4-3/4 inches, Model 55 style.

D) Hard rubber, checkered with Winchester logo, five inches, no rollover.

E) Hard rubber, checkered with Winchester logo, 4-3/4 inches, no rollover.

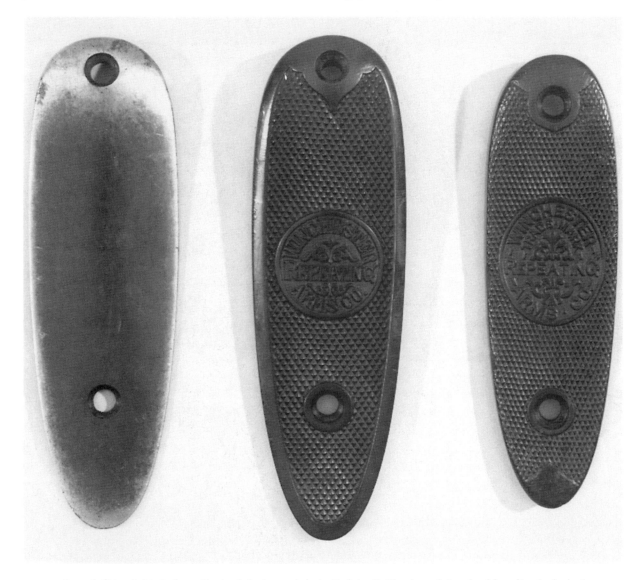

From left to right: 1. Smooth steel shotgun style buttplate. 2. Checkered, hard rubber five-inch shotgun style buttplate with logo. 3. Checkered, hard rubber 4-1/2-inch shotgun style buttplate with logo; used on some pre-war carbines.

F) Hard rubber, checkered with Winchester logo, 4-1/2 inches, no rollover – pre-war carbine.

G) Checkered flat steel, early World War II to early Post-64.

H) Checkered phenolic (same style and dimensions as the "flat" steel), mid Post-64.

I) Hard rubber (plastic) logo type (Winchester), late Post-64.

J) Hard rubber (plastic) logo type (USRAC).

K) Red rubber cushion type with logo, (Winchester), used on BigBore.

L) Red rubber cushion type with logo, (US-RAC), used on BigBore with Angle Eject.

SWISS STYLE

The cast, pronged, "Schuetzen" type buttplate. These are usually made of brass, nickel plated and may have an upper prong only, a lower prong only, or both. These buttplates, while closely resembling a "Schuetzen" type

From left to right: 1. Model 55 style, serrated steel buttplate used on pre-war/post-transitional carbines – 4-3/4 or 5-inches. 2. Flat checkered steel buttplate of the postwar or "Pre-64" carbines (actually in use through the mid/late 1960s until the same design made of phenolic plastic was adopted). 3. Checkered, hard rubber 4-3/4-inch shotgun style buttplate with logo.

Typical example of the cap used on most versions of the pistol-grip style buttstock. Note the use of a nicely decorated screw in the installation of this example. These decorative screws were also often used in attaching the buttplates on deluxe guns, but as with the grip caps, this practice follows no rule and the engraving style varies. The screws could also be blank.

plate, have shorter prongs and are generally less radical in design. An extremely rare special order feature on any Winchester – most unusual and valuable when documented to a Model 94.

RECOIL PADS

Recoil absorbing pads were available on special order on any Model 94. These were usually supplied from the factory with a Winchester logo but any available brand would be installed on request. Original Winchester pads on the Model 94 are very rare and especially hard to find with "condition."

CUSTOM

Almost any type of pad or plate could be made on special order to the customer's request/design.

GRIPCAPS

Gripcaps were made of hard rubber, had a Winchester logo and usually were fastened with decorative screws. In the Model 94 "family," the only pistol-gripped buttstocks that are uncapped are those on the standard Model 64 and some commemoratives. Inlays or caps made of any other material are definitely special order. As with buttplates, any custom features of the gripcap was per the customer's request/design.

Note: When a gripcap is used with a shotgun type buttstock, most often the gun will be found to have a hard rubber buttplate matching the design of the cap. The buttplate also may or may not be fastened with decorative screws.

A close-up illustration of the extremely rare and desireable "Swiss style" buttplate. Only 214 are noted in the available records. These are found in either original brass finish or plated with various other metals. (Author photo)

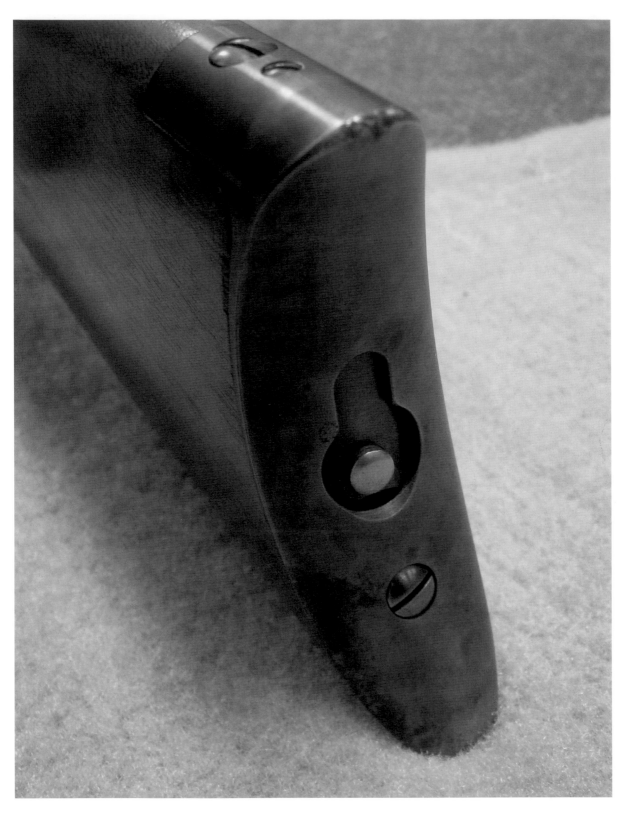

A fine illustration of the 'trapdoor" feature on a rifle-style buttplate. As mentioned elsewhere, this was used to house a multi-piece cleaning rod assembly. This is an extremely rare find on a Model 1894/94. (Klein photo)

A carbine-style buttplate with the trapdoor version. This is even more scarce on the Model 1894/94 than on the rifle type. (Klein photo)

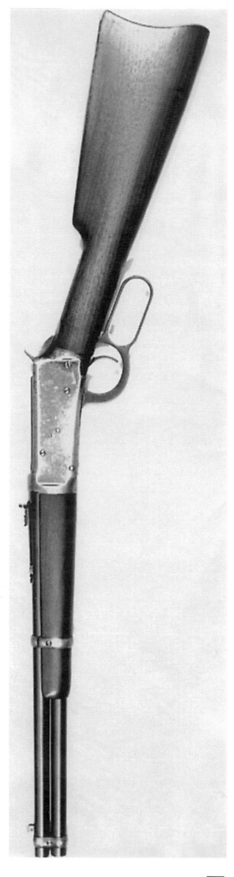

A very interesting trapper model with a 15-inch barrel is serial number 1,090,460. This is an extremely high serial number for a trapper with a barrel length of under 16 inches (carbines/rifles with barrels of under 16 inches were no longer manufactured and were not legal to own after the implementation of the 1934 National Firearms Act. This serial corresponds to late 1933/early 1934).

This specimen is the second highest serial numbered trapper model with a barrel length of under 16 inches to be certified by the BATFE as being originally manufactured in the short configuration, and is now redefined as a legal-to-own "curio and relic." This specimen shows all the "transitional" changes contemporary to its date of manufacture. It has a rifle type rear sight in the pre-war sight location of 3-1/16 inches from the receiver, but since it is a trapper, it does not have the ramp with hood front sights; it is in caliber 30 WCF (later trapper models, those with 15-inch barrels in particular, are commonly found in 30 caliber); it has no saddle ring and has the correct pre-war style barrel markings. It also has the typical, short 8-1/8-inch forend and a beautiful buttstock of perfectly straight-grained, quarter-sawn walnut.

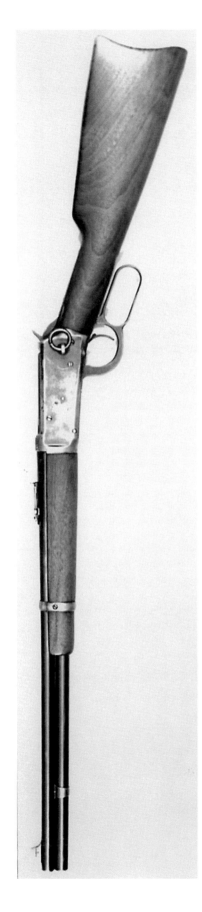

Featuring a nicely grained buttstock, carbine number 1,033,422 is one of only about 30 of this variant known to exist. This is the 20-inch barreled version of the "Model 94/95" variation.

Of these 30 examples, only 9 have ramp front sights with pinned blades, and this is one of them. Two of the seven 21-3/4-inch specimens have ramps with dovetails; all the remaining 20-inch examples have ramps with dovetails.

Except for the unusual front sight and the rifle style magazine retainer, this gun appears to be a completely standard saddle ring carbine. Its existence in this configuration is not definitively explained. (Author's collection)

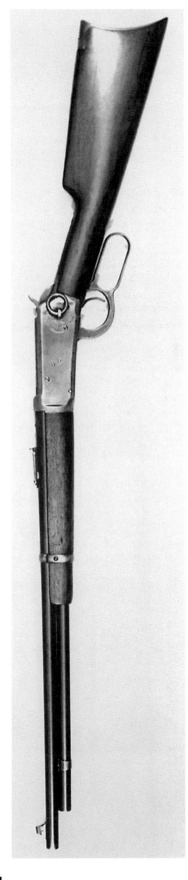

One of only 9 known to exist, carbine number 1,032,618 features the mysterious 21-3/4-inch barrel that is reputed to be a modified Model 95 NRA musket barrel. Note the rifle style magazine tube retainer. This is also the only one of the seven examples to have a rifle type buttstock. The magazine tube, while appearing to be shortened, is in reality a standard length carbine tube. Also note the unusual ramp front sight and pinned blade arrangement (most ramp style sights have a dovetail for the blade). Assembled around 1927/28, these four guns and about 30 known 20-inch versions have been highly researched and closely examined; however, no conclusive answers are forthcoming. (Author's collection)

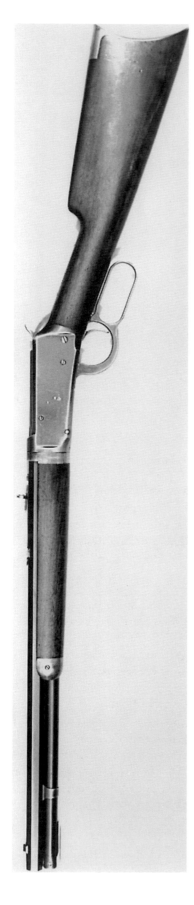

This is a very unusual and extremely rare rifle, even though it has only two special order features. Serial number 419,783, in caliber 30 WCF, has the takedown option and the seldom encountered 19-inch barrel length. Odd numbered barrel lengths of any Winchester are very rare, and on a rifle with a barrel length of under 20 inches, it is even more unusual. This fine example is standard in every other way. Notable is the shorter 8-1/8-inch forend common to most short rifles and the altered position of the rear sight (see Chapter 2).

An extreme rarity is serial number 288,514. This is a museum documented, 18-inch barreled, takedown rifle in caliber 30 WCF.

Also notable is the long, 9-1/8-inch forend that is less common on short rifles and the shotgun style buttstock with hard rubber buttplate. The sights are the standard rifle type.

Although the finish on this example is very worn from many years of service (there are 40 "notches" cut into the rubber around the perimeter of the buttplate), it was apparently well maintained and is still mechanically excellent. Model 94s with barrels of 18 inches are rarities in the extreme and considerably more so in a takedown rifle – this example, in "condition" or not, is a highly desirable collectible.

Number 288,514 was received in the warehouse on Jan. 30, 1906, and shipped on April 13, 1906.

MARKINGS

INTRODUCTION

The reader should by now have a good grasp of the many facts and facets of mass production. Remember the inevitability of overlaps in the introduction/discontinuance of engineering changes, and notice the gradual introduction of most new features. By all means, don't be too hasty in discounting as incorrect any unexplained variances that you will surely find. These variances commonly occur in all phases of the mass manufacturing process.

The "overlap rule" has never been more important to consider than when studying markings. The possibility of a discrepancy is greatly magnified by the fact that a great many parts, each possibly having more than one type of marking, are chosen for assembly from separate parts bins that may have been replenished at very different times.

Fortunately, standard grade Model 94s were produced in such quantity that there were very few old parts left to mix with the new parts, thus the discrepancy periods are usually rather short.

Special order guns, however, may have been assembled with unpopular or otherwise unusual parts that have been lying unused for years: odd barrel lengths, set triggers, the additional barrels for multi-barrel sets, etc. These items will often be found assembled on a receiver whose serial number does not necessarily coincide with the barrel markings, the hammer design or whatever. These specimens may very well be absolutely correct, but they most assuredly warrant a very close and very careful examination.

When examining any Winchester for possible acquisition, try to officially verify (with a museum/factory letter or a note from the original owner) all the options. Unfortunately, at times this is impossible, and you must rely solely on your experience to ascertain authenticity. This can be a very nerve-wracking experience, especially on the very expensive specimens.

Remember, go slowly and look carefully; let your experience guide you. While you may find many things on many guns which cannot be proven as correct, don't be overly hasty in making your decision. They may not be able to be proven as incorrect either. Keep a keen eye and an open mind – study the big picture – you may find a real "one off." There are plenty of them out there.

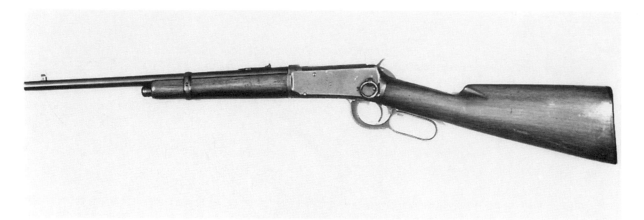

A wonderful example of a very rare, very unusual and seemingly 100 percent correct (albeit possibly factory re-barreled) 16-inch trapper carbine. If it was originally a trapper model, we will never know with absolute certainty; the serial number 887,084 is much too high to research. It does, however, have a 16-inch barrel at present, and some of the details noted while examining this gun are very interesting; actually they are rather astounding. Note: This gun has never been refinished and all the parts match in overall condition perfectly. Here are the details. The barrel on this specimen is in the very rare 16-inch length and is perfectly slotted for both the 1/2 magazine tube cap and the forend band screw. It also has the extremely rare August 14th "error" patent date in the barrel marking, which on this barrel is found just forward of the forend band.

In having the error date feature, this barrel had to be manufactured at least 15 years before the receiver. "Error date" barrels are found on guns with serials in the mid-300,000 to the early 400,000 range, corresponding to a manufacturing date of 1906/07, and this receiver with serial number 887,084 corresponds to a manufacturing date of about 1921.

In having the factory cut for the magazine cap and the forend band screw in the correct position to correspond with the short trapper forend, and to have the barrel markings forward of the forend band, it is undoubtedly an original trapper barrel. Could this barrel have been in stock for all those years before installation? Apparently it was. (If the gun is in fact a re-barrel, the barrel was probably in stock for even a longer period. The barrel also has a proofmark. Barrels this early may or may not be proofed, but this proofmark is also in a position befitting the likely era of the barrel – alongside the caliber designation. The receiver is not double proofed!

While there is a remote possibility that this is a re-barrel (if it is, it was definitely done by the factory), I feel this specimen was originally ordered as it appears: a 30 WCF, 16-inch barreled trapper model with a 1/2 magazine, three-bladed express rear sight and the smaller style shotgun buttstock with a hard rubber buttplate. The barrel was pulled from older existing stock at the time of assembly, and incredibly, just happened to be one of the very rare error date barrels.

This is the only trapper model known to exist with the incorrect Aug. 14 patent date.

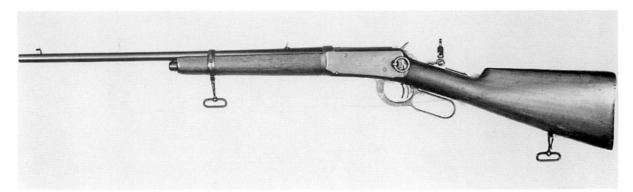

A rare and very collectible saddle ring carbine with six special order features. Specimen number 444,099 is a nicely optioned, caliber 32 Special example, with a list of extras that includes the extremely rare double-set trigger. Model 94s with set triggers are all considered rare, but to find this option on a carbine is indeed unusual. Additionally noted on this tastefully personalized specimen are a button-style magazine; a folding rear sight with white inlay; a Lyman tang mounted sight; a shotgun-style buttstock with a smooth steel buttplate; and sling swivels in original Winchester "eyes." (Author's collection)

A receiver close-up of serial number 444,099, showing some detail of the set trigger assembly (note the adjusting screw behind the rear trigger), and a nice illustration of the Lyman tang sight.

A. RECEIVER: SERIAL NUMBERS

All Model 94 serial numbers on pre-angle eject models (this includes the Model 55 and the Model 64) are placed on the lower part of the receiver between the forend and the lever link. At the introduction of the angle eject model, the serials were relocated to the lower left rail of the receiver next to the link. The numbering sequence was not disturbed when making this change.

Serial numbers begin with number 1, are consecutive and in the earliest versions the numbers are 5/32 inch in height and relatively lightly stamped. At serials in the very early 100,000 range, the size of the numbers decreases noticeably to 1/8 inch and at serials near 1,000,000 they are again reduced – to 7/64 inch.

This size remains in use. The depth of the stamping of all Model 94 serial numbers is

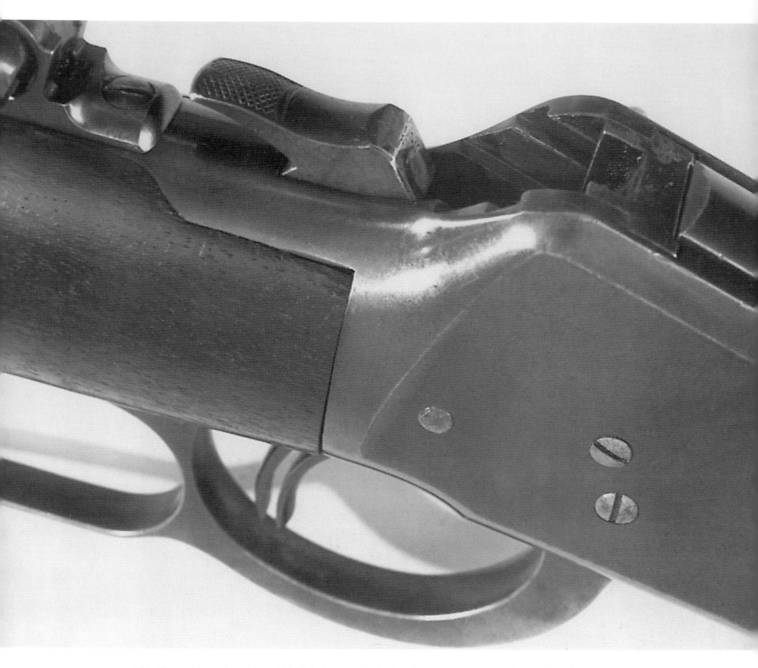

This illustration of number 444,099 shows clearly that in very rare cases, the early style hammer can be found on a gun that has a relatively high serial number. Note that the checkering on the hammer spur is of the first design, or "pointed top" style. These hammers are seldom seen in guns with numbers beyond the mid-100,000 range. This particular hammer is peculiar to the set trigger assembly, and the set trigger option is rarely ordered; apparently the entire trigger/hammer assembly sat in the parts bins for about 10 years before being ordered and installed on this gun.

somewhat variable and on many examples near the 100,000 range, the number 1, when used, appears to be inverted.

If a gun was returned to the factory for rework or refinish and the serial number was worn away or otherwise indiscernible, the factory would apply a "W.R.A. CO." or "WRACO" stamping to the area where the serial had originally been. This was also done at times to guns in need of a new receiver but most often these examples were returned with the later serial number that was on the receiver they pulled from stock.

This "W.R.A. CO." stamping practice effectively curtailed the fraudulent sale of refinished guns as new by unscrupulous dealers.

Note: Some Model 55s and all Model 64s are serial numbered into the Model 94 sequence.

This illustration shows the original 5/32-inch numbering style that was used for serials into the very early 100,000 range. Note what appears to be an inverted number (1) and the rather shallow "strike" of the numbering die.

This is the second style of serial number with the size changed to 1/8 inch. This type of numbering was used from serials beginning in the 100,000s and continued into the very late 900,000 range. Note the considerably heavier indentation of the numbers.

An illustration of the numbering style used from serials in the late 900,000 range to the introduction of the angle eject model. The size of the numbers is now 7/64 inch.

The pre-angle eject "BigBore" serial marking. The size and location of the numbers are the same as those on standard models, but the numbers have their own sequence and the "BB" prefix.

Very early examples of the angle eject BigBore series will also be found with the serial numbers in this location but prefixed by "AE" (serials from AE10001 to AE19000). This system was soon revised, and all angle eject specimens, including the BigBore models are now numbered sequentially in the original 94 series.

The style and location of the serial numbers since the introduction of the angle eject models. The size of the numbers remains the same as the previous models at 7/64 inch.

This is a fine specimen of what is commonly referred to as a serial number with inverted ones. Often encountered in serials near this range (note the illustration of serial 85,816), this is merely an example of the wearing out of the numbering dies. The upper "flag" on the number one has either broken off or worn off, and thus the number appears inverted.

As previously mentioned, the numbering size was changed at or about this serial range; this necessitated the use of new dies and the problem was solved.

B. RECEIVER: ASSEMBLY NUMBERS

Very early (first or second model) Model 94s will often, though not always, be found with numbers in the inverted position on the right side of the upper tang. These are always one-, two-, or three-digit numbers. Most people familiar with this unusual occurence have convinced themselves that these are in fact assembly numbers. I'm not so sure.

Assembly, rework and wood grading numbers or marks are usually found only on deluxe guns (the inverted numbers are found on standard guns as well as deluxe examples), and are almost always found on the left side of the lower tang but have been noted on the left upper tang; also, assembly numbered marks are not inverted.

These numbers have not been determined to follow any particular sequence, and quite often, but again not always, the same number will be found stamped in the upper tang inletting area of the buttstock. This practice could easily lead one to believe that these are in fact assembly numbers, but the prevailing explanations (or lack thereof) do not allow me to state this as indisputable.

As with the earlier Winchester models, the Model 94 as a deluxe or special order gun will often be found with assembly numbers and/or wood grading marks. Reworked guns may also have assembly numbers, and reworked deluxe guns will often be found with several sets of assembly numbers. Most often when encountering a gun with more than one set of assembly numbers, the previous set will be X'd out and only the latest numbers will remain unmarred. Occasionally, numbers may be found on some internal parts. These are usually an indication of a reworked gun and are most often stamped on the hidden surfaces of the lever, hammer and bolt.

Winchester was known to occasionally apply a second stamping of the serial number on the inside of the upper tang; this is extremely rare. Equally as rare is the word "refinished" found stamped in this location.

Along with the serial number, the proofmark and the upper tang markings, the only other visible markings on an assembled and stocked receiver would be the fitter's markings. (After serial numbers in the 4,500,000 range, receivers no longer carry a proofmark; only the barrel is proofed.)

Parts for Winchesters, mass-produced and proclaimed interchangeable, still required a certain amount of "fitting and filing." This critical phase of production not only assured perfect mechanical operation, but was also paramount in maintaining the highest degree of aesthetic quality. These are the reference marks made by the men who assured that quality.

Technically, these markings are not on the

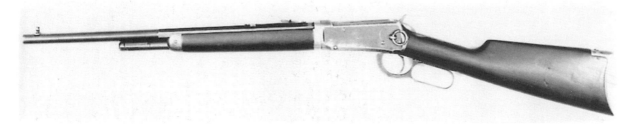

A rare and very unusual takedown rifle. Specially ordered by someone who knew precisely what he wanted, serial number 879,368 has now become a collector's prize. It has seven optional features that when found in concert make this specimen an absolutely outstanding oddity. Chambered in caliber 38-55 (which itself is rare in short rifles), this gem is a 20-inch barreled takedown short rifle, with the barrel in the half-round, half-octagon style; this style is especially rare in barrels as short as 20 inches. It also has a Beach combination folding front sight, a flat-top style sporting rear sight, a 2/3 length magazine tube, and a saddle ring.

While it is highly unusual to see a saddle ring installed on any rifle, it is even more of a rarity when seen in combination with a rifle style buttstock, as seen here – rifles with saddle rings are almost always short rifles and are almost always found in combination with a carbine style buttstock.

This particular specimen epitomizes the short, easy to carry, fast pointing, hard hitting, lever action sporting rifle.

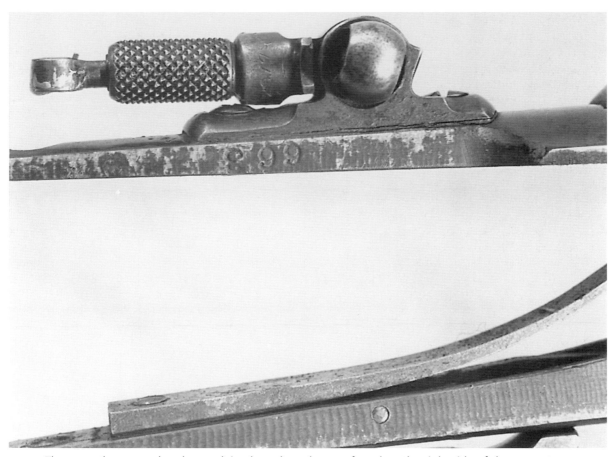

These are the unusual and unexplained numbers that are found on the right side of the upper tang on most first model Model 94s. Note that they are inverted. These numbers (663) are on a standard, round-barreled 38-55 rifle, serial number 764. Some first model takedown versions will also have this number on the forend side of the takedown flange. Some numbers are NOT inverted.

Also illustrated is a rather finely detailed shot of a Lyman "combination" tang sight. The combination type sight is notable by the hinged disk in the eyepiece that provided a second, smaller aperture for sharper sighting in good lighting conditions. This specimen carries the Pat. Jan 29/79 marking.

Sharp-eyed collectors will note that this particular example of the combination sight was not made for a Model 94. The mount pad is too short and therefore required the drilling and tapping of another hole in the upper tang to install.

The upper tang inlet in the buttstock from number 764, showing the same number (663) as found on the upper tang.

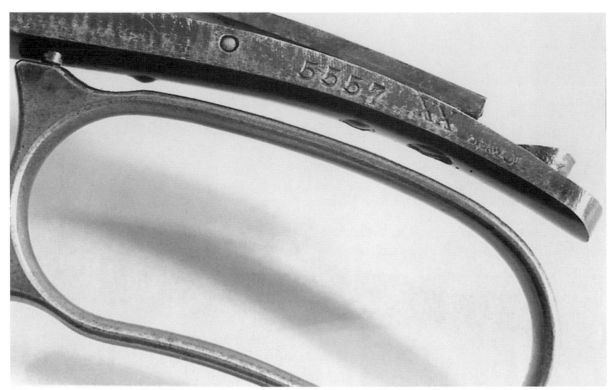

This is an example of a true assembly number. These numbers are found on the left side of the lower tang. Note also the XX wood grading stamp. These marks are less frequently found numerically marked such as, 2X, 3X, etc.

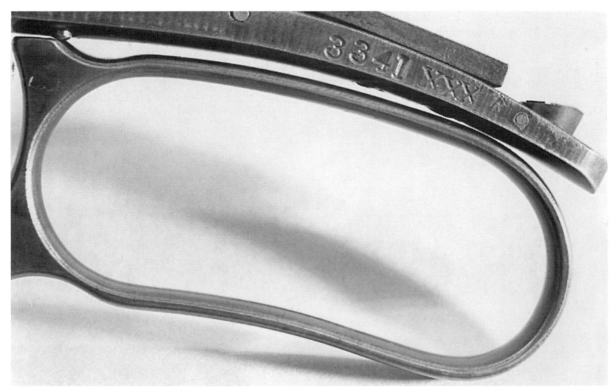

Another fine example of an assembly number, this one with a XXX wood grading stamp. A high grade indeed!

The fitter's marking. Note how it appears to be on the receiver but is actually on the forward end of the lower tang. The lower tang is technically NOT part of the receiver.

receiver, they are on the lower tang, but on an assembled gun they appear to be receiver marks. I feel this is the logical place to mention them.

On Pre-64 specimens, between the front of the trigger and the lever, small numbers or letters will usually be found (there are some specimens without marks, but these are uncommon). These markings were applied by either the fitter (assembler) or an inspector. If the markings are inside a square, a diamond, a circle, or if they are underlined, they were applied by an inspector. If the markings are standing alone they were the fitter's marks. While these markings were extensively used, they were randomly sequenced and followed no apparent pattern.

Occasionally a gun will be noted with "agency" or military markings, and even a few marked "experimental" are in public hands. There were about 1800 U. S.-marked Model 1894 carbines delivered to various government agencies during the WWI era and some *very* rare examples in the WWII era. These markings are not to be considered normal, and a collection of these oddly marked guns would certainly make an interesting display.

All references in this chapter, except where otherwise noted, apply equally to rifles and carbines.

A late model (post-4,500,000) receiver showing no proofmark. Notice the unusual "double-struck" proofmark on the barrel.

An angle-eject receiver showing no proofmark and the two forward holes (filled) for mounting a telescope base. This specimen also displays an extremely fine example of the definitive Winchester proofmark on the barrel.

Here is an example of a factory experimental or prototype marking. The "EXP." is obvious, but note the "X" before and after the serial number. This specimen is a prototype of the "Classic" series; the serial number (2,972,395) is approximately 35,000 numbers prior to the public introduction of the series.

This "Classic" series example and the "antique" models are actually commemorative style guns with nothing in particular to commemorate. Consequently they were numbered into the standard Model 94 serial sequence.

The typical U.S. acceptance marking on upper forward receiver section.

Another factory experimental marking. Note how the serial number was moved over slightly to allow room for the "X" suffix. This example is a prototype of the "XTR" series, and along with the special marking, it is accompanied by the appropriate factory documentation. The serial number (4,696,778) is approximately 100,000 numbers prior to the public introduction of the XTR guns.

There are many experimental guns found in this serial range; most were experiments with finishing methods and were not specially marked. They are interesting and collectible but to have any additional value they must have authenticating documentation.

This is a very rare and unusual example of a Model 94 without an actual serial number. EXP 94 is a mysterious specimen inasmuch as it appears to be a prototype of either the "Wyoming Jubilee" commemorative or the "Antique" series and has the scroll-engraved and casecolored receiver of both models. Complicating the identification, however, is the fact that this example is assembled with the later style (mid-1970s) stocks with a plastic logo-style buttplate, a blued rather than brass-plated saddle ring, and a barrel that is screwed only hand-tight into the receiver. With absolutely no substantiating records available, conjecture is that this is in fact a receiver prototype of the "Wyoming Jubilee" or the "Antique" model and was kept as an unassembled receiver in the factory for years. It was probably discovered and finally assembled during one of those "clear out the old junk" campaigns and auctioned around the time of the WW/Olin corporate change in 1981.

Typical Canadian acceptance and proofing marks. Note that these are on the barrel. There will also be a Canadian "broad arrow" (a circle with an arrow inside) marking on the receiver, usually on the left forward side, and another broad arrow marking on the buttstock and/or forend. Another Canadian variant, those with Canadian PMCR markings, are primarily found in the serial range pertaining to 1942 with the lowest number so far verified being 1,317,167.

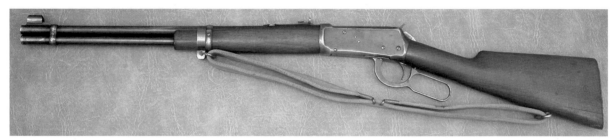

Typical example of the Canadian PCMR "Pacific Coast Militia Rangers" carbine of the mid-1940s. Note the special sling arrangement. Carbines of this type are marked "PCMR" on the top of the receiver as well as having the other Canadian acceptance proofmarks.

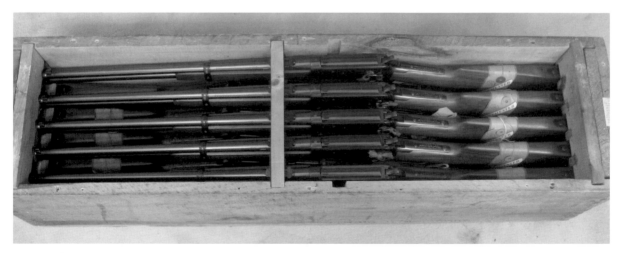

Shortly after WWI the United States Government began a program of "arsenal rebuilding" many of the weapons that had previously been in service and subsequently returned after the war, thereby building a fairly inexpensive stockpile of "as new" arms. They were then warehoused at a Government facility for possible future use. They also stocked up a limited supply of what were essentially brand new civilian arms. All were recorded as and considered U.S. Government inventory/property.

About two decades later WWII began.

Great Britain, being dreadfully lacking in the armament department, put forth a cry to the U.S. (and Canada) for whatever in the field of weaponry they could spare. They rightfully feared a visit from the once again uprising German forces and felt that they needed help in the self-protection department ASAP. To this end they quickly recruited a country-wide militia group, first called the Local Defense Volunteers and later known as the Home

Guard, and soon had personnel numbers nearing one million – but they needed arms, and they needed them immediately.

Along with countless thousands of donated guns from sympathetic American civilians, the very benevolent U. S. Government responded with shipments from the stock-pile they had so diligently accumulated. These may have been a part of the well-known "Lend-Lease" program but I am not able to confirm that. Apparently, included as part of these "relief" shipments were about 20 cases of brand new Winchester 94 and 95 carbines in calibers 30 WCF and 30-06 Govt., respectively. No actual records have been found regarding these guns, but ostensibly, recordkeeping was unnecessary due to the fact that these arms were being "donated" – they were not expected to be returned.

As we now know, the dreaded troop invasion never came.

Not following the usual pattern of governmental waste, some remaining guns were NOT destroyed after the war and instead were relegated back into storage. (Unlike arms of WWI that were largely returned and refurbished, in post-WWII it was deemed too much trouble to inventory and record most of the still usable weaponry and various other types of equipment for return to the U.S., and therefore, it was either destroyed, given away, or unceremoniously dumped into the ocean.) Discovered some time later, this unused cache of weapons was finally returned to the U.S. Upon arrival, no one knew exactly what to do with them so again they took up residence in a warehouse, this time on a pier at the Navy Yard in Brooklyn, N.Y.

After another prolonged period of time, the warehouse became slated for demolition. Upon clearing out of the place in anticipation of its demise, and along with much other "stuff," here were found the unopened and pristine cases of Winchesters that had been shipped to Great Britain some 40 years ago and then back to Brooklyn some 20 years prior to this inevitable discovery. As is usual with "uncovered" articles of this sort they found their way through a government auction to a privateer who promptly sold them to another privateer, etc., etc., etc. As the story goes, most of the cases were "broken up" for resale by the individual piece, but at least two cases of Model 94s and one case of Model 95s are known to have survived intact. This is one of them.

I, totally unexpectedly, was contacted and asked to perform the honor of personally inspecting, authenticating and appraising one of the remaining untouched cases. In it were 10 absolutely new and unmarred Model 94 carbines of a mid-1920s vintage, at this time being approximately 80 years old, complete with every piece of original paperwork, packing, tags, serial number listings, inspection records, and even 10 original wooden cleaning rods. They had NOT been foreign proofed or marked in any way – they were NEW and untouched!

Every piece and every position of every item in the case was carefully recorded as to the original place and position therein and was returned to rest exactly the way it left the factory. For me it was a lifetime experience; it was the proverbial " time-warp."

These guns are perfect. Not perfect "for being 85+ years old and having traveled many thousands of miles and survived 40+ years of unattended storage" – PERFECT.

I recently had the privilege of another visit with them. They reside comfortably in a very high-end collection in the American southwest and they still take my breath away. A fully detailed article on this sensational artifact titled "A Case History" and written by me after the initial inspection and appraisal appears in the 2002 spring issue of the "Winchester Collector" magazine. (Wes Adams collection)

C. RECEIVER: TANG MARKINGS

1) Type 1, 1A

All first model receivers and early second model receivers up to the serial range of 250,000 to 280,000 had the following tang markings but they *do* have the factory drilled tang sight mounting hole. *Note: Several specimens in the pre-serial 700 range have been found without any tang markings. These are randomly interspersed, and there is no explanation for the omission.*

Two versions of Type 1 tang markings. The upper example is of the earliest version (serials to about 10,000); notice the shallow lettering and the periods after both "1894"s. The lower example shows a deeper impression, a larger "Model 1894" and "Pat. Aug 21, 1894" and the omitted periods after both "1894"s.

2) Type 2

Serial ranges of approximately 250,000 to 500,000 will be found with the following tang marking.

The Type 2 tang marking. Notice how the "MODEL 1894" has been slightly spread out and that its lettering and numbering are all the same size. On the bottom line the words "trade" and "mark" have been substituted for the patent information.

3) Type 3

Serial ranges of approximately 500,000 to 765,000 will be found with the following tang marking.

The Type 3 tang marking. Basically the same as the Type 2, but there is the new bottom line designation "TRADE MARK REG. IN U.S.PAT.OFF."

4) Type 4

Serial ranges of approximately 750,000 to 950,000 will be found with the following tang marking.

The Type 4 tang marking. Again a bottom line change – "trade mark reg. u.s. pat.off.&fgn." Note that the word "IN" has been omitted and FGN. has been added.

---

5) Type 5

Serial ranges of approximately 950,000 to 1,100,000 will be found with the following tang marking.

The Type 5 tang marking. The same marking as Type 4 except that the "18" is missing from 1894.
Hereafter, all Model 1894s were officially designated the Model 94 – 1920s.

6) Type 6

Serial ranges of approximately 1,080,000 to 1,180,000 will be found with the following tang marking.

The Type 6 tang marking. Here we have an entirely new marking using "logo" style lettering for the word Winchester, and no model designation at all. This marking is also used on the Model 55.

7) Type 7

Serial ranges of approximately 1,150,000 to 1,300,000 will be found with the following tang marking. In this serial range we also find some receivers stamped with a "W" just below the serial number.

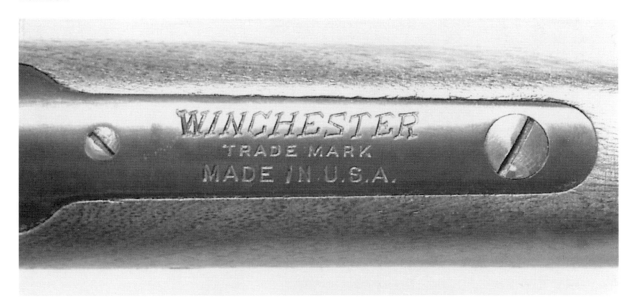

The Type 7 tang marking. Essentially identical to the Type 6 marking but with the dashes removed from before and after trademark and "MADE IN U.S.A." This is the final style of tang marking to be applied on the Model 94. There are examples of this marking with no tang sight hole.

This llustrates the tang marking change (blank) found after serials of about 1,350,000. This change prevailed on all standard issue specimens through final production.

This is a clear illustration of the "W" stamping found on most guns, including some Model 64s, near this serial range. One theory is that this marking designates a factory re-blued gun because a defective batch of chemicals was used for the original bluing attempt. This theory is feasible since all the guns with the "W" are in a very narrow serial range, but at this time it cannot be indisputably substantiated. A larger "W" stamped on the stock or receiver, or both, usually designated a factory exhibition gun. These markings were often filled in with red paint.

8) Type 8

Receivers bearing serials from approximately 1,300,000 (post-World War II) to present have no tang markings and *no* receiver sight holes. 1972-73 receivers built specifically for the 44 Magnum cartridge have an "M" after the serial number and the designation "MAG" directly below the serial number.

The 1972-73 receiver made specifically for the 44 Magnum cartridge. Note that the serial number has been moved over slightly to allow for an "M" suffix, and there is the designation "MAG" under the serial number. A few examples have been noted without the "MAG" marking and some will be found with a "right side" barrel marking as found on the commemoratives. (Author's collection)

BARREL MARKINGS

Because barrels are the most profusely marked of all parts, barrel markings are not only the most difficult but also the most interesting of all Winchester markings to completely and accurately document.

Barrels are made in lots – this is a very basic practice in mass manufacturing (the making of many identical pieces at the same time). It saves countless hours of unnecessary machinery re-setting. The quantity manufactured at any given time is proportionate to popularity/projected usage, and some of the governing factors include the caliber, the length, the weight, the style, etc.

Although the markings applied to barrels definitely follow a "period of manufacture" pattern, some of the more unusually featured specimens are also the most likely parts to sit for longer than normal periods of time in the parts bin. This explains how a specially made but years-old barrel could be found in stock, assembled on a much later receiver, and turn up now as a gun of questionable authenticity.

Conversely, but less commonly, an older receiver could be fitted with a later barrel (possible repair); receivers also were misplaced and lay unnoticed for extended periods. The serial sequence on the manufacturing of receivers was consecutive, but the assembly sequence for the entire gun definitely was not.

Custom orders were most often filled by pulling receivers from the assembly line and fitting them with pre-existing parts. These parts only had to match the customer's specifications, not their respective vintages. Winchester was not noted for throwing away perfectly good parts, and many stange specimens that are absolutely factory original have evolved from this phenomenon.

A keen eye and hard-earned experience are paramount in determining the originality of mismatched or otherwise unusual examples with serials too late to document (note specimen 2,137,XXX elsewhere in this book).

Lately, with the cooperation of the fine research staff at the Buffalo Bill Historical Center, additional and more accurate dating of serial numbering vs. final finishing and/or shipping has become available by comparing "polishing room" records with the "warehouse" records. This is yet another invaluable asset on the road to accurate historical research and documentation.

UPPER BARREL MARKINGS
(those visible on an assembled gun)

A) Type 1, 1A, 1B

Barrel markings corresponding with receivers with serial numbers in the 1 to 150,000 range are as follows:

The characters are 3/64 or 1/8 inch in height, are found on the top of the barrel, and are approximately three inches from the receiver on the carbine and seven inches from the receiver on the rifle. There is a version with dashes only on the bottom line and a version with dashes on both lines, as well as those with no dashes.

Note: Trapper carbines usually had the barrel markings ahead of the forend band or even partially under the forend band until the later serial ranges (after receivers with Type 5 tang

---

This is the barrel marking on a very early 18-inch barreled "trapper" carbine. Note that it is of the Type 1 design (pre-150,000 serial range) and it is partially covered by the forend band. This position of the marking/band is fairly common in early trapper models with 16- or 18-inch barrels.

Barrel markings for trapper models were applied at the same distance from the receiver on all barrels regardless of length, but – as mentioned earlier – 16-inch and 18-inch trappers were often assembled with the longer (standard 9-1/8-inch) style forend. The additional length of the standard forend placed the retaining band one inch farther forward, partially covering the marking in the position illustrated.

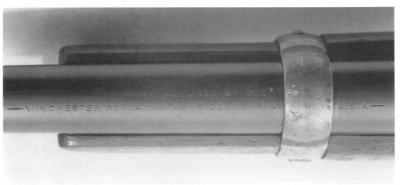

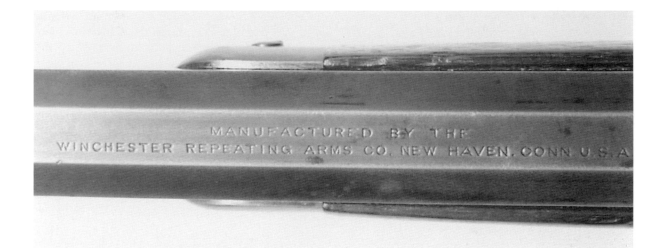

This is a clear illustration of the three types of early barrel markings (Type 1, upper photo; Type 1A, middle photo; and Type 1B, lower photo). On rifles, the no-dash Type 1 version is most often found with 3/64 inch lettering, while Types 1A and 1B usually have 1/8 inch lettering; on carbines, the 3/64 inch size will prevail in all types.

markings). After this they were marked in the same location as standard carbines. Barrel markings on rifles can vary *slightly* as to distance from the receiver; this is largely dependent on barrel length but generally follows no pattern.

The caliber designation is stamped on the top of the barrel at the receiver junction – 32-40, 38-55, 30 WCF, 32 Special, and 25-35 WCF.

The "nickel steel" designation on the left side of the barrel near the rear sight will be found on guns in 30 WCF and 25-35 after serials around 12,000 and 32 Special guns concurrent with the introduction of this caliber (at approximately serial 144,000 but there are many earlier serialed examples). If the nickel steel designation is found on 32-40 and 38-55 caliber guns, it is definitely a special order feature.

This is the first style of nickel steel barrel marking. Also note the early position of the caliber designation and the fine example of an early (serrated edges) "flat-top" rear sight. "extra" is substituted for "nickel" in the marking designating extra steel.

An illustration of the extremely rare and desirable (from a collector's standpoint) "extra steel" barrel marking. These are found in the serial range of 40,000 to 80,000 with some exceptions and precede the "nickel steel" designation. More detail on this marking is found in the text.

This is the earliest type of caliber designation. It is on the barrel top immediately forward of the receiver, and there is no proofmark. Later versions (beginning with serials around 300,000) have a proofmark on the receiver top and another on the barrel just forward of the caliber designation.

Another designation, "Extra Steel," will be found on some guns in the 40,000 to 80,000 range. The "nickel steel" and "extra steel" markings have a slight overlap in the serial sequence. Usually found on 30 WCF and 25-35 caliber guns, the extra steel option was short-lived and is therefore very rare (see Chapter 2 for further details). Extra steel barrels have been noted on guns with serials that date them into the teens (serials starting in the 650,000 range), but this must be attributed to a re-barrel or one of those "use up the old parts" campaigns.

The marking is exactly the same as the first style nickel steel marking substituting "extra" for "nickel."

Note: A factory re-barrel on receivers made after about 1906 (serials in the 300,000 range) will probably show a double proofmark on the receiver and a single proofmark on the barrel. If the receiver was of the older non-proof-marked variety, it will probably still be found without a proofmark. Winchester wasn't anxious to chance the blowing up of a customer's previously unproofed receiver while installing a new barrel. All barrels, however, will have a proofmark if the rebarreling took place after current production guns were routinely proofmarked, even if the barrel is of an early series (normally unproofed).

Again, we have one of those situations where almost anything could be correct – the only combination that will most assuredly be non-factory is an unproofmarked barrel on a proof-marked receiver.

B) Type 2

Barrel markings corresponding with receivers with serial number in the 100,000 to 300,000 range are as follows:

This is the Type 2 barrel marking. It once again has dashes only on the bottom line and now includes the patent date.

The characters are the same as the previous version as to size and location.

The caliber designation is the same as the previous version with caliber 32 Special appearing in normal production as early as serials near 144,000.

The nickel steel designation is the same as on the previous version and nickel steel is standard for 32 Special.

Proofmarks begin to appear near serial 300,000 and are located immediately forward of the caliber designation.

Proofmarks have been observed on a few guns with serials in the early 240,000s and have been seen located just forward of the rear sight on carbines in this range.

The earliest proofmark location.

C) Type 3

Barrel makings corresponding with receivers with serials in the 275,000 to 500,000 range are as follows:

This is the Type 3 barrel marking. Notable is the spelling out of the words "patented" and "august" which effectively eliminated the necessity of using lower line dashes to balance out the marking. This marking can be found in both 2-1/2-inch and 3-inch versions.

The characters are now 1/32 inch in height but the markings remain in the same location as the previous version. Note that the words "PATENTED" and "AUGUST" are spelled out and the dashes on the lower line have been omitted. Barrels with the previous markings will be found generously interspersed with this new version well into the 400,000s. Proofmarks predominate after serials in the early 300,000s, and the second type nickel steel marking with upper line dashes appears.

In the serial range of approximately 345,000 to the low 400,000s some barrels were inadvertantly marked with an Aug. 14 patent date; this is a true factory error and is quite rare. It's also a very easily overlooked variation and is frequently unnoticed by even the most experienced of collectors.

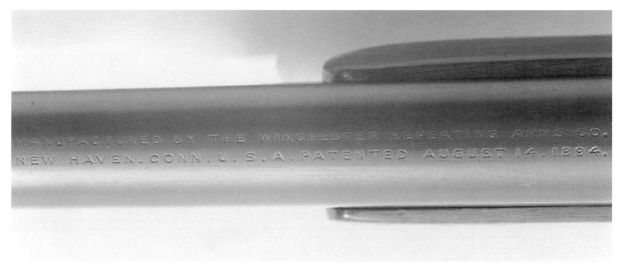

An exceptionally sharp example of the seldom noticed August 14, or "error" barrel date. Note also that this particular marking is forward of the forend band; this is the barrel of the error dated trapper model that is fully illustrated and detailed in the beginning of this chapter.

A rare example of the second-to-be-found "error date" on a Model 1894 barrel – October 14, 1884. This is actually the correct patent date for the Models 1886 and 1892. This is one of only two examples noted as of this writing; the other is on one barrel of a two-barrel set. Be on the lookout for more. The serial range is unknown but judging from the position of the marking and lack of proof-mark (not shown), it's most likely somewhere in the 300,000 to 400,000 range, coinciding with the other error date marking.

This illustration shows us a wealth of interesting features. This is the second type of nickel steel marking; note the dashes before and after the words" nickel steel barrel". Also seen are the second style and location of the caliber designation and the revised positioning of the proofmark.

Also note the finely pictured example of the optional but regularly encountered three-leaf "express" or Type 34 rear sight.

D) Type 4

Barrel markings corresponding with receivers with serials in the 450,000 to 760,000 range are as follows:

Here is the Type 4 barrel marking. Essentially it is the same as Type 3; note the size of the characters and the revised location of the marking.

The same 1/32 inch no-dash marking of the previous version is used but has been relocated to the left side of the barrel in various distances from the receiver. The caliber marking is also relocated to the left side of the barrel immediately forward of the receiver.

Proofmarks were still placed on the top of the barrel but now they are located immediately forward of the receiver and in line with the receiver proofmark.

The second type nickel steel marking with dashes before and after the words "nickel steel barrel" was fully integrated by this time. It remains in the original location on the left side of the barrel and is approximately 3/4 of an inch forward of the newly-positioned caliber designation. Double-marked barrels (i.e., Type 4 and Type 6) have been noted. There is no positive explanation.

The second location of the caliber designation beginning near serials in the 450,000 range. Note the position of the proofmarks.

E) Type 5

Barrel markings corresponding with receivers with serials in the 750,000 to 1,000,000 range are as follows:

These are two examples of the Type 5 barrel marking. The upper photograph illustrates the marking on a standard carbine and the lower photograph shows the same marking on a trapper model. The difference in the size of the characters is only 1/64 inch larger than a Type 4 marking but is readily noticeable.

A beautiful example of what Winchester would do for a price. A personalized inscription above the standard barrel marking. Very rare and unusual.

The previous no-dash version was used and was in the same location but had a character size change to 3/64 inch.

Also found in this serial range is a new nickel steel marking. There is now a dash between the marking and the caliber designation.

The third type of nickel steel marking. Essentially the same as the second type in size and location but there is an additional dash between the marking and the caliber designation.

Note the fine illustration of the carbine or "ladder" type rear sight – the graduation marks on these sights vary somewhat with the caliber/type of powder. The Winchester designation was Type 42 (early) or Type 44.

F) Type 6

Barrel markings corresponding with receivers with serials in the 960,000 to 1,100,000 range are as follows:

This is the Type 6 barrel marking. Note that it now includes the model designation and the nickel steel designation and is all on one line except for the words "trade mark." "STAINLESS STEEL" is substituted for the word "NICKEL STEEL" in the marking designating a stainless steel barrel.

Note that the entire marking except the words "TRADE MARK", including the nickel steel and calber designation, are on one line and the word "Winchester" is now in logo-style lettering. Also note the first use of the Model 94 designation on the barrel.

For the first time we also find a right-side barrel marking. It is in 1/32 inch lettering and located just forward of the receiver.

Illustration of the typical "stainless steel" barrel marking.

The right side barrel marking used with the Type 6 barrel marking and sometimes Type 7. When used with Type 7 it was slightly smaller and had a period (.) after "CO". It could also differ in size between a rifle ands carbine. It also appears on the Models 55 and 64.

G) Type 7

Barrel markings corresponding with receivers with serials in the 1,080,000 to 1,250,000 range are as follows:

The Type 7 barrel marking including the new designation of proof steel. Note the fine illustration of the optional Series 22 rear sight in the flat-top style and the 3C elevator.

H) Type 8

Barrel markings corresponding with receivers with serials in the 1,250,000 to 2,000,000 range are as follows:

Here is a late version of the Type 8 barrel marking (note the later "30-30 WIN" caliber designation versus "30 WCF".) Also illustrated is the intermediate, "shortnosed" style of the series 22 rear sight and a 32B elevator. The 32 W.S. marking also changes to 32 SPL. at this point.

Note the difference in distance from the receiver of this sight compared to the one illustrated with the Type 7 barrel marking – the dovetail for this sight is in the final location at four inches from the receiver while the previous distance was 3-1/16 inches.

The right side barrel marking is discontinued.

This particular marking will be found on a great many guns dating from the 1930s to the early

1950s. There were many different roll dies used, and consequently there will be noted a fair number of slight variations. The lines found adjacent to the words "Winchester proof steel" may appear broken on some examples, and the depth and sharpness of the lettering changes noticeably thoughout the series. This is not to be considered a point of collectibility; it merely illustrates the effects of wear and tear on the manufacturing machinery. The later specimens will definitely show a gradual yet unmistakable deterioration in overall quality.

At serials near 1,550,000 (post-flatband), there is a caliber designation change from 30 WCF to 30-30 WIN, and from 32 W.S. to 32 SPL. or 32 WIN SPL.

A very rare prototype receiver of the 10th anniversary "Friends of the NRA Commemorative." This was apparently a pass-around-the-boardroom-for-approval example. It has no serial number and is marked EXP inside the upper tang area. (Author's collection)

I) Type 9, 9A

Note: Type 9A has no dashes around the "TRADEMARK and "MADE IN U.S.A."

Barrel markings corresponding with receivers with serials in the 1,900,000 to 3,300,000 range are as follows:

This is the Type 9 barrel marking. Shown also is the late version of the series 22 rear sight with a 3C elevator – note how the mounting portion of the sight has been formed from a "stamping" rather than using the previous and much more expensive method of machining it from a solid piece of steel.

J) Type 10, 10A, 10B

Barrel markings corresponding with receivers with serials in the 3,300,000 to 5,100,000 range are as follows:

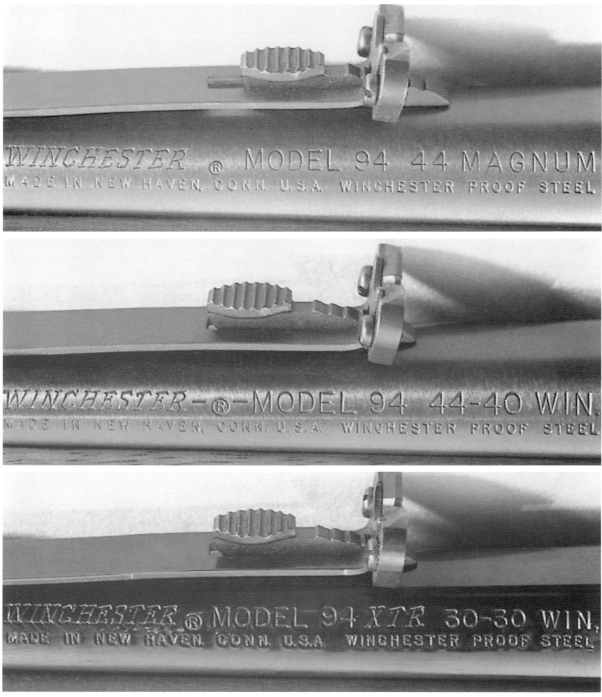

These illustrations are of the Type 10, 10A and 10B barrel markings that were used from the early 1970s to the introduction of the angle eject series in 1981. Note the dashes before and after the registered trademark "r" in the middle photograph. This is the only difference between the two upper illustrations and this practice follows no apparent pattern. There is also no "trademark", and there is now a reference to "New Haven, Conn."

The lower illustration is the Type 10B or "XTR" marking of the same period. XTR's have a higher quality metal finish and checkered wood.

K) Type 11 "BigBore" Barrel Marking

This is the Type 11 or "BigBore" barrel marking. It is found only on top eject guns that also have the "BB" prefix in the serial number. Note the use of dashes before and after the bottom line. These are used to balance the length of the bottom line in relation to the top, making up for the addition of the words BIG BORE and XTR; all BB series guns are XTR.

Ranger models in both pre-angle eject and post-angle eject carry a slightly modified barrel marking consisting of the substitution of the word "RANGER" for "MODEL 94" and adding a separate registered trademark (®) after the word "RANGER."

In addition to the above markings, there may be found any number of agency names and addresses or "made to order by Winchester Repeating Arms Co." stamped into the barrels or on the receiver. Model 94s with these types of markings are extremely rare and highly collectible if the markings can be verified as factory applied – see the illustration on page 137.

Also noted are some examples of specimens with the MODEL 94–WINCHESTER–TRADE MARK – marking on the right side of the barrel and only the caliber designation onthe left. The word Winchester is in "logo-style" lettering. These are found in the 900,000 serial range and are so far unexplained.

On some very late 32-40 and 38-55 specimens (post serials of about 975,000), this right side barrel marking (occasionally but rarely seen on the left side) may be encountered. The discoloration around the lettering is an indication that the marking was applied after the barrel was blued.

The barrels on these guns will also have the earlier style barrel marking, usually Type 4. These earlier barrels were supplied from existing stock and re-marked as illustrated when an order for a discontinued caliber was received.

L) Type 12, 12A

Barrrel markings corresponding with receivers in the 5,100,000 range to present are as follows:

This is the Type 12 or "angle eject" barrel marking. It is typified by the addition of the letters AE after the model designation and the abbreviation CAL, added before the caliber designation. Also notable is the inclusion of dashes before and after the bottom line to balance the longer upper line.

The Type 12A (lower photo) marking differs only by the inclusion of the letters "XTR" to designate the deluxe series. The dashes on the lower line are slightly longer than those on the Type 12 to make up for the additional three letters placed in the upper line marking. Some XTR series guns may also carry the word "Deluxe" (1987-1988 only) in a script style on the right side of the barrel immediately forward of the receiver.

The XTR designation was discontinued in 1989, and only the catalog designation "checkered rifle" is now used. The barrel marking is the same on the checkered rifle and the standard version. Checkered wood is standard on BigBore models.

There is no longer a separate barrel marking for BigBore models after the introduction of the angle eject design; this series also uses the standard Model 94 barrel markings. Several examples in the low 6,000,000 range have been noted with no barrel markings whatsoever, not even the caliber designation. These are definitely to be considered factory errors and are very collectible.

The final right side barrel marking introduced intermittently at the same time as the tang safety at about serials near 6,450,000.

LOWER BARREL MARKINGS
(those visible on a disassembled gun)

On the barrel under the forend wood there will be found many different markings. Most often found will be a model number, a year of manufacture, a caliber designation and various inspection and acceptance marks. All marks do not necessarily appear on all barrels.

The year of manufacture is often omitted and various unexplained marks are often noted. Treat these markings merely as curiosities and not as definitive proof of anything.

Other than a grossly mismatched barrel date/serial number range, nothing of consequence can be determined from these marks.

Typical lower (under the forend) barrel markings. Clearly seen are the model designation ("94," upper photo), the violent proofmark ("VP" in the oval), caliber designations, various inspectors' marks (an "I" in the triangle, a dash mark in the square) and assorted miscellaneous letters, etc.

The barrel top on this specimen shows the definitive proofmark and the "mail order" proofmark. Also note the absence of a proofmark on the receiver. This gun, serial number 4,762, is listed in museum records as a standard round barreled rifle, caliber 32-40, manufactured on June 29, 1895, but now it is not.

Perhaps not considered very collectible to a purist, number 4,762 is still a fine, solid, low-numbered "shooter" and a very interesting specimen.

Having four special order features, serial number 111,071, in caliber 30 WCF, is a worthy addidition to the finest collection. It has an ultra-rare 18-inch barrel with the correct standard length 9-1/8-inch forend (18-inch barreled guns may be correct with 8-1/8-inch or 9-1/8-inch forend); a 1/2 magazine tube (these two items in concert are quite rare); a three-leaf express sight; and the deleted saddle ring option (eastern style receiver).

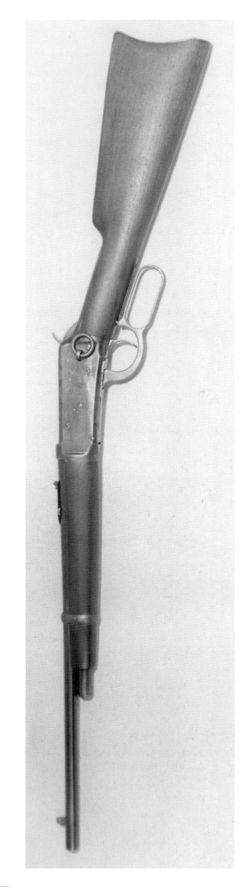

An extreme rarity is this carbine with serial number 312,264. It has two of the rarest options found on a trapper carbine: an 18-inch barrel (with the correct standard length 9-1/8-inch forend) and a 1/2 or button magazine tube. It is also chambered for the very scarce 38-55 caliber; this chambering is very rare in a standard carbine and by far the rarest caliber in the trapper variant.

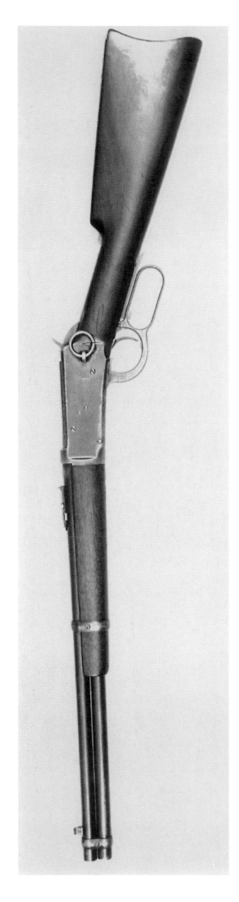

This early saddle ring carbine is completely standard except for this extremely rare 18-inch barrel. Serial number 42,749 in the rather hard to find (in a carbine) caliber 32-40, is a seldom encountered and highly collectible specimen. The forend on this gun is of the standard, 9-1/8-inch length can be correct on 18-inch carbines. The saddle ring is somewhat oversized, but appears to be original to the gun.

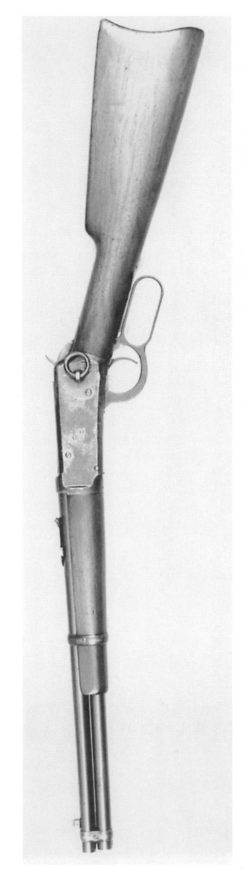

A fine and rare 15-inch barreled 30 WCF trapper carbine. This gun, serial number 887,409, is typical of the later trapper model. Observant collectors will notice that an unusual number of trapper carbines are equipped with the two- or three-leaf express Type 34 rear sights, as is this example. I have no explanation for this; it's merely an observation.

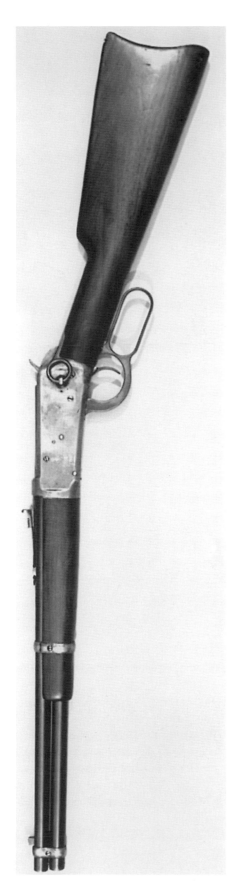

A very collectible Winchester, this trapper carbine, serial number 1,018,699, is a very late-production, seldom-seen variant. It has the very rare 16-inch barrel and is chambered in the hard-to-find 25-35 caliber. It is in the transitional period (note the rifle style rear sight) but is equipped with a saddle ring – saddle rings were beginning to become special order items around this time.

Another illustration of a typical but extremely rare factory "cut-away" or "salesmen's sample." Oddly, most Winchester cut-aways were left full size when most companies (Marlin in particular) were cutting them off at the wrist portion of the stock and just forward of the forend to make them more compact and easier to carry.

This is an early 70s version, serial number 3,477,674, and was used to show the improved lockwork that was introduced at this time. It is superbly crafted, came with several inert cartridges to demonstrate the action "in action," and is completely functional other than the lack of a firing pin.

Factory originality is assured by the absence of a proofmark on either the receiver or the barrel and the lack of a firing pin recess in the bolt.

CALIBERS

INTRODUCTION

Throughout the production of the Model 1894/94, there has been an ongoing and never-ending cartridge development program at Winchester. To try to compile and list the incredible amount of data generated by over 100 years of research would be nearly impossible. It is also irrelevent. What I will provide here is a list of the various calibers that were in production, giving dates of introduction and discontinuance, while including a few other incidental pieces of information that may be pertinent. There have also been many experimental, "mistaken entry" or otherwise strange entries found in the official records.

CHRONOLOGICAL LISTING

1894 – Initial production included 32-40 and 38-55 calibers only. Barrels in these calibers were made as standard in ordnance steel only (see Chapter 2) and any marked "nickel steel" are definitely special order.

1896 – 25-35 and 30 WCF introduced. All barrels made from nickel steel or extra steel until the introduction of "proof steel." Some early carbines may not be marked accordingly, but are definitely not plain ordnance steel.

1902 – 32 Special announced with some sporadic delivery.

1903 – 32 Special officially introduced. Nickel steel barrels only.

1929 (approx) – 32-40 and 38-55 discontinued. There were barrels remaining in stock after this date and guns continued to be assembled in these calibers until the supply was exhausted.

1952 – 25-35 discontinued as supplies ran out.

1967 – 44 Magnum introduced.

1972 – 44 Magnum discontinued.

1973 – 32 Special discontinued.

1976 – 44-40 (non-commemorative) introduced and 44 Magnum re-introduced. Canadian issues only; discontinued in 1980.

1978 – 375 Win. (Big Bore) introduced. Special new receiver utilized.

1982 – 32 Special re-introduced in the Wrangler model, later as regular production.

1983 – 307 Win. and 356 Win. introduced in the "BigBore," "angle eject" receiver. (All models now angle eject.) 375 Win. discontinued.

1985 – 7x30 Waters introduced (24-inch barrel only) and 45 Colt introduced (Trapper model only).

1986 – 44 Magnum once again re-introduced (third time, Trapper model only).

1992 – 357 Magnum introduced (Trapper

model only)

In the mid-1990s to the end of production other calibers have been noted such as the return of the 25-25, 38-55 and 44-40. There were also modern additions as well, e.g., 450 Marlin and 444 Marlin.

Note: Calibers for Commemorative issues are not consistent with regular production.

410 shotgun conversions for use with 2.5-inch shotshells have been noted in both Pre-64 and Post-64 models. These are strictly gunshop conversions, were never factory produced, and are not to be confused with the later Model 9410. They are really quite interesting nonetheless.

NEW .410 SERIES – THE MODEL 9410

In the years after the first edition of this book was released, many new variations of the Model 94 became available. Such variations would have earlier been called variants and relegated to the custom shop on special order only. But in this later bid for diversity and to improve overall sales, the factory wisely offered them as regular production variations – they were mostly cosmetic and caliber oriented and many (e.g., 45 Colt and 357 Magnum) were apparently aimed at the cowboy-action-shooting segment of the buying public. However, the latest (and last true variation of the Model 94) was a .410 shotgun version. It was first seen in 2001 and continued in regular production until the factory closed in 2006. This variation was officially designated the "Model 9410" (which I feel was a quite thoughtful and catchy designation) but it was actually only a very slightly modified Model 94 – as were the earlier introduced BigBore models.

It was produced with an interchangeable choke arrangement called the "Invector system," as well as a straight, cylinder-bored version. This is not an innovative choke system but it, and the introduction of a shotgun version itself, was innovative for the Model 94. Both were designed for the standard 410, 2-1/2 inch shotshells (3-inch cartridges will not feed properly and are definitely not recommended even for single shot usage) and both have a specially designed rear sight that appears as the same as a rifle sight but has a slightly different sighting notch and calibration. They also have a Model 9410-specific fiber-optic front sight with the fiber-optic piece being either fluorescent orange or fluorescent green. Some earlier versions may have a non-fiber-optic front sight. There were several stock options offered – laminated, checkered or uncheckered and pistolgrip or straight grip, a shortened "youth" version, two barrel lengths, 20-inch and 24-inch; and two magazine tube lengths. The 20-inch version has a total ammunition capacity of six rounds and the 24-inch version can hold 10 rounds.

Model 9410s are also found with factory cataloged cosmetic selections or even specially-ordered custom shop modifications. Some of these include inscriptions, engraving, a casecolored receiver or a large-loop lever. The large loop lever addition is quite scarce on this model but factory-installed originals have the styrofoam box insert cut out to fit the lever and the end label is usually marked accordingly; the more elaborate "custom shop" versions have the end label marked "CS".

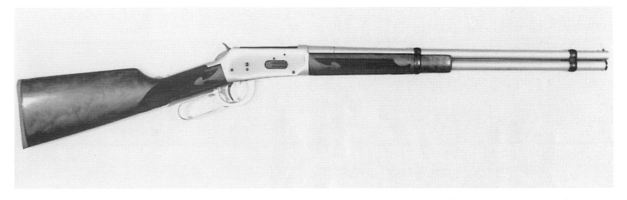

Professionally done conversion of a Post-64 Model 94 carbine into a 410 shotgun. This gun is designed to use 2-1/2-inch brass shotshells. Note the lack of a rear sight and the installation of a front bead. The use of a late model shotgun style buttstock with a thin rubber recoil pad completes this skillful and well thought-out conversion.

A plug was furnished for limiting the possibility of inserting ammunition to only two rounds in the magazine. One round in the chamber and two in the magazine when hunting migratory waterfowl has long been a federal mandate in this regard.

It appears that as many as 45,000 to 50,000 Model 9410s may have been produced but actual records are unfortunately nonexistent. This is a very interesting, very well-made and seemingly popular variation but its true potential was cut short by the closing of the factory. Model 94s of all eras have been found as gunshop conversions to 410 shotguns but this was a first for the Model 94 as a factory produced variation.

An illustration of the two barrel lengths and two stock styles on the recent (2001 to end of production) Model 9410. These models were also both available with a variety of stocks and with or without the Invector choke system. There were also laminated versions of the stocks and a shortened "youth" model.

An illustration of the barrel marking on the Model 9410. This is the marking for the model with the interchangeable Invector choke system and is in this case on the straight-gripped 24-inch barreled version.

The non-Invector barrel marking. This happens to be on a 20-inch pistol-gripped version. Specimens in either barrel length may or may not have a right side barrel marking below the rear sight (see Chapter 7).

The muzzle detail for the Invector choke system. The non-Invector muzzle looks similar, including the same front sight, but it obviously would have no screw-in choke tube and therefore appears as a plain, crowned muzzle in a large caliber. You can see in this illustration that one choke tube is installed – the gun comes delivered with three different choke tubes – modified cylinder, improved cylinder and full – marked accordingly, and with the necessary installation tool (the tubes are also marked with a "notching system" denoting the choke and this "tactile coding" is fully explained in the instruction manual – it can be seen if you look carefully at the illustration). Specialty tubes such as "skeet," and "extra full," etc., or those made for steel shot were/are available through a Winchester dealer. During the period of production up to seven different choke tubes were available.

The Model 9410 is one of the few Model 94 series guns with its own serial range. The SG (shotgun) prefix as shown in this illustration is a logical differentiation, but separate serial ranges (such as seen during the initial introduction of the Model 55) in the Model 94s history is unusual in a full-production variation (commemoratives and special interest versions, as earlier noted, usually had their own serial ranges). The last time out-of-serial-sequence numbering occurred in regular production Model 94s was the initial group of pre-angle eject BigBore guns and the first run of standard angle eject models. They each had a very short-lived period of separate serial ranges (see Chapter 1).

44

Cartridges Adapted To Model 1894 Rifle.

The cartridges described below are adapted to Model 1894 Winchester Repeating Rifles. For shooting big game, soft point bullets should always be used in preference to full patch bullets, as the effect of the former on animal tissues is much more deadly. Black powder cartridges cannot be used in .25-35 or .30 caliber Model 1894 rifles.

.30 Winchester Soft Point Bullet.   *.30 Winchester Soft Point Bullet.*

Before Firing.   *After Firing Into Soft Pine Boards. Penetration 11 Boards.*

Smokeless Powder, Soft Point Bullet.

Cartridges......................per 1,000, $33.00	Smokeless Powder....................		
Primed Shells..................." 15.00	Soft Point or Full Patch Bul-		
Bullets..........................." 5.00	lets..................................117 grains.		

Cartridges packed 1,000 in a case.

Cartridges*......................per 1,000, $30.00	Smokeless Powder.....................		
Primed Shells..................." 15.00	Lead Bullets..........................86 grains.		
Bullets..........................." 4.00	Cartridges packed 1,000 in a case.		

Smokeless Powder, Soft Point Bullet.

Cartridges......................per 1,000, $38.00	Smokeless Powder....................		
Primed Shells..................." 18.00	Soft Point or Full Patch Bul-		
Bullets..........................." 6.00	lets.................................170 grains.		

Cartridges packed 1,000 in a case.

Cartridges,* Lead Bullets......per 1,000, $30.00	Bullets, Full Patch or Soft		
Cartridges,* Full Patch or Soft	Point.........................per 1,000, $5.00		
Point Bullets............... " 35.00	Smokeless Powder.............		
Primed Shells.................. " 18.00	Bullets, Lead, Full Patch or		
Bullets, Lead.................. " 3.00	Soft Point.................. 117 grains.		

Cartridges packed 1,000 in a case.

* These cartridges require a different adjustment of sights from regular cartridges.

Available cartridges, technical information and prices from the 1916 salesmen's catalog.

45

Cartridges Adapted To Model 1894 Rifle.

Smokeless Powder, Soft Point Bullet.

Cartridges	per 1,000, $38.00	Smokeless Powder	
Primed Shells	" 18.00	Bullets, Soft Pt. or Full Patch, 170 grains.	
Bullets	" 8.25	Cartridges packed 1,000 in a case.	

Cartridges, Lead Bullet	per 1,000, $27.00	Bullets, Lead (165 grains)	per 1,000, $7.25
" Full Patch or Soft Point		Bullets, Full Patch or Soft Point	8.25
Bullet	28.00	Black Powder	40 grains.
Primed Shells	15.00	Cartridges packed 1,000 in a case.	

SMOKELESS CARTRIDGES, .32-40 Smokeless Powder, 165 grains Full Patch or Soft Point Bullet, per 1,000, $32.00.

WINCHESTER HIGH VELOCITY LOW PRESSURE SMOKELESS CARTRIDGES,* Full Patch or Soft Point Bullet, .32-40, per 1,000, $38.00.

Cartridges*	per 1,000, $27.00	Black Powder	13 grains.
Primed Shells	" 15.00	Cartridges packed 1,000 in a case.	
Bullets (98 grs.)	" 6.00		

SMOKELESS CARTRIDGES, .32-40 Short Range, 98 grains Lead Bullet, per 1,000, $28.00.
.32-40 MINIATURE, Smokeless Powder, 100 grains Full Patch Bullet, per 1,000, $35.00.

Cartridges, Lead Bullet	per 1,000, $33.00	Bullets, Lead (255 grains)	per 1,000, $9.50
" Full Patch or Soft Point		Bullets, Full Patch or Soft	
Bullet	34.00	Point	" 10.50
Primed Shells	18.00	Black Powder	48 grains.
	Cartridges packed 1,000 in a case.		

SMOKELESS CARTRIDGES, .38-55 Smokeless Powder, 255 grains Full Patch or Soft Point Bullet, per 1,000, $40.00.

WINCHESTER HIGH VELOCITY LOW PRESSURE SMOKELESS CARTRIDGES,* Full Patch or Soft Point Bullet, .38-55, per 1,000, $46.00.

Cartridges*	per 1,000, $33.00	Black Powder	20 grains.
Primed Shells	" 18.00	Cartridges packed 1,000 in a case.	
Bullets (155 grains)	" 7.00		

*These cartridges require a different adjustment of sights from regular cartridges.

Available cartridges, technical information and prices from the 1916 salesmen's catalog.

VARIATIONS

INTRODUCTION

In this section, I will attempt to put it all together and make a bit of sense out of the facts, figures and observations found throughout this book.

This section is divided into two parts: *variations* (major design changes) and *types* (significant changes within a variation that warrant detailed acknowledgement).

Please remember that every last bit of information and every detail of a change may not be in this chapter. If you refer to the appropriate chapters for further details and learn to use the ever-evolving experience you'll gain from the careful examination of many variant specimens, you'll soon become hard to fool.

VARIATION I

This variation is easily determined by the visible cartridge guide screw heads on each side of the receiver. (See Chapter 1, Receivers,

subsection A, and Chapter 7, Markings, "Receiver – Tang Markings.")

The serial range is from 1 to 7400 +/-. Remember, serial ranges for all variations, types, changes, etc., are never totally inclusive and will almost always have some overlap.

In this variation there is only one type and in it we may find the following:

A) Rifles and carbines (only seven carbines known so far).

B) Calibers 30 WCF, 32-40 and 38-55 only but 32-40 unknown, and examples in 30 WCF are very rare, with only one as verified.

C) Round or octagon barrels (octagon more common at about 9:1).

D) The controversial assembly numbers inverted on the right side of the upper tang on most examples (see marking section B).

E) Takedown models (extremely rare).

F) First design hammers.

G) Deluxe models (very rare).

H) Shorter than standard barrels (very rare).

I) Marking section (A) 1, 1a or b barrel markings.

J) No proofmarks.

K) Color finished hammers, levers and buttplates.

L) Color finished receivers (extremely rare).

In this variation it is very important to verify anything that is considered non-standard. Factory records of the first few thousand guns show almost all options as available and in production; they cannot tell us, however, if a particular serial numbered gun is a first or a second variation. There is an approximate 3,000 gun overlap. I have not yet seen or heard of first model guns that are <u>verifiable</u> with:

A) Longer than standard barrels.

B) Other than 30 WCF or 38-55 caliber.

C) Half-round, half-octagon barrels.

D) Trapper carbine option.

This is not to imply that none of the above are in existence. Factory records may prove yours to be correct. You may have or find the one that "letters."

Consult the respective chapters/sections for exact details.

VARIATION II, TYPE 1

This variation and type is determined easily by noting the absence of the outside/in guide screw, and the continuation of the earliest style tang markings. (See Chapter 1, Receivers, and Chapter 7, Markings, "Receiver – Tang Markings.")

The serial range is from the 500s to near 300,000.

All options become available.

In this variation and type we will find in addition to the full option list:

A) Calibers 30 WCF, 25-35 WCF and 32 Special introduced.

B) Marking section (A) 1, 1a or b, or (B)

C) First or second design hammers.

D) Proof marks introduced in later serial ranges.

E) Nickel and extra steel markings first appear.

F) Receivers may be thickened by 3/64 inch near serials of 150,000.

Consult the respective chapters/sections for exact details.

VARIATION II, TYPE 2

This variation and type is distinguished by the change to marking section (C) 2 tang markings.

The serial range is from approximately 250,000 to 500,000.

In this variation and type we will find in addition to the full option list:

A) Marking section (C) barrel markings.

B) Second design hammers used exclusively. Note: First design hammers may be noted with the "double set trigger" option on some guns with very high serial numbers.

C) Several examples of muskets are known to exist in this serial range but only one has been verified.

Consult the respective chapters/sections for exact details.

VARIATION II, TYPE 3

This variation and type is distinguished by the change to marking section (C) 3 tang markings.

The serial range is from approximately 500,000 to 765,000.

In this variation and type we will find in addition to the full option list:

A) Marking section (D) or (E) barrel markings.

Consult the respective chapters/sections for exact details.

VARIATION II, TYPE 4

This variation and type is distinguished by the change to marking section (C) 4 tang markings.

The serial range is from approximately 750,000 to 960,000.

In this variation and type we will find in addition to the full option list:

A) Marking section (D) or (E) barrel markings.

B) Introduction of the stainless steel barrel option (near 950,000).

C) Some musket models seen with serial ranges corresponding to the World War I era (near 850,000). The existence of one has been verified.

Consult the respective chapters/sections for exact details.

VARIATION II, TYPE 5

This variation and type is distinguished by the change to marking section (C) 5 or 6 tang markings.

The serial range is from approximately 950,000 to 1,100,000.

In this variation and type we will find in addition to the full option list:

A) Marking section (F) barrel markings.

B) Carbines appear with ramp front sight-hoods (late). "Transitional" model. The true "transitional" model has a ramp front sight, a carbine buttstock and a 3-1/16-inch rear sight slot measurement (about serial 1,100,000). Some versions of this front sight have been noted with no sight hood slot. It is unknown if this is an error or deliberate.

C) Forend bands on carbines change from "milled" to "stamped." This was one of the changes found on the "transitional" model but either style may be found on early ramp sighted guns.

Rifles become increasingly scarce after serials around 1,000,000.

Consult the respective chapters/sections for exact details.

VARIATION II, TYPE 6

This variation and type is distinguished by the change to Marking section (C) 6 or 7 tang markings.

The serial range is from approximately 1,000,000 to 1,300,000.

This is commonly known as the "pre-war" model.

While there is still a "full" option list, only a very few of the last production rifles and even fewer of the carbines in this serial range will be seen with options.

Optional sights, a shorter than standard magazine tube, and perhaps a shotgun butt-stock will be the most common.

In this variation and type we will also find:

A) Marking section (G) or (H) barrel markings.

B) Saddle rings omitted from all carbines (available on special order).

C) Rollover carbine buttplates replaced by the serrated steel Model 55 styles (except "transitionals" on overlap).

D) Rifles phased out at approximately 1,090,500 except Model 64.

E) Ramp front sights on all carbines with marking section (C) 7 tang markings.

Consult the respective chapters/sections for exact details.

VARIATION II, TYPE 7

This variation and type are distinguished by the change to marking section (C) 8 tang markings.

The serial range is from approximately 1,300,000 to 2,600,298 (2,600,298 is reportedly the last Pre-64 Model 94).

This is commonly known as the "flatband" model (to approximately serial 1,550,000).

After the "flatband" version it is commonly known as the "Pre-64" model (after approximately serial 1,550,000).

In this variation and type we will also find:

A) No options (except custom shop orders).

B) Marking section (I) or (J) barrel markings.

C) Third design hammers.

D) Omission of the tang sight screw hole and tang markings.

E) The front barrel band is changed from the original rounded "milled" style to a "flat" style with the inner area still being "milled" (serials from approximately 1,300,000 to mid 1,550,000).

F) The front barrel band is again changed. It reverts to a rounded contour like the pre-flatband style but it is stamped, not milled. This change occurs around serial 1,550,000.

G) Two receiver sight holes are provided on the left side of the receiver and the stock comb is blunter in contour beginning at serials near 1,790,000.

H) There is a noticeable degradation of the quality of the rear sight at serials around 2,000,000.

I) Two lower tang designs. (See Receivers, Chapter 1).

Consult the respective chapters/sections for exact details.

VARIATION III, TYPE 1

This variation and type is the first of the "Post-64" varieties. There are several distinguishing design changes that are readily visible on even a casual inspection. (See "Receivers," Chapter 1, and "Markings," Chapter 7.)

The severe decline in the overall quality of the product is readily apparent.

The serial range is from somewhere after number 2,600,298 to approximately 3,400,000 (see "Receivers," Chapter 1).

In this variation and type we will find marking section (I) or (J) barrel markings.

Consult the respective chapters/sections for exact details.

VARIATION III, TYPE 2

This variation and type is essentially identical in appearance to Type 1, but you will immediately notice the upgrading of product quality (see "Receivers," Chapter 1).

The serial range is from approximately 3,400,000 to 4,700,000.

In this variation and type we may find the following:

A) Marking section (K) barrel markings.

B) The change in buttplate material from steel to phenolic.

C) Introduction and discontinuance of the Model 64A.

D) Introduction and discontinuance of the first Model 94 to chambered for a handgun cartridge (44 Magnum).

Consult the respective chapters/sections for exact details.

VARIATION III, TYPE 3 AND 3A

This variation and type are essentially the same as the previous two but there are some distinguishing changes. The fit and finish continue to improve and there is a totally revised hammer spring/lower tang assembly design (see receiver section D - Type 3A see receiver section E).

The serial range is from approximately 4,700,000 to 5,290,000.

In this variation and type we may find the following:

A) A smooth lower tang, showing only the end of the stock screw and the hammer block

plunger (see receiver section D).

B) Type 3 - marking section (K) barrel markings.

C) Type 3A (BigBore) - marking section (Ka) barrel markings.

D) XTR introduced.

E) BigBore introduced.

F) Trapper models reintroduced.

Consult the respective chapters/sections for exact details.

VARIATION IV, TYPE 1 AND 1A

This variation and type is the latest evolution for the Model 94. This is the "angle eject" model (see receiver section F).

In this variation and type we may find the following:

A) Type 1- marking section (L) 12 barrel markings.

B) Type 1A (BigBore) - marking section (L) 12a barrel markings.

C) Forged steel receivers.

D) Some carbines with dovetailed front sights (1987-89).

E) Rifles re-introduced (actually a long-barreled carbine).

F) Laminated stocks introduced.

G) A Monte Carlo stock (angle eject BigBores – 1983).

H) Hammers are drilled and tapped for a screw-in hammer extension beginning in 1986.

I) A special model designated "DELUXE" on the right side of the barrel (1987-88).

J) Link pin with locking screw reintroduced (1990).

K) Hammerblock safety introduced (1992).

L) The barrel band on the Ranger model is repositioned to the same area (2-1/16 inches from the muzzle) as on the standard model (1992).

M) Heavier barrels appear on trapper versions (late 1991).

Consult the respective chapters/sections for exact details. This variation continued with very slight changes, mostly in the availability of many previously special-order features such as different barrel lengths, stock configurations, and calibers until the end of production on March 31, 2006.

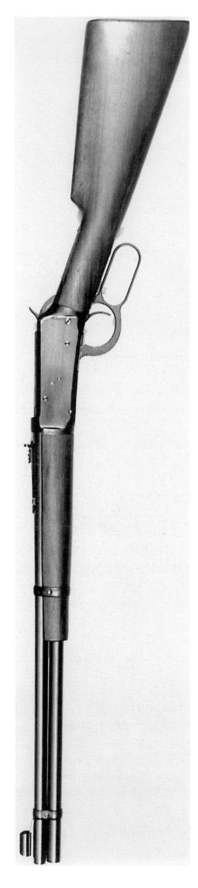

This specimen, serial number 1,240,596, in 30 WCF, is a new, unfired example of what is commonly referred to as a "pre-war" carbine. This gun is still in its original box and retains all the original pre-war paperwork. The ramp with hood front sight has now been fully incorporated, and the buttstock style has been changed to the semi-shotgun type with the Model 55 buttplate. Forend bands all now all stamped. Some examples can still be found with the earlier carbine-style rear sight, but the rifle ight is now the norm. The rear sight dovetail remains at the 3-1/16-inch distance from the receiver – notice how close the end of the rear sight is to the receiver. Specimens of this configuration have been authenticated through 1946.

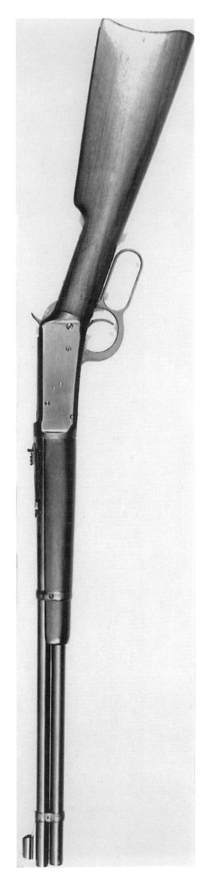

A fine example of the so-called "transitional" variant. This specimen, serial number 1,115,394, is a typical, standard 30 WCF caliber carbine, showing the early signs of the changes that would occur during the 1930s.

The transitional variant is easily identified; it has a ramp style front sight and a "behind the sight' barrel band on an otherwise standard carbine with the original style carbine buttstock. To avoid fakery, one should be aware that the serial range for this variant is very narrow and falls very close to that of this specimen. These variants may have either a rifle type rear sight or the standard "ladder style" carbine sight, but both sights are mounted at the 3-1/16-inch dovetail location; the four-inch location is incorrect for this variant (see Chapter 2). This particular specimen has the optional flat-top style of rifle sight. The forend band on some of these guns changes from the milled style to the stamped style. This is a random change. (W. Raymond collection)

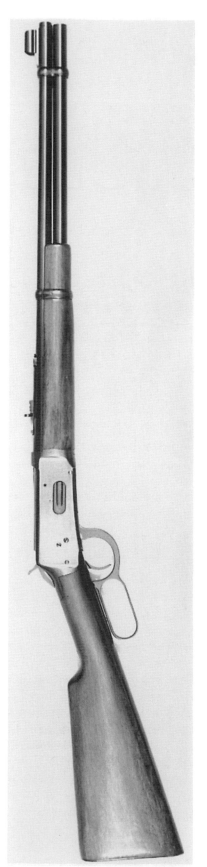

A post-war or early Pre-64 carbine. This example, serial number 1,678,033, in 30 WCF caliber, is typical. The only significant difference between this and the flatband model is the return to the rounded style front barrel band (this band is also now a stamping) and the change in the caliber designation from 30 WCF to 30-30. The caliber change is only in the designation; the 30 WCF cartridge is identical to the 30-30. (Author's collection)

This 30 WCF carbine, serial number 1,465,894, is a new unfired example of a typical wartime production "flatband" carbine. Clearly seen is the flat style front barrel band.

Many other subtle changes may also be noted in guns of this period. The hammer design is changed from the checkered type to the ribbed style; the buttplates are of the flat checkered type; and the measurement from the receiver to the rear sight dovetail has now been standardized at four inches. Notice the increased clearance between end of the rear sight and the receiver/barrel junction and the use of the longer 32B style elevator. The upper tang is now devoid of any markings and the tapped hole for mounting a tang sight has also been eliminated. These specimens are routinely found with the different lower tang configuration (See Chapter 1).

PACKAGING

INTRODUCTION

Boxes, tags, booklets, wrapping paper and filler material specifically designed for the packaging of the Model 1894/94 follow the same general manufacturing progression as that made for other models in the Winchester line.

I have decided to include a chapter on these items, but none of the following should be considered more than a superficial appraisal of the most obvious differences encountered.

The importance placed on these items by a collector is a matter of personal preference, as would be the addition of related cartridges, posters, display items, etc., to any gun collection.

The importance placed on these items by a dealer/seller, however, is another story altogether.

The "boxed, complete with papers and tags" examples are sometimes looked upon with an air of reverence that is, in my opinion, far beyond any logical reasoning. Some dealers, being acutely aware of this phenomenon, exploit it; consequently these specimens are usually found carrying a substantial monetary premium.

Unfortunately, because there is such a lack of accurate information on these items and because having a box to put a nearly flawless specimen into can be so lucrative, a good deal of fakery or "imaginative packaging" has been taking place. A good deal of extra cash has been spent for nothing more than plain cardboard. *Do not* spend a lot of extra money for a boxed example if it can't be indisputedly proven that the gun and the box and the paperwork actually left the factory together.

There are many variations in box design, end labels, hang tags, filler material, wrapping paper and instructional/promotional booklets. Most of these items will show changes that appear concurrently with the various changes in corporate ownership: Winchester Repeating Arms to Winchester Western – Winchester-Western to Winchester Olin, etc.

The most reliable and most logical way to determine authenticity with at least some assurance of accuracy would be to match the year/serial number on the gun to the corporate markings on the box and/or packaging material. You shouldn't, for example, find a nice pre-war carbine nestled comfortably in an Olin-marked box. Olin took over as a division of W.R.A.C. in late 1944, well into the post-war (flatband) era.

Also beware of similarly mismatched packaging items themselves. End labels, boxes, tags, booklets, etc. should all have the same corporate markings. There is a slight possibility of a transitional overlap, but corporations are usually very anxious to get their name/logo on everything they produce, and this is accomplished almost immediately.

Below is a list of the changeover dates relating to different corporate takeoversof the Winchester line. Once again, caution and prudence are paramount when paying a premium for what is represented as original packaging.

CORPORATE CHANGEOVERS

Original WINCHESTER REPEATING ARMS CO. to WINCHESTER REPEATING ARMS CO./ DIVISION OF WESTERN CARTRIDGE CO. – December 1938.

To WINCHESTER REPEATING ARMS CO. - DIVISION OF OLIN INDUSTRIES INC. – December 1944.

To WINCHESTER - WESTERN DIVISION - OLIN INDUSTRIES INC. – January 1952.

To WINCHESTER - WESTERN DIVISION - OLIN MATHIESON CHEMICAL CORP. – September 1954.

To WINCHESTER WESTERN - OLIN – September 1969.

To U.S. REPEATING ARMS CO. – July 1981.

To F.N. CORPORATION – December 1990 to closing of factory.

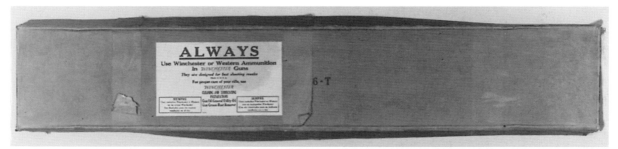

Packaging for a pre-war Model 94 carbine marked Winchester Repeating Arms. Co.

Packaging for a Pre-64 Model 94 carbine, typical of the post-war through early 1960s period. This example is an early 50s type, marked Olin Industries Inc.

Packaging for a Model 94, 44 Magnum carbine, circa 1971, typical of the style used in early 1960s to the mid 1970s. This example is identified by the caliber/serial number of the gun, and the Winchester Western-Olin marked literature on the tags and booklets inside. The outside of the box is marked C.1961, Olin Mathieson Chemical Corp.

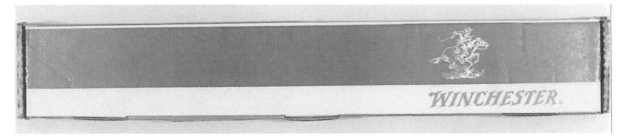

Packaging for a Model 94 carbine of the mid 1970s to 1981. The outside of the box carries no corporate markings other than the name Winchester on the end label. The underside of some examples will be seen with "made in Canada" markings (Cobourg, Ontario) and very late examples (mid-1981) may be marked "USRAC."

Packaging for a Model 94 carbine typical of the style used until the "licensee" box was introduced. This design was introduced in mid-1981 and is marked U.S. Repeating Arms Co.

This is the final "to end of production" packaging for the Model 94 and the Model 9410. In the earlier 6,000,000 range it can be found in red and without the horse and rider. Later it is found as shown with the addition of the word "licensee" in the printing. The end labels, as before, give all the pertinent information including the crossbolt to tang safety change. The imported "historical" models from Japan are almost always seen in red boxes. They carry the "Olin" markings on the bottom.

Serial number 2,041,780 is a new-in-the-box and unfired example of the final version of the Pre-64 Model 94. This example illustrates the shortwood type of forend (the term "shortwood" denotes the amount of wood forward of the barrel band as compared to previous models. This 7-5/16-inch forend length is found on all standard Model 94s from serials in the 1,790,000 range to date except for later special issues.

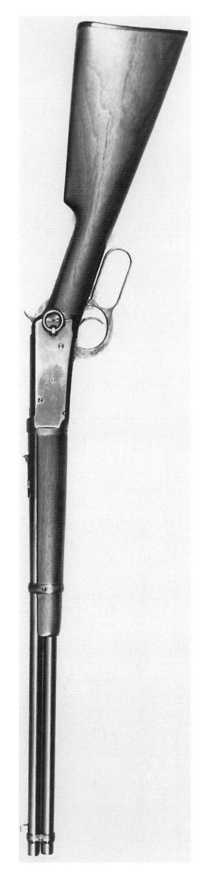

An early saddle ring carbine, serial number 314,870, chambered in the rather unpopular 32 Special caliber. This interesting specimen has two very basic but classy options: a three-bladed express type rear sight and a shotgun style buttstock with a checkered hard rubber buttplate. A fine collectible in its own right, but making this gun even more collectible is the fact that it appears to be unfired.

Sent to the warehouse on Sept. 11, 1906 and shipped the next day, this gun (except for the discolored area on the receiver that is evident in the photograph) remains absolutely pristine. The bluing on the discolored area is not worn, but has turned to a brown color, perhaps from a handprint that was left unwiped; the wood is unmarred and there is little other evidence to show any use or handling whatsoever. Even the casecoloring on the lever and hammer are perfect. A wonderful old Winchester and a collector's dream.

Winchesters are classified as collectible for many reasons. Usually, a combination of rare options and/or unusually fine condition will be a factor, and sometimes only a notable history will be the sole criteria. Here with specimen number 666,175, we have an interesting combination of condition, rarity and history.

In 1978, a bank in the Boston area relocated one of its branch offices. During this move, in a large walk-in vault, between the wall of the vault and a file cabinet was discovered what appeared to be a canvas gun case. It was stuck in place, muzzle down, resting on the floor. While the floor end of the case was badly rotted, a look inside revealed a nearly pristine Model 94 carbine. No one at the bank had any recollection of, or any explanation for, its existence.

Rarity: The caliber of this fine example is 38-55, which is quite scarce in a carbine.

Condition: Except for some spotty receiver discoloration and some rather serious external pitting at the muzzle, the gun is nearly mint. The bore remains perfect and the stocks (gumwood) are for the most part unmarred. The gun appears to be in a virtually unused condition and is very possibly unfired.

History: There is a letter from an involved bank officer, attesting to the validity of the story.

A wonderful Winchester collectible – assembled in mid 1913, it was protected from the ravages of time by spending most of 65 years hidden in a bank vault. (W. Ford collection)

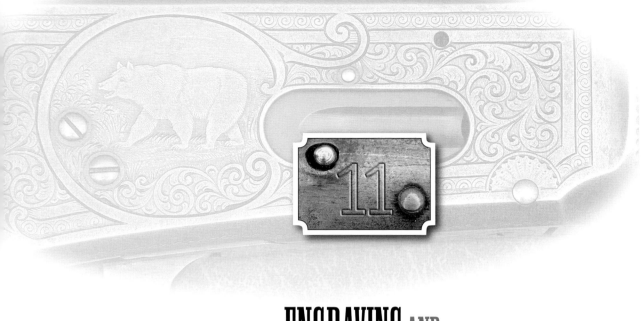

ENGRAVING AND SPECIAL ORDER FEATURES

INTRODUCTION

Standard or basically equipped guns predominate by far, but some special order features are not uncommon. Extras were added routinely both at the factory and by outside gunsmiths, and often by the owners themselves. Any Model 94 with factory-installed special order features is a collectible; more and more specimens with added features are disappearing into private collections, and unusual configurations or highly optioned original guns bring substantial monetary premiums over standard or non-factory original specimens.

While we are not very interested from a purist/collector's point of view on those guns with options that are known to be non-factory, many later-added features can be both aesthetically appealing and quite functional. The hardcore collector may frown on anything that isn't strictly original, but the hobbyist/shooter type of collector may delight in finding a special set of sights installed or a nicely upgraded set of stocks.

There are many bargain priced non-original Model 94s on the market and some of these are as beautiful and appealing to the eye as any factory original.

Some options were actually deletions, such as leaving off the saddle ring on a carbine or not milling the rear sight slot on a gun with a tang mounted rear sight; there was only a nominal charge of a dollar or so for these requests.

The offering and availability of options declined very rapidly at the beginning of World War II, and very few guns manufactured after this period will be so equipped. After this time non-standard guns were no longer normally kept in stock, and all requests for special order items now had to go through the Custom Shop. The added expense of special options, especially in those troubled times, and the extra delay in delivery incurred by the special order having to go through the Custom Shop, effectively kept the manufacture of higher grade guns to a minimum.

As most optional features have been commented on and detailed in their respective chapters, and many have been illustrated and explained in the photographs/captions, further discourse is unnecessary.

In this chapter I will focus lightly on engraving as it pertains to the Model 94 and provide some interesting catalog excerpts from different eras showing the availability and pricing structure of most optional/special order features.

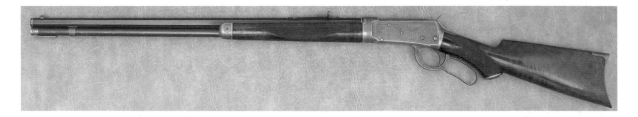

The first engraved and monogrammed Model 1894. Serial number 1835, a second model receiver, has the following options: a 26-inch octagonal barreled rifle with takedown frame; pistolgrip and fancy walnut stocks monogrammed (jnlaid in gold) with "MWS" on the buttstock; steel buttplate; engraved $16.00 with relief engraving; and gold inlays on scrollwork on the forend cap, buttplate and barrel tip. Sent to the warehouse on March 5, 1895 and shipped on the same day. This is one of only two known "relief" engraved Model 1894s documented to be factory work. (Rob Kassab collection)

Right side detail of serial 1835.

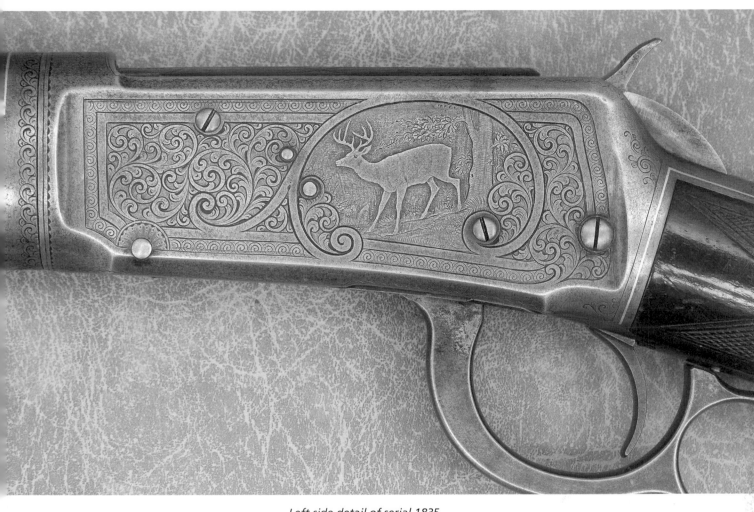

Left side detail of serial 1835.

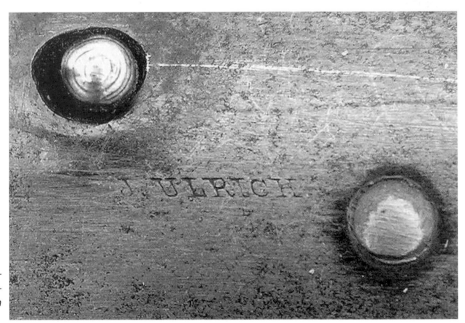

The typical engraving signature of Winchester's master engraver John Ulrich on serial 1835.

ENGRAVING

Engraving was at one time a very popular adornment for firearms, and Winchesters were far from being an exception. But as the cost of labor and consequently the prices increased, this popularity decreased. By the introductory date of the Model 94, the cost for even modest coverage was rapidly becoming prohibitive. By the end of World War I, the pricing for factory engraving had very nearly quadrupled – hence the extreme rarity of engraved Model 94s and the resulting astronomical cost of collecting these beautiful specimens.

Originally Winchester offered only three basic types of engraving, amounting mainly to different degrees of coverage. The customer could somewhat alter each style by asking for slightly more or less coverage than the catalogs dictated (this would be priced accordingly), but not much else from the standard design could be changed.

Plaques and inscriptions would also be provided as per request, but even though this option was accomplished by the engravers, it was considered a somewhat separate operation from the decorative engraving itself.

These early styles of engraving cost anywhere from a few dollars to about $100, depending on the coverage, with the engraver usually only getting a dollar or two per gun. The ability to tailor-make the final price by ordering a specific degree of coverage (usually ordered as $5 worth or $10 worth, etc.) greatly enhanced the chance that even a "working gun" might be treated to a little embellishment. This is particularly noticeable by the amount of lightly engraved "working" Henrys, Model '66s and even Model '73s that are encountered.

This engraving policy was phased out before the introduction of the Model 94.

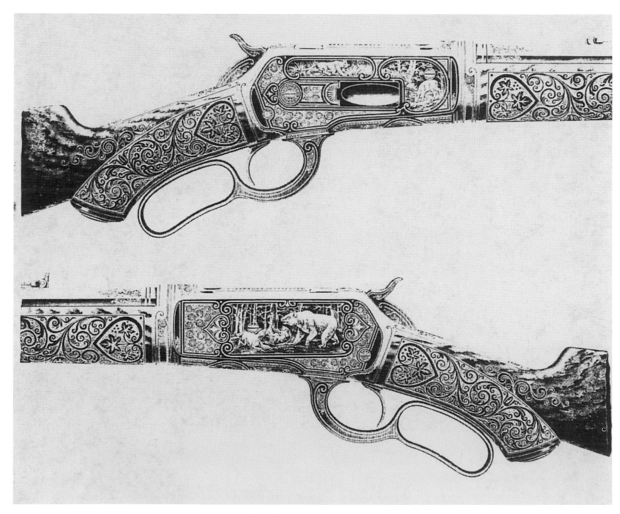

Engraving style 1 from an early 1930s sales catalog.

The later offering, and the one pertaining mainly to the Model 94, was of a standard group of patterns numbered from one to 10 and ranging in price from a low of about $5 to wonderfully artistic creations costing hundreds.

Again the patterns were variable upon the customer's request for more or less coverage (it was still possible to order by specifying the price to be paid), but now the patterns or vignettes could be changed significantly or the customer's own designs would be duplicated.

The standard Winchester factory engraving was a base design of what was known as American/Germanic style scroll, but English style scrolls could easily be substituted and often were.

Places for inscriptions with or without the inscription itself would be provided, and unusual border designs would be applied. The possibilities were almost unlimited. A nicely varied group of game scenes and vignettes was also available to choose from.

The only unwavering feature of factory engraving, regardless of the price, was the dedication to uncompromising quality and the perfect proportioning of the scrollwork and vignettes in relation to the size of the gun to which it was applied.

Essentially unchanged for centuries were the many different tools and methods used in the engraving operation. There were special tools for the different tasks such as scrolling, background work, shading, highlighting, etc.

Most of the work was, of course, done by the principal engraver, but quite often an apprentice would be used when the time came for the more mundane jobs such as polishing, background work or bordering.

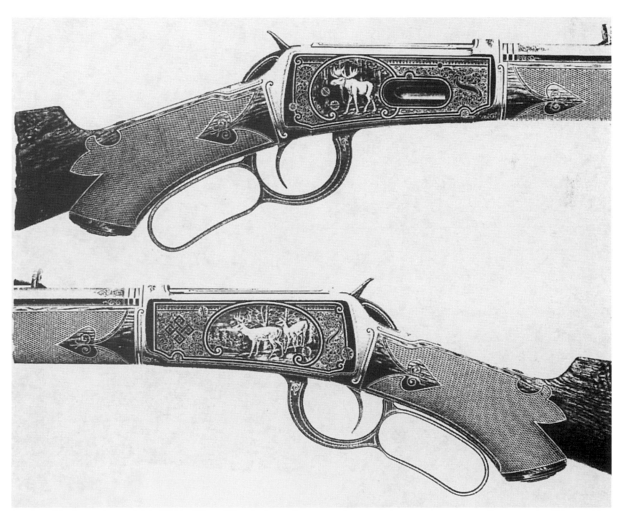

Engraving style 2 from an early 1930s sales catalog.

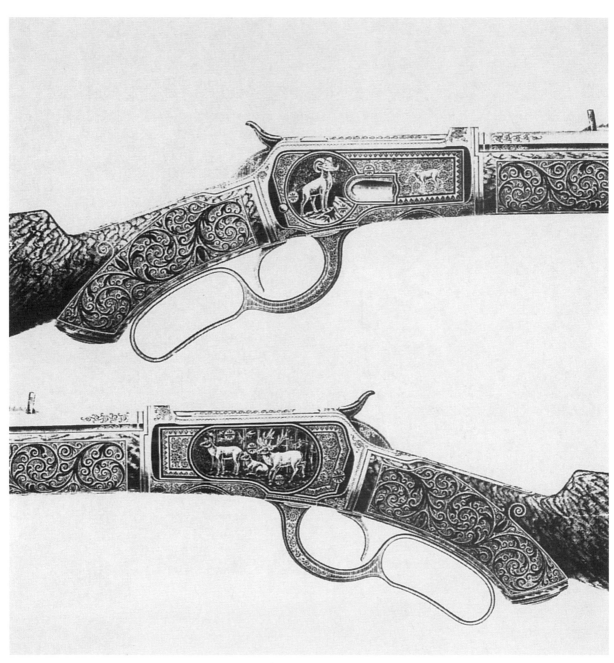

Engraving style 3 from an early 1930s sales catalog.

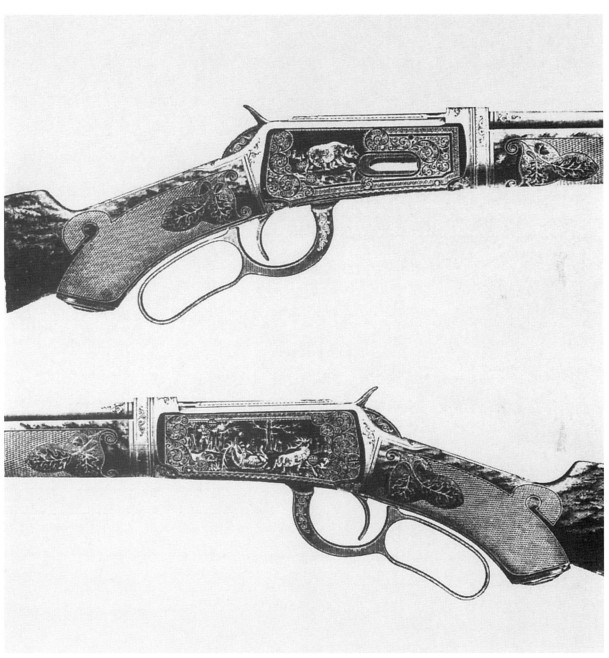

Engraving style 4 from an early 1930s sales catalog.

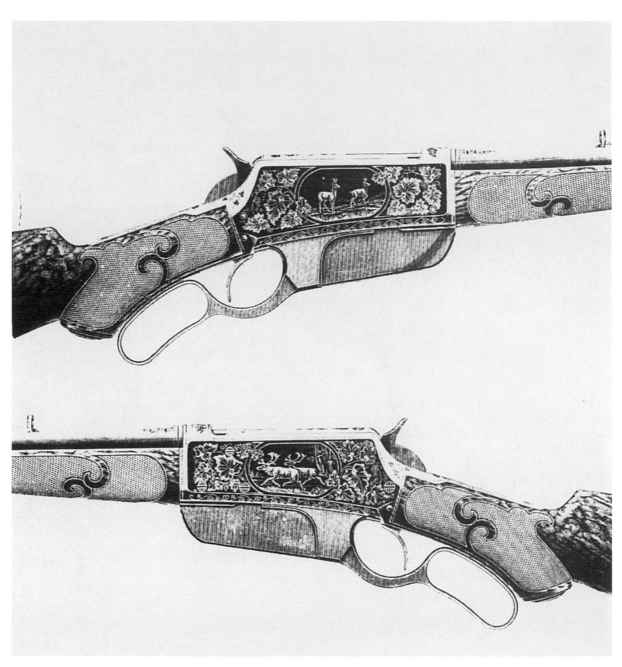

Engraving style 5 from an early 1930s sales catalog.

Engraving style 6 from an early 1930s sales catalog.

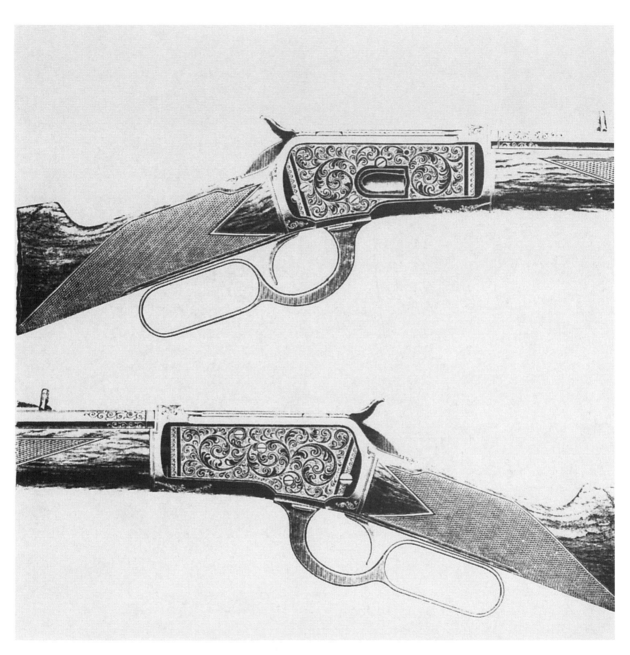

Engraving style 7 from an early 1930s sales catalog.

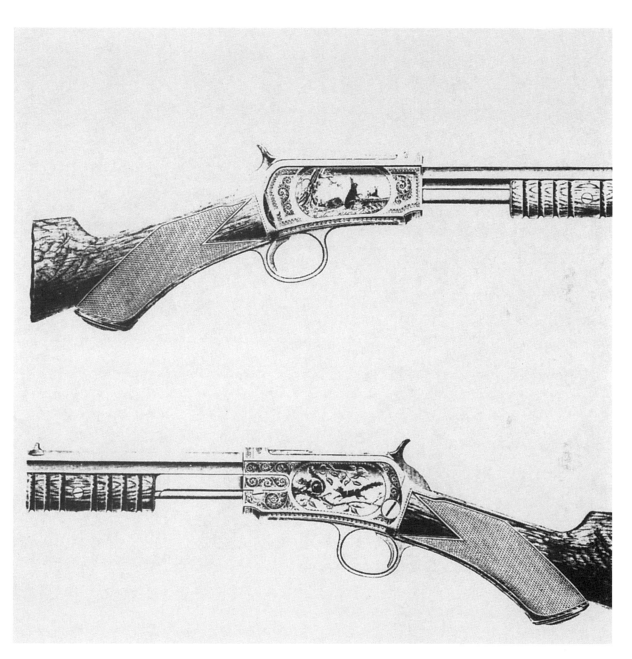

Engraving style 8 from an early 1930s sales catalog.

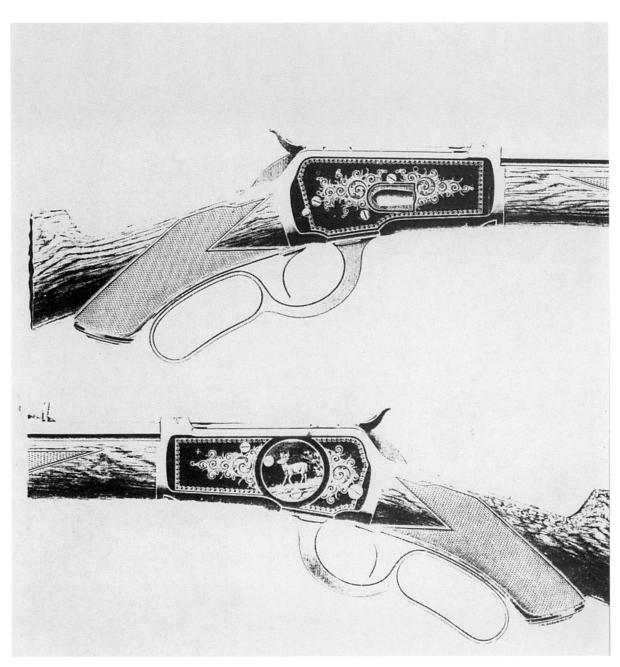

Engraving style 9 from an early 1930s sales catalog.

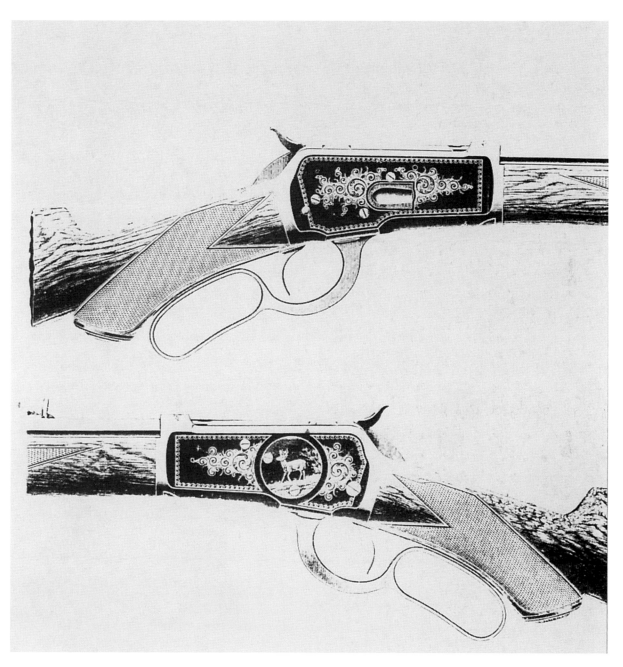

Engraving style 10 from an early 1930s sales catalog.

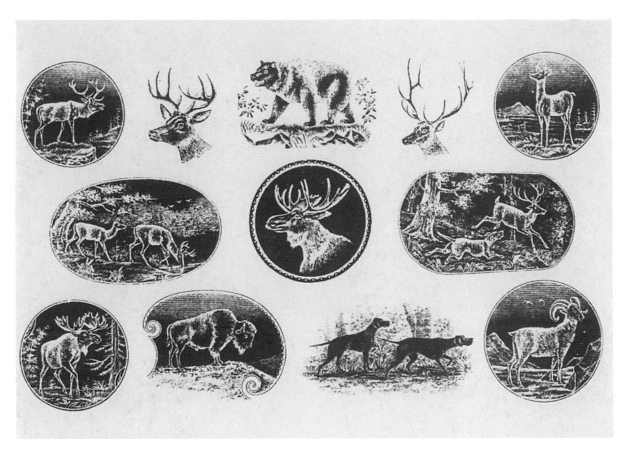

Appropriate Scenes and Vignettes for reproduction on ornamented rifles.

A detailed study of many engraved guns is absolutely essential if one hopes to become proficient at distinguishing factory from non-factory work or identifying specific engravers from their individual style. This is particularly true if the example has been well-used.

Referring to other examples of factory engraving is of little help either; even original factory-applied patterns are never 100 percent identical. Although the base design was often applied with a transfer pattern, the cutting was done by hand, and variations from piece to piece were inevitable.

Due to myriad technical complexities and the lucrativeness of fakery evidenced by phenomenal prices that are commanded for even moderately decorated specimens, I have only touched lightly on the subject of engraving. If engraved Model 94s pique your fancy, a serious study from a singularly devoted source is not only wise – it is imperative.

Caution cannot be too strongly stressed – an engraved gun can be a very expensive mistake. A wonderful and very comprehensive reference on this subject, and highly recommended, is R.L. Wilson's book, *Winchester Engraving*.

This is a reasonably well done contemporary copy of Winchester's Style 10 engraving. It is shown here on a completely restored pre-war carbine. While this is not a bad job of engraving and the gun is extremely attractive overall, it certainly shows the lack of "crispness" and quality of a factory effort

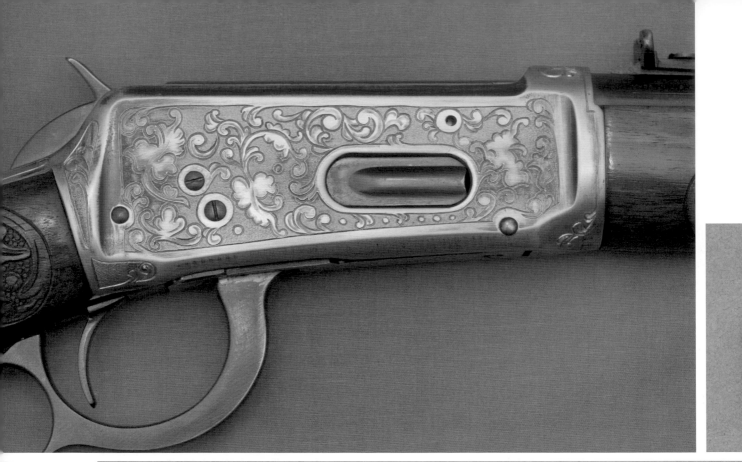

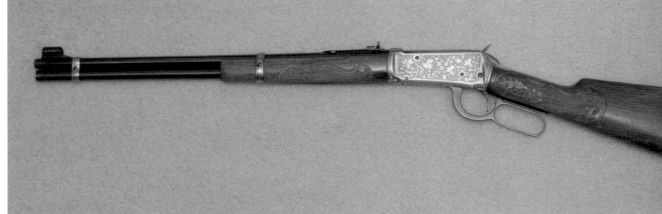

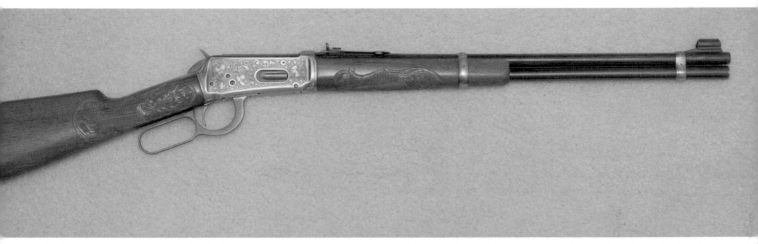

A fine contemporary engraved "transitional" carbine (See Chapter 9) with beautifully carved stocks. This specimen is an example of superior non-factory work. (Author's collection)

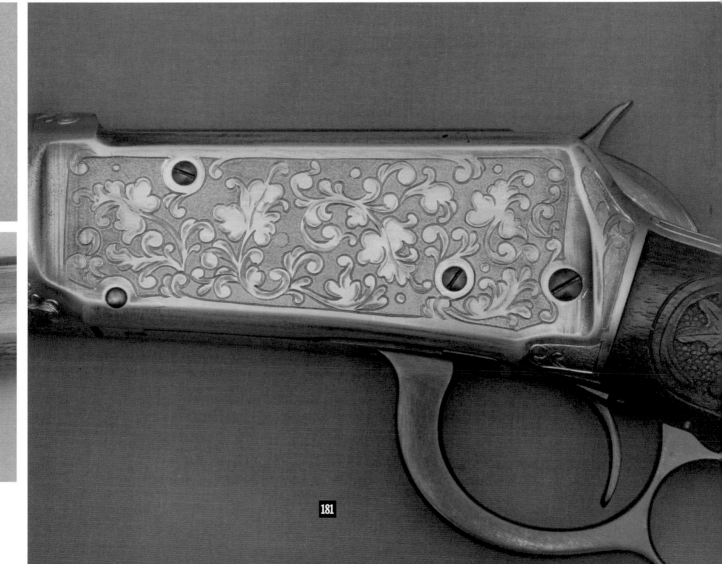

WINCHESTER FRONT SIGHTS

21 Sight Series

Adapted to Models 73—S.S.—86—90—92

		Retail Price Each	Wholesale Each
21-J	Sporting front sight, rifle, .271 high	$ .40	$ .30
21-B	Sporting front sight, rifle, .296 high	.40	.30
21-A	Sporting front sight, rifle, .358 high	.40	.30
21-C	Sporting front sight, rifle, .381 high	.40	.30
21-H	Sporting front sight, rifle, .435 high	.40	.30
21-F	Sporting front sight, rifle, .486 high	.40	.30
23	Express front sight	.60	.45

53 Sight Series

Adapted to Model 95 Carbines

53-A	Blade front sight, .298 high	.40	.30
53-B	Blade front sight, .326 high	.40	.30
53-C	Blade front sight, .362 high	.40	.30
53-D	Blade front sight, .400 high	.40	.30

61 Sight Series

Adapted to Models 73—86—92 and 94 Carbines

61-A	Blade front sight, carbine, .374 high	.40	.30
61-B	Blade front sight, carbine, .450 high	.40	.30
67-A	Globe front sight, rifle, with large and small aperture and post disc, (interchangeable)	1.50	1.13
69-A	Windgauge front sight rifle, without spirit level, with large and small aperture and post disc (interchangeable)	3.60	2.70
69-B	Windgauge front sight rifle, without spirit level, with large and small aperture and post disc (interchangeable)	4.75	3.56
71-A	Beach combination front sight, rifle, Adapted to models 73—92—94 and S.S.	1.25	.94
73-A	Knife blade front sight, rifle, steel blade, .380 high for black powder rifles	.60	.45
73-B	Knife blade front sight, rifle, ivory blade, .380 high for black powder rifles	.60	.45
75-A	Front sight, .292 high, Models 90 and 04	.40	.30
75-B	Front sight, rifle, .292 high, Model 03	.25	.19
75-C	Front sight, rifle, .33 high, Model 56	.40	.30

77 Sight Series

Adapted to Models 02, 03, 04, 06 and 90

77-B	Front sight, rifle, .235 high	$ .40	$ .30
77-A	Front sight, rifle, .290 high	.40	.30
77-C	Front sight, rifle, .310 high	.40	.30
77-D	Front sight, rifle, .335 high	.40	.30
77-E	Front sight, rifle, .370 high	.40	.30
77-F	Front sight, rifle, .405 high	.40	.30

79 Sight Series

Adapted to black powder rifles

79-A	Front sight, rifle, .300 high	.60	.45
79-B	Front sight, rifle, .340 high	.60	.45
79-C	Front sight, rifle, .375 high	.60	.45
81-A	Front sight for shotgun, .123 bead	.10	.08
81-B	Front sight, for shotgun, .140 bead, (for matted rib)	.15	.12
83-A	Front sight for shotgun, .180 bead, brass, Model 97 riot	.15	.12
87-A	Front sight for shotgun, 3/16" bead, matted rib	.15	.12
93-A	Front sight, .368 high, Model 57	.40	.30
93-B	Front sight, .350 high, Model 52	.40	.30
95-A	Front sight, .265 high, Model 58	.15	.12
	Pins for carbine front sight, each	.10	.08
	Aperture disc large, .085 for 67-A, 69-A and 69-B front sight	.40	.30
	Aperture disc small, .267 for 67-A, 69-A and 69-B front sight	.40	.30
	Post disc, for 67-A, 69-A and 69-B front sight	.40	.30
	Key, for 67-A, 69-A and 69-B front sight	.30	.23
	Spirit level complete for 69-B front sight (Key with bulb and (2) cap screws)	1.25	.94
	Windgauge screw and head for 69-A and 69-B front sight	.30	.23
	Base for 69-A and 69-B front sight	.90	.68
	Binding screw for front sight	.10	.08

WINCHESTER REAR SIGHTS

Give model, caliber and kind of ammunition used.

Rear Sights

		Retail Price Each	Wholesale Each
50-B	rear sight, musket and carbine, Model 95	2.40	1.80
82-A	rear sight, Model 52	5.00	3.75
	Elevator cap, 82-A Rear Sight	.15	.12
	Sporting peep cap, 82-A sight	.20	.15
22-C	flat top rear sight with elevator, all rifles	.95	.71
22-E	Rocky Mountain rear sight with elevator, all rifles	.95	.71
24-B	flat top rear sight with slide and elevator, all rifles	.95	.71
26-A	California buckhorn rear sight with elevator, black powder rifles	.95	.71
26-B	California Buckhorn rear sight with elevator, smokeless powder rifles	.95	.71
30-B	rear sight, Models 90, 04 and 06	.75	.56
32-A	rear sight with elevator, Models 90, 04 and 06	.75	.56
34-B	Winchester express rear sight, black powder rifles	1.80	1.35
34-C	Winchester express rear sight, smokeless powder rifles	1.80	1.35
38-A	midrange vernier peep sight, S.S., 86, 90, 92 and 04	4.75	3.56
	Rear sight, 40-A, 03, 04 and 56	.75	.56
44-A	rear sight for carbine, Models 73, 86, 92, 94	1.50	1.13
66-A	rear sight (open), Model 02	.30	.23
68-A	rear sight (peep), Model 02	.30	.23
70-A	leaf rear sight, Model 94, all calibers, and rifles handling smokeless powder cartridges and Winchester high velocity ammunition. Also 05, 07, and 10 rifles	4.75	3.56
72-A	shotgun rear sight, for barrel with matted rib; size of bead .10", Model 12	.15	.12
78-A	rear sight, Model 41	.15	.12
94-A	shotgun rear sight, Model 12	.15	.12
1-A	elevator to be used with No. 22, No. 24 and No. 26 sights, black powder	.30	.23
1-B	elevator to be used with No. 22, No. 24 and No. 26 sights, smokeless powder	.30	.23
1-C	elevator to be used with 22-C, Models 05, 07, 10	.30	.23
2-B	elevator to be used with 32-A, Models 90, 04, 06	.15	.12
3-C	elevator to be used with 22, 24 and 26 sights when used on carbine and Model 54 rifles	.30	.23
	Rear sight blank when rear sight is removed, Models 73, 86, 92 and 94	.35	.27
	Rear sight blank when rear sight is removed, Models 90, 06 and 04	.35	.27
	Rear sight blank when 82-A sight is removed, Model 52	.50	.38
	Elevator cap screw, 82-A sight	.10	.08
	Windgauge screw, 82-A sight	.20	.15
	Windgauge screw spring, 82-A sight	.10	.08
	Elevator complete, 50-B	1.00	.75
	Disc for 38-A sight	.90	.68
	Elevator stop screw, 44-A sight	.10	.08
	Leaf guide screw, 44-A	.10	.08
	Elevator, 44-A	.20	.15
	Elevator spring, 44-A	.10	.08
	Connecting screw, 30-B sight	.10	.08
	Adjusting screw, 30-B sight	.10	.08
	Adjusting screw, 40-A sight	.10	.08
	Binding screw, 22-sight series	.10	.08
	Slides, 22-sight series	.20	.15

Sighting equipment from an early Winchester sales catalog.

WINCHESTER SIGHTS ADAPTED TO WINCHESTER RIFLES

No. 30-D Rear Peep Sight

No. 32A Rear Sight with Elevator

No. 30-B Rear Sight

No. 70A Four Leaf Rear Sight

Express Rear Sight
No. 34B for black powder
No. 34C for smokeless powder

Carbine Rear Sight No. 44A
for Models 73, 86, 92 and 94
Black Powder Cartridges

40A Rear Sight

22E Rocky Mountain Rear Sight

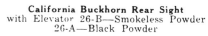

California Buckhorn Rear Sight
with Elevator 26-B—Smokeless Powder
26-A—Black Powder

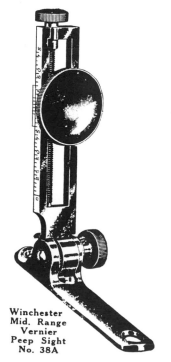

Winchester
Mid. Range
Vernier
Peep Sight
No. 38A

22-C Flat Top Rear Sight
with Elevator

22-F Sporting Rear Sight
with Improved Elevator adapted to Model
54 Rifle and Carbine

Sighting equipment from an early 1930s Winchester sales catalog.

WINCHESTER
TRADE MARK

WINCHESTER SIGHTS ADAPTED TO WINCHESTER RIFLES

No. 21 Sight Series

No. 93 Sight
Not adapted to Model
94 .30 Caliber or .32
Winchester Special
Rifles

No. 77 Sight Series

No. 79 Sight Series

No. 75 Sight

**No. 61 Sight Series
Blade Carbine Front
Sight**
Adapted to Carbines
Models 73, 86, 92 and
94

**No. 53-D
Blade Front Sight**
Adapted to Model 95
Carbine and .30 Army
and .303 British
Rifles

**No. 69-B Windgauge Front
Sight**
with Spirit Level and large
and small Aperture and
Post Discs
(Interchangeable)

No. 67-A Globe Front Sight
with large and small Aperture and Post Discs
(Interchangeable)

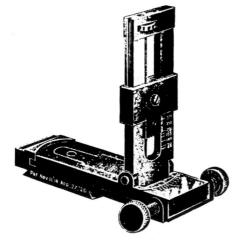

No. 82-A Rear Sight
Adapted to Model 52 Rifle

**No. 23 Express
Front Sight**

**Sporting Peep Cap
Rear Sight**

For use on No. 82-A rear
sight for hunting purposes

No. 50-B Rear Sight
Adapted to 95 Musket and
Carbine

Sighting equipment from an early 1930s Winchester sales catalog.

184

LYMAN SIGHTS ADAPTED TO WINCHESTER RIFLES

**Lyman No. 4
Hunting
Front Sight**

**Lyman No. 3
Front Sight**

**Lyman No. 5-B
Combination
Front Sight**

17A with Eight Interchangeable Inserts

17G same as 17A except with high base for Model 52 rifle with heavy barrel.

**Sight
Folding Leaf
Lyman No. 6**

**Lyman No. 6-W
Single Leaf Sight
Adapted to Models
56 and 57**

**Lyman No. 6-W
Leaf Sight
Adapted to
Model 54 Rifle**

**Lyman Sight No. 66-W
for
Model 54 Carbine
and Rifle**

**Lyman No. 26
Carbine Front Sight,
Models 92 and 94**

**Lyman No. 26
Adapted to Model
95 Carbine, .30 Army
and .303 British
Rifles**

**Lyman No. 26-W
Baby Jack Gold
Bead Front Sight**
Adapted to
Model 54

**Lyman Rear Sight
No. 42-W**
Adapted to
Models 56 and 57

**Lyman No. 1-A
Combination Rear
Sight**

**Lyman No. 48-W
Micrometer Windgauge
Receiver Sight
Adapted to Model
54**

**Lyman No. 21
Receiver Sight**

Sighting equipment from an early 1930s Winchester sales catalog.

MARBLE SIGHTS

Adapted to Winchester Rifles

Flexible Rear Sight

Sheard Gold Bead Front Sight

Marble Standard
Front Sight

Marble Improved
Front Sight

**Special Base Flexible Joint
Rear Sight**

Marble Reversible Front Sight

Marble Duplex Sight

Marble Adjustable Leaf Sight

Marble Blade
Front Sight
for Models
95 and 54

Marble Blade
Front Sight
for Models
92 and 94

Marble V-M Front Sight

Sighting equipment from an early 1930s Winchester sales catalog.

A very early (serrated edges) flat-top sporting rear sight with the 1A elevator. This sight was particularly popular on short rifles but was available on all variations of Model 94s.

This is a standard or "Rocky Mountain" type rear sight and 1A elevator. This is a very early example with the serrated edges.

The typical Winchester-installed and so-called "fancy filler" that is sometimes installed when an optional rear sight is used and the rear sisght slot is not needed. Blanks of other manufacturers are seen as well. The "fancy" style is is most often found on deluxe guns.

This is an example of an aftermarket or non-Winchester bolt peep sight. While of some quality, it is not in any way the same as the factory version. An illustration of the factory type can be found in the Model 64 section.

This is an illustration of the rarely-encountered "Daniels" rear sight. It is mounted in the original rear sight slot and works much like a receiver peep sight but without need for extra holes being drilled in the receiver. It is quite rare.

This is a striking example of the very graceful and beautiful "full California buckhorn" type of rear sight with a 32B style elevator. Not very often encountered, this sight is an eye-catching addition to any fine rifle.

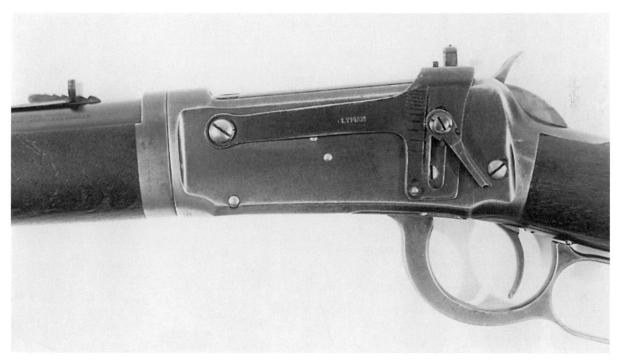

The unusual and quite rare Lyman side-mounted receiver sight, often referred to colloquially as the "Climbin' Lyman." An attractive and interesting option, this sight may be encountered on rifles or carbines with almost equal frequency. They have even been found on engraved models, covering a good portion of the engraving – very strange!

41

Winchester Repeating Rifle.

MODEL
1894

Price List Of Model 1894 Rifles.   Full Or Half Magazine.   Solid Frame.   .32-40 And .38-55 Calibers.

Carbine, Barrel 20 Inches Long, Weight about 6¼ pounds,....................$17.50
Rifle, Round Barrel 26 Inches Long, Weight about 7¾ pounds,............... 18.00
Rifle, Octagon Barrel 26 Inches Long, Weight about 8 pounds,................. 19.50
Rifle, Half Octagon Barrel 26 Inches Long, Weight about 8 pounds,........... 20.00
Rifle, Extra Light Weight, Round Barrel 26 Inches Long, Weight about 7¼
   pounds, ... 23.00
Rifle, Extra Light Weight, Octagon Barrel 26 Inches Long, Weight about 7¼
   pounds, ... 24.50
Rifle, Extra Light Weight, Half Octagon Barrel 26 Inches Long, Weight about
   7¼ pounds,... 25.00

"Take-Down."

Rifle, Round Barrel 26 Inches Long, Weight about 8 pounds,..................$25.00
Rifle, Octagon Barrel 26 Inches Long, Weight about 8 pounds,................. 26.50
Rifle, Half Octagon Barrel 26 Inches Long, Weight about 8 pounds,........... 27.00
Rifle, Extra Light Weight, Round Barrel 26 Inches Long, Weight about 7½
   pounds, ... 30.00
Rifle, Extra Light Weight, Octagon Barrel 26 Inches Long, Weight about 7½
   pounds, ... 31.50
Rifle, Extra Light Weight, Half Octagon Barrel 26 Inches Long, Weight about
   7½ pounds,... 32.00

.25-35, .30 Winchester, And .32 Winchester Special Calibers. Solid Frame.

Carbine, Nickel Steel Barrel 20 Inches Long, Weight about 6½ pounds,.........$21.00
Rifle, Round Nickel Steel Barrel 26 Inches Long, Weight about 8 pounds,....... 23.00
Rifle, Octagon Nickel Steel Barrel 26 Inches Long, Weight about 8 pounds,..... 24.50
Rifle, Half Octagon Nickel Steel Barrel 26 Inches Long, Weight about 8 pounds, 25.00
Rifle, Extra Light Weight, .25 and .30 calibers only, Round Nickel Steel Barrel
   26 Inches Long, Weight about 7¼ pounds,.............................. 28.00
Rifle, Extra Light Weight, .25 and .30 calibers only, Octagon Nickel Steel Barrel
   26 Inches Long, Weight about 7¼ pounds,.............................. 29.50
Rifle, Extra Light Weight, .25 and .30 calibers only, Half Octagon Nickel Steel
   Barrel 26 Inches Long, Weight about 7¼ pounds,....................... 30.00

"Take-Down."

Rifle, Round Nickel Steel Barrel 26 Inches Long, Weight about 8 pounds,.......$28.00
Rifle, Octagon Nickel Steel Barrel 26 Inches Long, Weight about 8 pounds,..... 29.50
Rifle, Half Octagon Nickel Steel Barrel 26 Inches Long, Weight about 8 pounds, 30.00
Rifle, Extra Light Weight, .25 and .30 calibers only, Round Nickel Steel Barrel
   26 Inches Long, Weight about 7½ pounds,.............................. 33.00
Rifle, Extra Light Weight, .25 and .30 calibers only, Octagon Nickel Steel Barrel
   26 Inches Long, Weight about 7½ pounds,.............................. 34.50
Rifle, Extra Light Weight, .25 and .30 calibers only, Half Octagon Nickel Steel
   Barrel 26 Inches Long, Weight about 7½ pounds,....................... 35.00

Interchangeable Barrels.

Model 1894 "Take-Down" rifles can be furnished with interchangeable barrels of any caliber in which these rifles are made.

Extra Barrels, complete with magazine, forearm, etc., .32-40 and .38-55, Round, $12.00; Octagon, $13.50; Half Octagon, $14.00.

Extra Barrels, complete with magazine, forearm, etc., .25-35, .30 Winchester or .32 Winchester Special, Nickel Steel, Round, $15.00; Octagon, $16.50; Half Octagon, $17.00.

Rifles to be fitted with interchangeable barrels must be sent to the factory. See page 66.

Extras from a 1916 Winchester salesmen's catalog.

EXTRAS

Extras For Winchester Rifles.

All deviations from standard styles and sizes involve a large proportional outlay for hand labor, and, when ordered, will be subject to the following charges, which should be added to the list price of a rifle:—

Butt stocks of special shape, involving change in either length or drop from standard, $10.00.

Engraving from $5.00 to $250.00 additional, according to style and quality. See page 99.

Full Nickel Plating, ... List,	$4.00
Nickel Plating Trimmings, ...	2.50
Silver Plating Trimmings, ...	4.00
Gold Plating Trimmings, ...	10.00
Set Triggers on Repeating Rifles, Model 1873,*	3.00
Double Set Triggers on Models 1886, 1892, and 1894,*	3.00
Regular Set Triggers on Single Shot Rifles,*	2.00
Schuetzen Double Set Triggers on Single Shot Rifles,*	6.00
Fancy Walnut Stock and Forearm, except on Models 1905, 1907, and 1910 Rifles,	10.00
Fancy Walnut Stock and Forearm on Models 1905, 1907, and 1910 Rifles,	13.00
Checking Fancy Walnut Stock and Forearm, ...	5.00
Fancy Walnut Stock and Forearm checked, except on Models 1905, 1907, and 1910 Rifles,	15.00
Fancy Walnut Stock and Forearm checked, on Models 1905, 1907, and 1910 Rifles,	18.00
Pistol Grip Stock and Forearm, Fancy Walnut checked, ...	18.00
Pistol Grip Stock of Plain Walnut, not checked, ...	3.00
Checking Plain Walnut Stock and Forearm, except Models 1905, 1907, and 1910,	2.00
Checking Plain Walnut Stock and Forearm on Models 1905, 1907, and 1910,	5.00
Palm Rest on Single Shot Rifle, ...	6.00
Spur Finger Lever on Single Shot Rifle, ...	4.00
Schuetzen Butt Plate on Single Shot Rifle, ...	4.00
Swiss Butt Plate, ...	2.00
Cheek Piece on Fancy Stock, ...	4.00
Leaving off Rear Sight Slot, or changing position of Rear Sight,	1.00
Blank Piece to fill Rear Sight Slot, ...	.25
.30 Caliber Barrels fitted to Krag-Jorgensen or Springfield Military Rifles,	20.00
Sling Strap, ...	1.35
Sling Strap with Screw Eyes, Swivel Hook and Button, ...	2.25
Sling Strap N. R. A. Style, ...	2.25
Silver's Recoil Pad fitted to Rifles with Shotgun Butt Stocks, ..	7.00
Matting Barrels, ...	5.00
Interchangeable Barrels, complete with Magazine, Forearm, etc., Model 1886, all calibers (except .33), 1892 (.38 and .44 calibers), and 1894 (.32-40 and .38-55 calibers), for "Take-Down" Rifles, Round Barrel,	12.00
Octagon Barrel, ...	13.50
Half Octagon Barrel, ...	14.00
Interchangeable Barrels, complete with Magazine, Forearm, etc., Model 1894, .25-35, .30 W. C. F., and .32 Winchester Special calibers, for "Take-Down" Rifles, Round Barrel,	15.00
Octagon Barrel, ...	16.50
Half Octagon Barrel, ...	17.00
Interchangeable Barrels for "Take-Down" Single Shot Rifles, Round Barrel,	9.00
Octagon Barrel, ...	10.50
Round Interchangeable Nickel Steel Barrels for "Take-Down" Single Shot Rifles, except .35 and .405 W. C. F. calibers,	12.00
Round Interchangeable Nickel Steel Barrels for "Take-Down" Single Shot Rifles, .35 and .405 W. C. F. calibers,	14.00
Hickory Cleaning Rods (one piece), ...	.10
.22 Caliber Metal Cleaning Rod, ...	15
Rifle Butt Stocks equipped with jointed rod on Models 1886, 1892, 1894, 1895, and on Single Shot Rifles of .25 caliber or larger,	.90

*See page 98 for Directions for use of Set Trigger.

Extras from a 1916 Winchester salesmen's catalog.

Set Triggers

Set Triggers For Winchester Rifles.

Winchester Rifles, which can be equipped with set triggers, take the following styles: Model 1873, Single Set Trigger only. Models 1886, 1892, and 1894, Double Set Trigger only. Single Shot Rifles, except those chambered for rim fire, .22, .32, .38, and .44 W. C. F., .25-20, and .32 Ideal Cartridges, the Double Set Trigger, or Schuetzen Double Set Trigger only. Single Shot Rifles chambered for rim fire, .22, .32, .38, and .44 W. C. F., .25-20, and .32 Ideal Cartridges, can be equipped only with the Single Set Trigger for Single Shot Rifles unless made with a No. 3 barrel, in which case they can be equipped with the Double Set Trigger, or Schuetzen Double Set Trigger.

How To Use A Set Trigger.

After the gun is closed and cocked, if the trigger is a single set, push the trigger forward with the thumb until a click is heard and the trigger sets in a forward position. If it is a Double Set Trigger, push the rear trigger forward until a click is heard. If it is a Schuetzen Double Set Trigger, pull the rear trigger back until a click is heard. The trigger is then set, and a very slight pull will fire the gun. The trigger must be set after each shot. If it is desired to make the set finer, turn in the small screw directly back of the trigger. By turning it in just to the right point, the trigger can be made to pull very fine indeed.

We advise parties having guns with plain triggers, who desire to have them changed over to set triggers, to send the guns to us and let us adjust and set triggers to them. Where plain trigger guns are sent to the factory to be changed to set triggers, $3.00 will be charged for making the change on magazine guns, $6.00 for replacing with Schuetzen Double Set Trigger, and $2.00 for the other set triggers on single shot rifles.

Special Parts For Winchester Single Set Trigger For Single Shot Rifles.

423 S. S. T. Catch Hook,......................$0.15	116 S. S. T. Sear,........................$0.25
424 S. S. T. Catch Hook Spring,......... .05	87 S. S. T. Trigger,...................... .50
276 S. S. T. Knock Off Spring,.. .... .20	425 S. S. T. Trigger Adjusting Screw,... .05

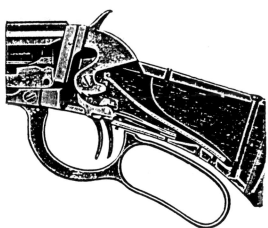

Parts Necessary To Change From Plain To Model '86, '92, And '94 Double Set Trigger.

426 D. S. T. Front Trigger,...............$0.70	
427 D. S. T. Front Trigger Pin,.......... .05	
428 D. S. T. Front Trigger Spring,....... .05	
62 D. S. T. Hammer, complete with Fly and Stirrup,....................... .85	
83 D. S. T. Lower Tang, M. '92, M. '94, or M. '86,........................... 1.75	
70 D. S. T. Mainspring,................. .30	
429 D. S. T. Rear Trigger,........ ... . 1.00	
430 D. S. T. Rear Trigger Pin,.. .... .05	
431 D. S. T. Rear Trigger Spring,..... . .10	
432 D. S. T. Rear Trigger Stop Pin,..... .05	
116 D. S. T. Sear,.. .... .50	
118 D. S. T. Sear Spring,............... .05	
119 D. S. T. Sear Spring Screw,........ . .05	
433 D. S. T. Trigger Guide Pin,....... .. .05	
434 D. S. T. Trigger Adjusting Screw,.. .05	

Extras from a 1916 Winchester salesmen's catalog.

WINCHESTER
MODEL 94 LEVER ACTION REPEATING RIFLE
Order by number shown at left of each item.
SOLID FRAME

No.	Caliber	Retail Each	Wholesale Each
G9405C—	.25-35 Winchester, round barrel	$33.00	$23.10
G9407C—	.25-35 Winchester, octagon barrel	34.90	24.43
*G9419C—	.30 Winchester (.30-30), round barrel	33.00	23.10
G9417C—	.30 Winchester (.30-30), octagon barrel	34.90	24.43
G9425C—	.32 Winchester Special, round barrel	33.00	23.10
G9429C—	.32 Winchester Special, octagon barrel	34.90	24.43
G9435C—	.32-40, round barrel	33.00	23.10
G9439C—	.32-40, octagon barrel	34.90	24.43
G9445C—	.38-55, round barrel	33.00	23.10
G9449C—	.38-55, octagon barrel	34.90	24.43
	One-half, two-thirds or three-quarter magazine additional	3.00	2.10
	Shotgun butt stock with either metal or rubber butt plate additional	2.00	1.40

TAKE-DOWN

	For take-down rifles with one-half, two-thirds, three-quarter or full magazine, round or octagon barrel add to solid frame price	8.00	5.60
	Shotgun butt stock with either metal or rubber butt plate, additional	2.00	1.40

MODEL 94 CARBINE

No.	Caliber	Retail Each	Wholesale Each
G9401C—	.25-35 Winchester, 20 inch, round barrel	$31.00	$21.70
*G9412C—	.30 (.30-30) Winchester, 20 inch, round barrel	31.00	21.70
G9411C—	.30 (.30-30) Winchester, 15 inch, round barrel	31.00	21.70
G9423C—	.32 Winchester Special, 20 inch, round barrel	31.00	21.70
G9433C—	.32-40, 20 inch, round barrel	31.00	21.70
G9443C—	.38-55, 20 inch, round barrel	31.00	21.70
	Attaching sling ring to receiver on carbine, add	2.00	1.40

MODEL 55 LEVER ACTION REPEATING RIFLE
Order by number shown at left of each item.
SOLID FRAME

No.	Caliber	Retail Each	Wholesale Each
G5504C—	.25-35 Winchester	$34.00	$23.80
*G5505C—	.30 (.30-30) Winchester	34.00	23.80
G5506C—	.32 Winchester Special	34.00	23.80
	Furnished with rifle butt instead of shotgun butt, additional	2.00	1.40

TAKE-DOWN

No.	Caliber	Retail Each	Wholesale Each
G5502C—	.25-35 Winchester	39.00	27.30
*G5501C—	.30 (.30-30) Winchester	39.00	27.30
G5503C—	.32 Winchester Special	39.00	27.30
	Furnished with rifle butt instead of shotgun butt, additional	2.00	1.40

*Will be furnished if order does not specify caliber.

MODEL 86 LEVER ACTION REPEATING RIFLE
Order by number shown at left of each item.

No.	Caliber	Retail Each	Wholesale Each
*G8607C—	.33 Winchester	$42.50	$29.75
G8609C—	45-70	42.50	29.75

Prices shown on this model are special close-out prices and no variations from standard rifle will be accepted.

*Will be furnished if order does not specify caliber.

From an early 1930s Winchester sales catalog.

EXTRAS FOR WINCHESTER RIFLES

All deviations from standard styles and sizes involve a large proportional outlay and considerable hand labor and when ordered will be subject to additional charges. The following list presents an outline of the various extras which can be furnished for Winchester rifles:

Making stocks of special dimensions, either straight or pistol grip, (except for Models 52, 54 and 57).

Changing standard dimension stock from straight to pistol grip, (pistol grip rubber cap not included).

Making stock and forearm of specially selected walnut to standard dimensions, either pistol grip or straight grip, with or without pistol grip cap, (except Models 07, 10, 52, 54 and 57).

Making stock and forearm of specially selected walnut as above for Models 07 and 10.

Making stock and forearm of specially selected walnut as above for Models 52, 54 and 57.

Plain checking stock and forearm, except Models 07, 10 and 52.

Fancy checking stock and forearm.

Checking stock only on Model 90 or 06 (Plain)

Checking stock only on Model 90 or 06 (Fancy)

Engraving and special ornamentation according to style and quality.

Full nickel plating.

Nickel plated trimmings.

Silver plated trimmings.

Gold plated trimmings.

Rubber pistol grip cap.

Checking triggers.

Telescope sight mount bases.

Leaving off rear sight slot or changing position of rear sight.

Blank piece to fill rear sight slot.

Attaching screw eyes for sling strap.

Stainless steel barrels for rifles.

High polished finish on stock and forearm.

Oil finish on stock and forearm.

Parts necessary to change from single trigger to double set triggers on Models 92, 53, 94 and 55.

Supplemental Chambers

Permit the use of popular pistol cartridges in high power rifles chambered for .30 Winchester, .30 Army, .30 Government Model 1906, .303 Savage, .303 British, .32-40, and 32 Winchester Special Cartridges without change or readjustment of the rifle except the sights. Inserted in the rifle same as the cartridge.

Made in the following sizes:
Caliber .30 Winchester, for use with .32 Smith & Wesson Cartridges.
Caliber .30 Army, for use with .32 Smith & Wesson Cartridges.
Caliber .30 Gov't Model 1906, for use with Smith & Wesson Cartridges.
Caliber .303 Savage, for use with .32 Smith & Wesson Cartridges.
Caliber .303 British, for use with .32 Smith & Wesson Cartridges.
Caliber .32 Winchester Special, for use with .32 Short Colt and .32 Long Colt Cartridges.
Caliber .32-40, for use with .32 Short Colt and .32 Long Colt Cartridges.

We recommend the use of Smokeless Powder Lead Ball Cartridges only, with the Winchester Supplemental Chamber. Cartridges carrying metal patch bullets should not be used with this device. Black powder cartridges soon foul barrels having such quick twists as the above.

From an early 1930s Winchester sales catalog.

EXTRAS FOR WINCHESTER RIFLES

Extras for Winchester Rifles	Retail Each	Wholesale Each
Making stocks of special dimensions, either straight or pistol grip (Except for Models 52, 54 and 57)	$20.00	$14.00
Changing standard dimension stock from straight to pistol grip (pistol grip rubber cap not included)	6.00	4.20
Making stock and forearm of specially selected walnut to standard dimensions, either pistol grip or straight grip, with or without pistol grip cap, (except Models 07, 52, 54, and 57)	25.00	17.50
Making stock and forearm of specially selected walnut as above for Models 07 and 10	30.00	21.00
Making stock and forearm of specially selected walnut as above for Models 52, 54 and 57. Prices on application.		
Plain checking stock and forearm, except Models 07, 10 and 52, which take fancy checking price	4.00	2.80
Fancy checking stock and forearm	8.00	5.60
Plain checking stock only, M/90 or 06	2.00	1.40
Fancy checking stock only, M/90 or 06	4.00	2.80
Engraving and special ornamentation according to style and quality. Prices on application.		
Full nickel plating	7.50	5.25
Nickel plated trimmings	5.00	3.50
Silver plated trimmings	7.50	5.25
Gold plated trimmings	17.50	12.25
Rubber pistol grip cap	2.00	1.40
Checking trigger	2.00	1.40
Recoil pads fitted to rifles with shotgun butt stocks (see detail under recoil pads).		
Telescope sight mount bases	1.00	.70
Leaving off rear sight slot or changing position of rear sight	2.50	1.75
Blank piece to fill rear sight slot	.50	.35
Attaching screw eyes for sling strap	.50	.35
Stainless steel barrels for rifles, exept Models 52 and 54. Prices on application.		
Highly polished finish on stocks and forearms	5.00	3.50
Oil finish on stock and forearm	2.00	1.40
Parts necessary to change single trigger to double set trigger	8.00	5.60
Stock of standard dimensions other than standard semi-beavertail type for Model 52	20.00	14.00

RECOIL PADS

	Retail Each	Wholesale Each
Winchester small pad	$ 3.60	$ 2.25
Winchester large pad	3.60	2.25
Noshoc pad	3.60	2.25
For attaching any of above pads	1.00	.70
Hawkins pad	3.25	2.44
Jostam Hy-gun pad	3.00	2.25
Jostam Sponge Rubber, 1-ply pad	1.50	1.13
Jostam Sponge Rubber, 2-ply pad	2.00	1.50
Jostam Sponge Rubber, 3-ply pad	2.50	1.88
Jostam Anti-Flinch, small	3.25	2.44
Jostam Anti-Flinch, medium	3.25	2.44
Jostam Anti-Flinch, large	3.25	2.44
Jostam Air Cushion pad	3.00	2.25
D-W No. A, large pad	3.25	2.44
D-W No. B, small pad	3.25	2.44
Goodrich Air Cushion pad	3.25	2.44
For attaching any of above pads	2.00	1.40

Prices of stainless steel barrels furnished on application.

SLING STRAPS AND GUN SLINGS

	Retail Each	Wholesale Each
Winchester Sling Strap	$ 1.30	$ .91
N.R.A. Improved Shooting Gun Sling	2.50	1.75
Kerr Webb Sling Strap, 1¼-inch	1.25	.88
Kerr Webb Sling Strap, 1-inch	1.00	.70

Extras from an early 1930s Winchester sales catalog.

WINCHESTER

WINCHESTER
Cleaning Rods

.22 caliber iron cleaning rod for Model 06	$ .15	$ .11
.22 caliber iron cleaning rod for Model 90	.15	.11
.22 caliber iron cleaning rod for Model 03	.15	.11
.30 caliber wood cleaning rod — long	.15	.11
.30 caliber wood cleaning rod — short	.15	.11
.38 caliber wood cleaning rod — long	.15	.11
.38 caliber wood cleaning rod — short	.15	.11
.22 caliber flexible cleaner, 24 inches	.50	.35
.22 caliber flexible cleaner, 30 inches	.50	.35
.22 caliber flexible cleaner, 36 inches	.50	.35
6 m/m U.S. Gov't. cleaner	.50	.35
.30-351 U.S. Gov't. cleaner	.50	.35
.38-44 U.S. Gov't. cleaner	.50	.35
.45-50 U.S. Gov't. cleaner	.50	.35
6 — Jointed Winchester cleaning rod	1.50	1.05
.22 caliber brass rod for Model 52, 37½ inches	.50	.35
.22 caliber brass rod, 27½ inches	.50	.35
Jointed shotgun cleaning rod with swab and brush, 10 to 20 ga.	.50	.35

WINCHESTER
Cleaning and Lubricating Preparations

	Retail Each	Wholesale Per Doz.
Gun Oil, in 3 oz. patent oil cans	$ .25	$ 2.00
General Utility Oil, in 3 oz. patent oil cans	.25	2.00
Crystal Cleaner, in 3½ oz. bottles	.25	2.00
Gun Grease, in collapsible tubes	.15	1.20
Rust Remover, in collapsible tubes	.25	2.00
	Each	Each
Gun Grease, in 5 lb. cans, per can	$ 3.50	$ 2.33
Gun Oil, in gallon cans, per can	3.00	2.00
General Utility Oil, in gallon cans, per can	3.00	2.00

Wholesale price subject to 5% discount in six dozen lots.

WINCHESTER
Cleaning and Lubricating Preparations Assortment

No.	Retail Per Asst.	Wholesale Per Asst.
G1098V	$ 6.60	$ 4.41

WINCHESTER
Gun Covers

	Retail Price Each	Wholesale Each
Style A Take-Down Canvas Cover	$ 4.35	$ 3.04
Style B Full-Length Canvas Cover	4.35	3.04
Style C Take-Down Canvas Cover	2.45	1.70
Style D Full-Length Canvas Cover	2.45	1.70
Style 15W	13.25	9.10
Style 25W	18.50	12.75
Style 35W	17.50	12.12
Style 45W	23.50	16.38

Extras from an early 1930s Winchester sales catalog.

WINCHESTER GUN COVERS

A selection of leather and canvas gun cases adapted to various models of Winchester rifles and shotguns is available. These cases are excellently made of the finest materials and afford an ideal protection to the gun as well as convenience for the use of the shooter. Please specify model and length of barrel when ordering.

Style A—Winchester take-down cover of heavy brown Army duck for rifle or shotgun. Strongly made. Lock and muzzle protected with heavy orange leather sewed ends. Straight heavy handle. Made in 20, 22, 24, 25 and 28 inch sizes.

Style C—Practically the same as style A, but made of heavy olive drab canvas. Made in 20, 24, and 26 inch size.

Style B—Winchester full length cover of heavy brown Army duck. For rifle or shotgun. Extra heavy combination sling and handle. Lined with flannel. Sewed ends. Made in 14, 15, 16, 26 and 30 inch.

Style D—Practically the same as style B, only made of heavy olive drab canvas. Made in 16 inch size.

Model 25W—A large roomy case of heavy russet leather strongly stitched. Will take a rifle or shotgun and extra barrel. Has patent hinged partition. Lined with maroon colored flannel, finished with solid brass trimmings. Sling strap and handle of finest grade leather. Made in size to hold 30 and 32 inch barrels.

Model 15W—A compact, finely made case of heavy russet leather for Winchester take-down rifles or shotguns. Maroon colored flannel lining, patent hinge partition. Heavy brass trimming, lock buckle, handle and sling. Made in 20, 24, 25 and 26 inch sizes.

Model 35W—Winchester take-down shotgun or rifle case, straight line style, hand sewed. Made of heavy russet leather, maroon colored flannel lining. Case opens at both ends, with hinged partition. Case has sling and handle. Brass lock, buckle and brass trimming throughout. Made in 25, 26, 28, 30 and 32 inch sizes.

Model 45W—Same style case as 35W but made large enough to carry two barrels. Made in 26, 30 and 32 inch sizes.

Extras from an early 1930s Winchester sales catalog.

WINCHESTER RECOIL PAD

Furnished in two sizes, a small pad which is furnished regularly on orders and a larger size adapted to Winchester Model 97 shotguns and other large size shotgun butt stocks.

Recoil pads other than Winchester which are carried in stock are listed below.

Noshoc pad
Hawkins pad
Jostam Hy-gun pad
Jostam Sponge Rubber, 1-ply pad
Jostam Sponge Rubber, 2-ply pad
Jostam Sponge Rubber, 3-ply pad
Jostam Anti-Flinch, small

Jostam Anti-Flinch, medium
Jostam Anti-Flinch, large
Jostam Air Cushion pad
D-W No. A, large pad
D-W No. B, small pad
Goodrich Air Cushion pad

STAINLESS STEEL BARRELS

Stainless steel barrels for Winchester rifles and shotguns are available on special orders. Bored and rifled with Winchester precision and exactitude, these barrels virtually do away with the threat of rusting and pitting whether from powder residues or from climatic conditions. In addition they give greatly increased resistance to erosion and the action of hot gasses so that their length of service is materially increased and their original accuracy is retained over a greatly lengthened period.

Extras from an early 1930s Winchester sales catalog.

PART II:
The Model 55

A fine example of the very scarce "solid frame" Model 55. Note the super high grade but uncheckered wood – at least a Winchester grading of XXX – on an otherwise standard model. There are XXXs on the lower tang. (P. Cammarata collection)

A standard and typical early variation Model 55 takedown model. (Author's collection)

THE MODEL 55

INTRODUCTION

The Model 55 was the first introduction of a "sibling" variation into the Model 1894 line. Appearing in late 1924 in its own serial range, it was configured as a lightweight takedown sporting rifle with a 24-inch barrel (conveniently shorter than the Model 94's standard 26-inch barrel), a half-length magazine tube and chambered in only one caliber, 30 WCF. (Although this model was originally offered in only the one landmark caliber, 30 WCF, caliber 25-35 WCF and 32 Special were offered and available within a year or so at no extra cost; several specimens in uncataloged calibers have been authenticated.)

The Model 55 supplanted the Model 94 version in that configuration. If customers wanted something other than what was cataloged for the Model 55, they were referred to the wide variety of options for the Model 94. Hopefully, the factory would still accommodate special orders for the soon to be discontinued Model 94 in the rifle version – I feel that Model 94 rifles and Model 55s in limited quantities and variants likely were assembled into the very late 1930s or very early '40s from parts on hand. However, at this time there is no indisputable

proof of this.

Beginning its existence in only one caliber and with so little offered as options, one had to wonder as to the corporate reasoning for a new model designation (only stocking options were listed in the 1925 catalog) but many optioned-out specimens in even the earliest serial ranges have been encountered. (Winchester would rarely turn down a lucrative special order.) In reality, the earliest Model 55s were nothing more than specifically appointed Model 94s with a different serial number sequence and only the barrel marking slightly changed to designate the gun as a "Model 55."

Before long however, the situation became an evolution.

Catalogs soon began referencing the complete Winchester option list for the Model 55, and special order specimens with many different features began to appear with more regularity. Wisely, by strictly maintaining the half-length magazine feature and the shorter lightweight barrel but adding some new calibers to the line and once again "officially" allowing the customer to special order almost anything else they could afford (even as far as double-set triggers and any style of engraving that they deemed appropriate), the Model 55 soon earned its place as a completely distinct and separate new model. It became the lightweight sporting rifle of the Winchester 94 series lineup. After serial numbers of all but the first 12,000 specimens or so (at dates of about 1927 and Model 94 serials of about 1,010,000), Model 55 serial numbers became integrated with the Model 94's sequence. This is a very close approximation of where the company data for the Model 94 rifle ceased to exist. There are some examples of very early Model 55s serial numbered mistakenly in the Model 94 sequence; conversely there are examples of very late production Model 55s having Model 94 barrels and the late first series Model 55 five-digit serials.

When it finally was phased out in about 1932, there were originally estimated to be about 21,000 Model 55s produced. Assembly and delivery of "parts-on-hand" guns, however, likely continued into 1934-35; again, no accurate factory data has been found so far. Accurate production estimates were, and are, made difficult by the integration of serial numbers into those of the Model 94. There are no factory records in existence for this period of manufacture other than some of the records surviving from the "polishing room," and they do not always designate a Model 55 receiver from a Model 94 receiver. With further research and analysis, revised estimates indicate that production totals are nearer to 31,000 units and possibly as high as 35,000; these later figures are most assuredly more accurate than those earlier compiled. One hundred percent accuracy is, as usual with all Winchester models, impossible.

The original list price for a standard Model 55 at introduction was $44.

RECEIVERS

Receivers used for the Model 55s were identical to those of the Model 94. The same alloys, the same machining processes and the same finishing methods were used. It is no wonder that it is very hard to find a Model 55 without a seriously flaked receiver. The high nickel content of the alloys used as receiver material during this era (as on most Winchester models in the lever action line that were concurrently produced) quickly rejected the bluing methods then in use (see Chapter 1). Very slight amounts of use were enough to trigger this rejection and even some obviously unhandled or new-in-

the-box specimens may show various degrees of flaking. This phenomenon is also seen on forend caps, barrel bands and buttplates that were likewise manufactured using the same high nickel content steel as the receiver but not on barrels or magazine tubes; these were of a different alloy. Many "silvered receiver" guns are seen with almost 100 percent blue barrels and magazine tubes. Rare indeed is a completely pristine Model 55. Model 92s and 94s of this era used the same alloys and had the same problems but the production numbers for these

Illustration of the typical early or "Model 55 only" serial numbering style. The lowest (verified by a very reliable source) serial number known so far in the Model 55-only serial range is number 4. (Klein photo)

models far exceeded those of the Model 55. For this reason we find many more "still pristine" Model 92s and 94s than 55s. Model 55s, 64s and Model 94s were known to be "confused" on the assembly line, as we will read about later in this chapter.

There are three distinct production variations of the Model 55 (not to be confused with variants – variants are differences due to special ordering).

VARIATION I

The first issue specimens were serial numbered in a sequence separate from the Model 94 and were all takedown models. (There is, as of this writing, one known solid frame Model 55 numbered in the early 55 only serial sequence [6856]. It is theoretically a Model 94 receiver that inadvertently became serialized with the earlier Model 55 grouping. It was apparently stashed away and later modified if necessary and assembled as a solid frame gun after the Model 55 takedown version had been long discontinued. As usual - Winchester wasted nothing.)

As also suspected, as with the Model 92's sibling version the Model 53, the different serialization was likely somewhat of a ploy by Winchester to make this newly designated model appear to be more distinctly "new" even though it was virtually identical to existing variations and could be duplicated fairly easily by attempting to special order an officially "discontinued" Model 94 with the same specifications: only the standard wood style and buttplate were Model 55-specific and it too could be special ordered on a Model 94. This individual serial range is consecutive from serial number 1 to about serials around 12,000. (Serial number 11467 is marked and verified as a Model 55 and serial number 11985 has an octagon Model 94 barrel.)

There is an overlap period of about one year (1927-28 at serials of about 11000 in the Model 55 range and 1,019,800 in the Model 94 range) when the first group of receivers that were serial numbered in the Model 94 sequence appeared, and for a while both types were produced concurrently. Serial number 1,019,769 appears to be the first Model 55 in the Model 94 sequence. The mistaken 55-94 designations earlier mentioned in the introduction likely happened here. All were takedown models and

An illustration of the typical serialization of the Model 55 in the intermingled Model 94 sequence. Note the flaking of the receiver bluing. (Klein photo)

none had the tapped holes for a receiver sight. Tangs were all marked the same as the Model 94 in the Type 6 style (See Chapter 7).

VARIATION II

The second issue specimens are readily identifiable by being numbered in the same seven-digit range as the then-current Model 94 but with a Model 55 barrel designation. The theory for the numbering change is that the company wanted to hide the fact that sales of the Model 55 were less than stirring. And still, only takedown versions were offered.

The first Model 55s to be numbered into the Model 94 sequence begin at serials about 1,019,800 with the lowest specimen verified so far at number 1,019,769. The final Model 55s with serial numbers in the 94/takedown sequence are in the 1,070,000 range with serial 1,085,754 being the last number for a takedown version recorded in the polishing room records. Caliber 30 WCF was still standard and by far the most prevalent and 25-35 and 32 Special were offered as a no-cost option. There were no (standard) factory drilled and tapped receiver sight holes; any guns found with them could have been "mixed up" with the production very early Model 64 receivers of that serial range (the period of concurrent manufacture of Models 55 and 64 is very short – only about 2,000 numbers could mix). I'm unsure of the possibility of this error actually occurring during this period due to the fact that all Model 64s are solid framed guns and the 55s were still only takedowns, but we can't be 100 percent sure. Chances are that any Model 55 found with receiver sight holes was done outside the factory. Tang markings continued in the Variation I style.

VARIATION III

The third and final variation of the Model 55 is also numbered into the Model 94/64 sequence but now it was only offered as a solid framed version. The final serial range for the Model 55 is approximate – from 1,075,504 (the first verified solid framed gun) to 1,085,754 (the last verified solid framed gun). One hundred percent accuracy, as usual, is impossible. This is the range where the earliest Model 64s appeared. Caliber 30 WCF was still standard with 25-35 and 32 Special remaining as a no-cost option. Calibers other than 30 WCF in any version of the Model 55 can be considered "scarce" with the 32 Special being the next most common of the three.

Again, on this variation, there were no standard factory-drilled holes for a receiver sight, and any Model 55 with this feature still cannot be verified as factory work. However, if such an example is found and falls into the serial range of the earliest Model 64s (remember, this would be a Model 55 solid frame only), it could very well be a production mix-up.

Tang markings could be Chapter 7C, Type 6 or 7, with the Type 7 pattern showing up intermittently on the later and final versions.

BARRELS

Barrels on standard issues of all variations are of the lightweight, rapid-taper style with a length of 24 inches. Takedown versions measure 23-1/4 inches to the front edge of the takedown flange, the remaining 3/4 inch being the measurement from the receiver/flange face to the bolt face. The nominal measurements of the muzzle and the receiver end are 9/16 inch and 7/8 inch respectively. All Model 55 muzzles are uncrowned. At 3/4 inch from the muzzle (measured to the center of the sight dovetail)

is a ramp style front sight pad. The pad is approximately one inch long with a centered 3/8 inch dovetail for mounting a sight of choice.

There is an ongoing controversy regarding the attachment of the sight pad to the barrel; this controversy persists through many Winchester models. One theory is that the pad is made integral, machined with the barrel, and the other is that the pad is "sweated" onto the barrel and is cleaned and finished before bluing. I am 95 percent in the sweated-on camp. I will concede to the possibility and even the probability that several of the bolt action models were completely machined as part of the barrel but I will reserve judgment either way on some of the lever guns. I am, however, adamant on my "sweating" theory regarding all early carbines and the later ramp-and-hood sighted Model 94 carbines and all Model 64s. As for Model 55s and lightweight 1894/94s with ramp type pads, I just don't know. I have hammered the front sights off many a scrap carbine barrel of various models and vintages to prove my point but never any of the other styles. It seems illogical, considering Winchester's penchant for "frugality," that they would go through the extra machining and subsequent waste of time and material just to end up with an integral barrel pad for the front sight that could have been more easily, quickly and inexpensively sweated in place. The arguments from both sides on the issue continue and as I expect, the controversy will remain quite active for the foreseeable future. Anyone ready to beat on some Model 55 or lightweight Model 94 barrel sights? How about a nice lightweight '86 barrel? I didn't think so.

The rear sight slot, also a 3/8 inch dovetail, is standardized at about five inches from the receiver, again, measured to the center of the dovetail. This measurement will vary very slightly from takedown frame to solid frame models. As of this writing, few shorter-than-standard, factory installed barrels have been noted and none have been known to have been checked for a different (four inch) rear sight slot location or shorter forend wood as is commonly found on the Model 94 (See Chapter 2). I have yet to see any shorter-than-standard or longer-than-standard barreled Model 55s although I have heard of their existence from many sources – only one verified. A very close inspection and several measurements would indeed be required to authenticate such a specimen.

These are Winchester carbine posts for front sights. One is well used and taken from a Model 94. The other is new and judging from its size I'd have to say it was for a Model 1886. Both have obviously not been machined with the barrel. (Author photo)

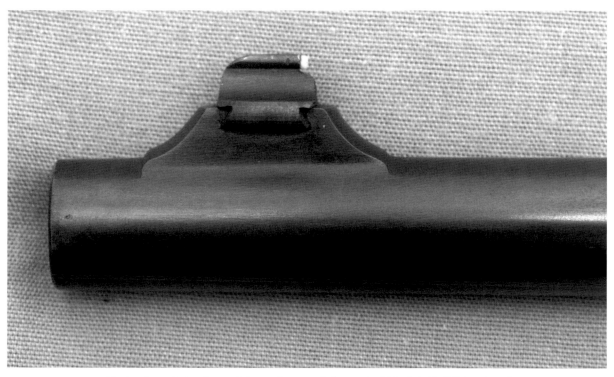

Illustration of the front sight and ramp of the typical Model 55. (Klein photo)

MAGAZINE TUBES

The magazine tubes are what are known as "half-length" or, in the case of the solid frame guns, a "button" magazine. In the takedown models only enough of the magazine tube to be able to accommodate the takedown lever extends beyond the forend retaining cap – about 2-3/16 inches. The solid frame versions have the true "button" type cap arrangement, ending as flush with the forend retainer, thus appearing as a "button" with no part of the magazine tube itself visible beyond the retainer. This type of cap required a specially designed forend-cap/retainer to hold the tube's end cap in place. The tube cap itself was also a special design to positively mate by way of a groove and ridge system within the forend retainer. The forend retainers of either type are not interchangeable and are upon disassembly noticeably different. The true button style was available as an option for all solid framed Winchester lever action rifle models but is quite uncommon on the Model 94 and most others. On the Model 55 solid frame version it was standard.

The ammunition capacity of solid frame or takedown models in any of the available calibers is four rounds – three rounds in the magazine and one round in the chamber. Optional magazine tube lengths were not advertised for the Model 55; of course, that is not to say that there are none in existence.

Shortly after production and distribution be-

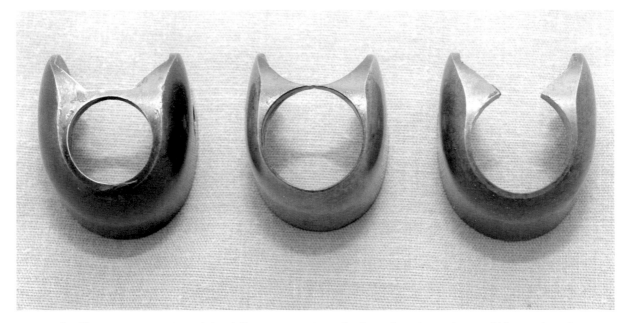

This illustrates a grouping of the different magazine tube/forend retainers that could be used on the Model 55. These are also used optionally on most other Winchester models and their appearance is typical of all, but the application for different models could vary as to actual engineering measurements due to differing barrel diameters. On all models, they are also internally different regarding their use on a round or octagon barrel and are not interchangeable between the two.

On the left is the retainer typical of the" true" button type magazine. Notably, it has a solid ring of metal that ultimately completely surrounds the "button" that covers the end of the tube and has a groove on the inside to accommodate and hold the button in place. It is machined differently (internally) than the other types and again, is different for round or octagon barrels.

In the middle, with a noticeably thinner metal ring, is a very early retainer for a takedown model. These could accommodate a magazine tube of any length except the "true button" type. Of course, there are no true button magazine takedown models – they are known as 1/2 magazines.

On the right is the retainer typical of all solid framed guns (again round or octagon barreled versions are different) with the obviously open design that will only partially surround the magazine tube. These are also seen on most takedown models other than the very earliest versions. These retainers are also NOT interchangeable with the button type. (Klein photo)

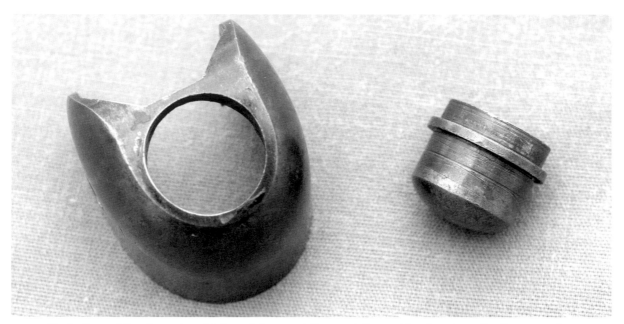

Illustration of the forend and tube retainer and the specially machined end cap for the magazine tube noted previously as the "true button" type. Notice the machined ridge on the end cap – it mates with a machined groove in the retainer, thus supporting and holding the tube in place. An illustration of the assembly on an assembled gun can be found in Chapter 3. (Klein photo)

gan, pretty much the entire Winchester option list for the Model 94 became available for the Model 55. Although there were no carbines or musket versions, there were options aplenty. (The Model 94/95 pictured and described in Chapter 2 is thought by some to be an experiment in producing a Model 55 carbine. Again, this is an unsubstantiated theory.) 22-inch and 26-inch barrels have been reported as well as those of the octagon or half octagon, half round style – all are unverified as existing as of this writing. Stainless steel barrels on the Model 55 are regularly encountered but cannot be considered common. Factory original stainless barreled specimens were usually made in the 1926 to 1930 era but later versions could and did have barrels from earlier stock installed upon request but at no extra cost. They were originally offered as an $8 option. Stainless barrels on the very early models, those produced prior to 1926, are likely re-barreled. There is no indication of when the factory may have run out of stainless barrels for any given model but they were officially discontinued from production in 1930. Any Winchester with a stainless steel barrel is quite rare and thereby very collectible even though the painted (japanned) finish is usually gone (see Chapter 2).

It is not unheard of to find a Model 94-marked barrel on a Model 55. Such specimens are readily identifiable as a Model 55, especially on the first variation due to the serial number sequence, but not as easily on the second and third types. All are most likely to be re-barreled examples, either factory or gunsmith installed. Gunsmithed installations usually have the mail order proofmark on the barrel if the barrel was a new factory-made replacement (see Chapter 7).

Model 55 barrels have also been noted on Model 94s. These can sometimes be detected as originally being Model 94s by the serial number but not always. A solid frame Model 94 with a Model 55 barrel or a solid frame Model 55 with a Model 94 barrel could be hard to determine as to originality, especially if the installation was made purposely to create a rare or unusual specimen and care was used to only use a receiver in a viable serial range. Another clue could be the configuration of the wood: Model 55s had their own style of buttstock and a very thin forend. At any rate, 94 barreled 55s or 55 barreled 94s are of little consequence to the value of shooter grade guns. There are many factory-correct possibilities and many almost-indistinguishable reworks. We must rely on careful observation and experience to separate the authentically unusual from the "gunsmith special."

STOCKS

The Model 55 was cataloged as standard with the same thinly contoured, standard length (9-3/8 inches) forend as used on the Model 92 and 94 rifle and had a straight-gripped, fluted comb, semi-shotgun style buttstock. The buttstock for this particular model (as well as the later Model 64) was designed by Col. Townshend Whelen in concert with the N.R.A. and retains the standard (nominal) Winchester rifle dimensions of 1-3/4 x 2-1/2 x 13 inches. Some say this buttstock design was originally a precursor for the Model 64 but no proof of this is on record. The Model 55 preceded the Model 64 by about 10 years and when the Model 64 ultimately arrived, it came equipped with a pistol-gripped buttstock with a matching curved lever but still had the tell-tale "Whelen" fluted comb. Model 55s could be ordered with a plain/uncheckered pistol-gripped stock but unlike those on the Model 64 even the standard grade pistol-gripped versions had a lettered, logo-style gripcap. They are rather easily authenticated by the having the standard Model 55 serrated buttplate although they could possibly be equipped with a hard rubber alternative. The Model 55 style buttstock did, however, show up on many Model 94s, both rifles and carbines; perhaps as a special order or more likely due to current availability. In fact, those Model 94s designated as "the pre-war model" had stocks and buttplates identical to the Model 55 in all ways except for the deletion of the "flutes" in the comb (see Chapter 5).

Available stocking options were as extensive as those offered on the Model 94 and any Model 55 ordered with a pistol-gripped and checkered buttstock immediately took on the basic appearance of the forthcoming Model 64 "deer rifle." Perhaps there was some "pre-Model 64" experimentation going on. Most deluxe versions of the Model 55 have nicely checkered and finished straight-gripped or pistol-gripped buttstocks with matching checkered forends, but with nothing more than a slightly higher grade of wood colloquially known as "extra grain." The pistol-gripped deluxe versions also have a gripcap that is virtually identical to those found on most deluxe Winchester models and later on the Model 64 deer rifle. (See Chapter 6.)

Higher grades of walnut such as XX or XXX or any other firearm-suitable wood could be special ordered but any specimen found to be so equipped must be expertly evaluated and authenticated – remember, there are no official records available. Any authenticated deluxe Model 55 can be considered very rare and very collectible as can any standard version with a stock option; there are rifle stocked versions, shotgun stocked versions, carbine stocked versions and pistol-gripped versions without checkering. Rare indeed, and they must be authenticated to be of any extra value – but they are out there!

For further stocking information, see Chapter 5.

A typical Model 55 buttstock. Notice the pronounced "Whelen" flutes on the comb (Klein photo)

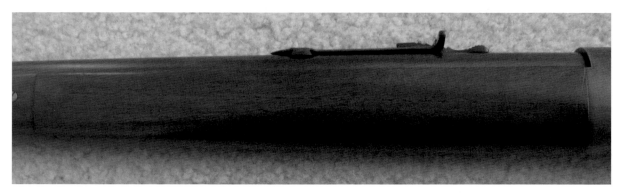

A typical Model 55 forend. These forends are essentially the same as those used on the Model 92, 94 and the standard Model 64 including the same nominal dimensions. (Klein photo)

BUTTPLATES

The buttplate is similar in design and size as that found on the Model 53 and the aforementioned short run of pre-war Model 94s. It is made of steel and basically smooth and slightly rounded both horizontally and vertically with no rollover onto the comb. It has a section of horizontal ribbing or "serrations" between the mounting screws (see Chapter 6). As usual, any Winchester buttplate option was available for the Model 55 and would be installed to complement any optional stock configuration.

MARKINGS

All Model 55s had proofmarks on the receiver as well as on the barrel.

BARREL MARKINGS

Barrels of all Model 55s had the Type 6 barrel markings of the Model 94, substituting 55 for 94, with the right side marking being slightly intermittent, specification-wise, regarding the sizing of the entire marking and the period after "Co."

TANG MARKINGS

Tang markings are also of the Model 94 Type 6 variety with the occasional late production specimen being found with Type 7 markings. When the Type 7 tang marking is found, the right side marking may or may not have a period (.) after "Co." This is usually where the difference in sizing of the right side marking is very slightly smaller than that used with the Type 6. (See Chapter 7)

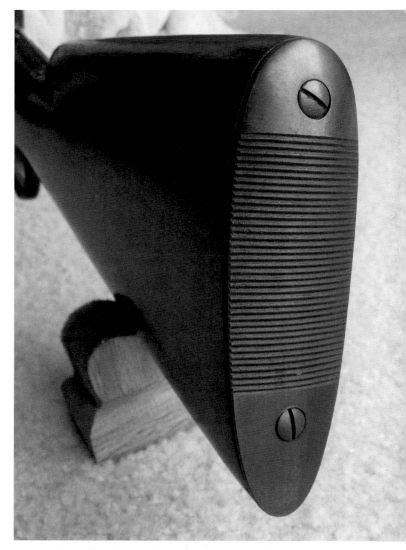

A standard Model 55 buttplate. All other Winchester stocks and buttplates were available on special order. (Klein photo)

The barrel marking of a Model 55 and typical of both the Model 55 and the Model 94 of the same era – the only difference being the "55" and the "94". Note the fine example of the (usual for a Model 55) "flat-top" model 22 rear sight and 32B elevator. (Klein photo)

The right side barrel marking of a Model 55 and also typical of the Model 64s and Model 94s of the same era. Any of these models may or may not have a period (.) after "Co." (Klein photo)

HAMMERS

All Model 55s had the second design hammers of the Model 94 (see Chapter 4).

SIGHTS

The standard front sight was typical of many Winchesters of the day: a Lyman gold bead installed in the aforementioned 3/8 inch dovetail in a barrel mounted front sight ramp. A substantial number of specimens with optional front sights have been noted and could be factory or aftermarket installations. There is no collectible consequence either way.

The standard rear sight is a Winchester Type 22 in either the sporting (semi-buckhorn) or the flat-top style. The flat-top is seen more frequently in absolutely untouched factory guns. The standard elevator for the rear sight is a 32-B.

All factory-made and aftermarket sights were available as extra cost options on the Model 55. Installations other than those other than mentioned above are very scarce but they are nearly impossible to verify as original. Any extra value derived from non-standard sights can be marginal but also can be substantial if authenticated or if it's a rare and unusual sight assembly. Many illustrations of different and available sights are seen throughout this book, especially in Chapters 7 and 11.

PACKAGING

All Model 55 packaging follows that design of all Winchester models of the era (see Chapter 10).

PART III:
The Model 64

A standard version of the Model 64. This example is in caliber 219 Zipper and has the apparently longer 26-inch barrel.

A deluxe version of the Model 64. This rare example is in caliber 25-35 and has the standard-length 24-inch barrel.

THE MODEL 64

INTRODUCTION

Further along the evolutionary line of "sibling" models we find another addition to the Model 94 group designated as "The Model 64."

A markedly handsome variation, the Model 64 was designed to replace both the Model 55 and the rifle version of the Model 94 (the Model 94 in the rifle version was already in the phase-out stage and the Model 55, though fairly recently introduced, wasn't far behind). The Model 64 was introduced in about 1932 in the Model 94 serial sequence at approximately serial number 1,087,000 (the lowest verified number so far is 1,087,281 and there are no Model 64s in a separate serial range from the Model 94, although during the period they were produced they do seem to have been made in "batches"). For a very short time, however, during transition, the three differently designated but basically identical (receiver-wise) models were produced simultaneously. Due to this overlapping of models many oddities are found in this model/serial range but are not to be considered a variation or an oddity worthy of "value enhancement." So many like-but-different parts for three different models mixed in the same parts bins or assembly areas could easily get confusing and thus result in a large variety of possible "mismatches." You get the idea.

The original list price for the standard Model 64 at introduction was $42.85 and the deluxe or "deer rifle" was $59. Short barreled models were the same price. Pricing for the 219 Zipper was about the same as the standard or deluxe version but the bolt mounted peep sight was about $5 extra.

RECEIVERS

The receivers on the Model 64 are nearly identical to those used on the Model 55 and Model 94 and absolutely identical to those used on the Model 94s after serials of about 1,790,000, when at last the Model 94 was also factory drilled and tapped for mounting a receiver sight – a very welcome "standard" inclusion. Early catalog text refers to "refinements" such as making the action smoother and the trigger pull lighter but other than the inclusion of the receiver sight holes, the refinements have not been noticeable.

The actual differences in the Model 64, the Model 1894/94 and the Model 55 are merely visible and aesthetic, such as the curved lower tang that is standard on all Model 64 variations and the inclusion of the aforementioned factory drilled and tapped holes for the installation of the optional Lyman Number 56 receiver mounted sight. The lower tang is technically not part of the receiver; the mismatch of replaced lower tangs on Model 64s, as well as Model 55s and Model 94s with a non-factory "upgraded" pistolgrip, is usually apparent and the same mismatch is commonly found and noticeable on amateurishly-installed, non-original set trigger assemblies.

The Lyman 56 was an option an all Model 64s (about $6) but is most often seen on the 20-inch "carbine" versions to increase the shorter sight radius. When installed at the factory, the Lyman 56 (or the 66A) is also usually accompanied by a rear sight dovetail filler similar to that illustrated in other areas of this book – specimens with installations of both barrel and receiver sights, or barrel and bolt peep sights have been noted – with no logical explanation. Later versions (post-1954) will most often be seen with the Lyman number 66A receiver sight. These two Lyman sights are interchangeable in both mounting and usage and were both cataloged until about 1959; the 66A was merely a more up-to-date version of the 1935 introduced Lyman 56, and finding one or the other on a specimen of any vintage is no cause for alarm. However, to be completely original and authentic, a collector-grade pre-1954 Model 64 should have the Lyman 56.

As mentioned earlier in Part II (the Model 55 section), there could conceivably be an early (serials of about 1,080,000 - 1,090,000) Model 64 receiver without the factory drilled receiver sight holes, and again, this could be a mix-up during the early manufacture of the Model 64 at a time when Model 55s and Model 94s were in production but were being produced as undrilled. Likewise, Model 64s found without these holes that are serialed anywhere prior to 1,790,000 could be production mix-ups with Model 94 receivers that were also being manufactured concurrently with the Model 64 but at that time were still not drilled and tapped as standard procedure. After serials of about 1,790,000 all Model 94-64 receivers were drilled and tapped from the factory and the problem becomes moot.

In other words, receivers for Variation III (solid frame) Model 55s could have correctly drilled holes from the factory (although none are so far listed as such); Model 64s prior to serial 1,790,000 might not have factory drilled holes; and Model 94s prior to serial 1,790,000 might have factory drilled holes (some, but very few, earlier than serial 1,790,000 Model 94s are listed as drilled as per the original polishing room records that have recently become available, as are several Model 64s without holes – there are no Model 55s either takedown or solid frame listed as factory drilled at this time). Considering these myriad possibilities, only those guns found with receiver sight holes that were made prior to the introduction of the Model 64 can be considered to be a special factory order or a gunsmithing job and not necessarily a factory error. Such an error, however, would glean no additional value or detraction to the specimen except to the real die-hard collector – and then only if the specimen is in otherwise near new condition.

Confusing? You betcha. Let careful observation and the quality of the work be your guide. Hint: if the interior of the holes are blued it is more likely that the holes were factory drilled.

Model 64s in the 1.2 million serial number range will often be seen with the same "W" marking below the serial number just as the Model 94 and some other Winchester models of this era. (See Chapter 7.)

The receiver of the Post-64 version, the Model 64A, is an identical receiver as that of the same period Model 94 except again, like the original Model 64, it has a curved lower tang requiring a pistol-gripped style stock.

VARIATION I

Like the Model 55, the Model 64 as originally cataloged was also introduced as a model of rather limited optional latitude. There was no cataloged option to the two-thirds magazine tube length or the pistol-gripped stock configuration (different stocks were, as usual, available on special order) and in this model there were no takedown versions offered. However, unlike the earliest Model 55s, there were far more catalog-noted options. It was available from the start in the three calibers of the Model 55, two barrel lengths, and two grades: deluxe (checkered) and standard (uncheckered).

Note: A 24-inch barrel was standard and after, or even during, the first year of production a 20-inch barrel was made available as a no-cost option. No longer-than-standard barrels were offered on the Model 64 except for those versions in 219 Zipper (see below), and in this caliber at 26 inches it wasn't really special order, it was standard.

It is in reference to the deluxe version of this model, mainly seen in caliber 30 WCF (by far the biggest seller; also known as 30-30 in later issues), that Winchester coined the term "the deer rifle." Slight cosmetic (and unfortunately, quality) changes to the receiver were made through the years to lower production costs and they follow the same changes as are seen on the Model 94. At serials around 1,350,000 (this could be called Variation II but I will resist the temptation because only the tang marking and the hammer are different), the upper tang no longer had markings of any kind nor did it have the second (drilled and tapped) hole for installing a tang-mounted rear sight. The hammer design was also changed at this time from the second model checkered type to the third model ribbed style. (See Part I, Chapter 4, Type 3A for the hammer and Chapter 7, Type 8 for an illustration of the tang marking.)

The deluxe grade guns came complete with a nicely checkered walnut buttstock (usually showing a quarter-sawn grain pattern), a slightly wider semi-beavertail forend (also checkered), a typical logo-styled pistol grip cap, beautifully inletted rear sling mounts and a quality sling with deluxe quick-disconnect sling swivels. (These upscale swivels are getting premium prices on the collector market today and will also be found on some specimens of the Models 70 and 71. They are also found in two widths, 1 inch and 1-1/2 inches, with the 1-inch version being correct for the Model 64.)

The forend cap on the deluxe version was also special to the gun and had a built in provision for the front sling swivel. The standard version was identical in all respects to the deluxe, including the usual quarter sawn wood, except it lacked the fancier checkered stocking, pistol grip cap and the sling and swivels. The forend cap was plain with no provision for a sling swivel. In a similar progression as noted with the Model 55, more and more optional features became available as time progressed, even to the point where double set triggers and engraving have been authenticated.

In 1937 another caliber, the 219 Zipper, appeared. The 219 Zipper was a centerfire 22. As could probably be expected, for ease of development and manufacture, the Zipper cartridge was loosely based on a necked-down 25-35 casing making use of a 22-caliber bullet. As previously mentioned, it came standard with a 26-inch barrel. 22-inch barrels original from the factory are known to exist and, due to their extreme rarity, a verifiable example is very high on the collector's want list. Consequently, when discovered, they are usually tucked away in a collection and rarely seen. I have never encountered such an example. The Zipper will often be seen with optional sights such as the Type 98A "bolt mounted" peep sight with changeable aperture sizes, which was also available for the Models 71 and 65 but is rarely seen on the Models 53, 92 or 94.

Bolts specially milled for the installation of the 98A sight are sometimes found on guns without the sight itself. In cases such as this it is felt that either the original sight was removed or Winchester needed a bolt at that time of assembly and only a milled version was available. Other than the milling for the 98A sight installation, the bolts are identical and the barrels were dovetailed for a standard rear sight anyway.

Note: Barrels on guns with factory installed receiver or bolt-peep sights could be ordered with the aforementioned "sight slot delete" option (see Chapter 2). These specimens are extremely rare. The 98A was discontinued around the WWII era and is most common on specimens in the 1.3 million serial number range. It is nevertheless still found on later production examples. The Type 22H rear sight could also be ordered on the Zipper and was standard for a time. However, it was installed with a specially calibrated Type 32B sight elevator.

In the 1938 Winchester salesman's catalog there was a reference to the discontinuance of the calibers 32-40 and 38-55. Examples of the 32-40 and 38-55 specimens are the rarest of the Model 64s, and indeed, many very prominent and long-time Winchester collectors have no knowledge of their existence. Few are those who have actually seen such a specimen but there is at least one example of each that has been examined and authenticated. From my personal observation, these calibers were listed in the 1937 catalog. Why they are so unknown is a mystery; why they are so scarce is not.

The 219 Zipper variant became obsolete and dropped from production as did the 25-35WCF in 1941 but some were assembled with parts on hand and in fairly abundant quantities into the early 50s. The Model 64 continued on, with the same progressive degradation in quality post-war as the Model 94, until it was finally dropped from production and left out of Winchester promotional material in 1956-57. Production figures are somewhat of a mystery, with total production numbers unknown due to the serial sequence being the same as the Model 94 and the total lack of period records. Estimates put it at a very wide variable of 50-100,000 units – frequency of encounter seems to corroborate the higher estimate range. A speculative standard vs. deluxe ratio is about 70 percent standard/30 percent deluxe with the shorter barreled versions the exception. Authenticated special-ordered examples are extremely rare. Serial numbers at the time of discontinuance were in the 2,200,000 range.

Note: There is an ongoing dispute as to the availability of the deluxe version in any caliber other than 30 WCF and 32 Special even though deluxe examples in caliber 25-35 are routinely encountered. Smaller calibers in the deluxe version were not cataloged. After all, the deluxe version was termed the "deer rifle" and although the 25-35 was definitely up to the task, perhaps the powers-that-be felt the smaller calibers should be left out of that genre (deluxe versions of the 32-40 and 38-55 are unknown as of this writing and guns in these chamberings would certainly not be regarded as an ineffective deer caliber). Despite the caliber vs. deer theory, many examples of deluxe 25-35 specimens exist in both the 24-inch and 20-inch versions with the 20-inch version being an extreme rarity and very high on the collector's want list. This is true of the deluxe 20-inch version in any caliber mainly due to the extra features and the aesthetics even though the standard versions of the 20-inch barreled specimens are noticeably rarer. Oddly, all "carbines" in all calibers are rarer in the standard version than the deluxe. No examples as of this writing have been seen of a caliber 32-40 or 38-55 specimen in a deluxe version of either barrel length, and these as well as the other aforementioned rarities, if in existence, are suspected to be hidden away in very advanced collections.

The bottom line regarding the three concurrently manufactured models is that all Model 64, 55 and 94 receivers are essentially and technically the same.

VARIATION II

There was a brief resurgence of the Model 64 with a Post-64 type receiver (see Chapter 9, Variation III, Type 2C) that came out in 1970-71. It was manufactured in the standard uncheckered version only. It also had a 24-inch barrel as standard (no 20-inch versions were offered or have been seen) with a pistol-gripped, noncapped buttstock, and common type sling swivels (screw in rear, non-inletted) but no sling was included. This variation, however, even though there was no deluxe option, had a specially designed forend cap to allow for the front sling swivel to be attached with no gunsmithing or "tube mounting" necessary. It was made only in caliber 30-30 (32 Special versions have been rumored but none verified) and it was cataloged as the Model 64A. It appeared in the 3,400,000 serial range and again was serialed into the Model 94 sequence. This variation had the same hammer and markings as the concurrently manufac-

tured Model 94. See Chapter 4 for the hammer and Chapter 7, Type 8 for the tang marking and Chapter 7, Type 10 for the barrel marking, substituting 64A for 94.

Despite being a rather attractive rifle as was its predecessor, and having the "improved" version of the Post-64 receiver (See Chapter 1C, third model), it was nonetheless found to be unpopular, and production ceased in 1972-73. Production numbers are unknown but are estimated to be about 4500. Collector interest is markedly on the rise for this variation despite its "Post-64" roots.

BARRELS

The original barrel length on the Model 64 and the Model 64A was standardized at 24 inches. It was made in a similar rapid taper style and with the same nominal dimensions of the Model 55 at 9/16 inch for the muzzle and 7/8 inch at the receiver. All Model 64 and 64A barrels are crowned. This length is standard for all guns in all calibers except the earlier mentioned 219 Zipper. A 20-inch barrel was offered as a no-cost option on all grades and calibers somewhere between the first and second year of production; however, the 20-inch barrel was not offered for the 219 Zipper or the Model 64A.

The muzzle diameter of the 20-inch versions is slightly larger at 19/32 inch. These short-barreled variants have acquired the colloquial name "carbine." This was not a factory designation and they were never cataloged as such. A third standard barrel length of 26 inches was applied to guns in caliber 219 Zipper when it was introduced. The standard Zipper barrel also had a slightly smaller muzzle diameter of 17/32 inch. No barrel length options were actually cataloged for the Zipper but there have been authenticated examples of 22-inch barreled specimens and at least one example with a 28-inch barrel. The 32-40 and 38-55 models had the standard 24-inch barrels of the others and no shorter or longer length barrels are known for these variants. The 20-inch barrels, and as far as is known at this writing, all non-standard length barrels, were discontinued in 1941. Guns produced later than 1941 may be found with non-standard barrel lengths but they were assembled from parts remaining in inventory – some were made into the 1950s.

Front sights were of the ramp and hood style, sweated on to the barrel, and this style was consistent through all periods of manufacture including the later Model 64A. It was definitely distinct from those on the Model 55 and this sight/hood arrangement was the same as that found on the later Model 94s (post serial numbers of about 1,100,000) and some very late issue Model 92 carbines. The length of the ramp base varied with the barrel length. The standard barrels had a base approximately 2-3/4 inches long with a very few being noted as 2-1/2 inches. The 20-inch versions had 1-3/4-inch bases and all had the same style "sight-protecting" hood that was slipped into a groove machined into the sight base. The true length of the bases will vary slightly but there will be a noticeable difference between those on the short version and those on the standard or longer barrels. The 3/8-inch dovetail for the sight blade was pretty much centered within the horizontal portion of the ramp. The sight blade inserts and the hoods were interchangeable between the ramp lengths (sometimes with a different height calibration for the sight blade depending on the caliber) and are consistent with those found on the Model 92s and 94s.

Rear sight dovetails were milled 3-1/16 inches from the receiver on 20-inch versions and some of the earliest 24-inch specimens. Later,

only the 20-inch barrel had this measurement; the standard barrels had the sight slot cut 5 inches from the receiver. The standard rear sight was the Type 22H including the 219 Zipper, but as previously mentioned, the Zipper had a unique-to-the-caliber elevator.

MAGAZINE TUBES

All Model 64s have a two-thirds length, five-round magazine tube. The designation "two-thirds" is based on the standard barrel length of 24 inches (2/3 being 16 inches, more or less) but the tube length and cartridge capacity is constant for all barrel lengths. It's noteworthy that the Model 64 and the Model 64A are two of the few Winchester models with a shorter-than-barrel-length magazine tube that has a rifle-type tube retainer. A few other examples will be found among the Commemoratives. The 3/8-inch dovetail for the magazine tube retainer on the bottom side of the barrel was located at 3-1/4 inches from the forward end of the forend cap to the center of the dovetail and was consistent for all barrel lengths and calibers. No optional magazine tube lengths were available or have been seen as of this writing.

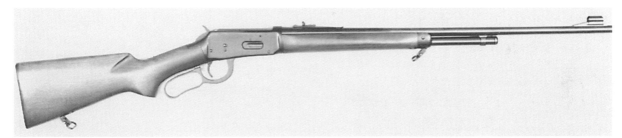

This photograph of the short-lived and rare Model 64A illustrates one of the few examples of the use of a retainer on a magazine tube of less than full length. Other examples are found among the commemoratives.

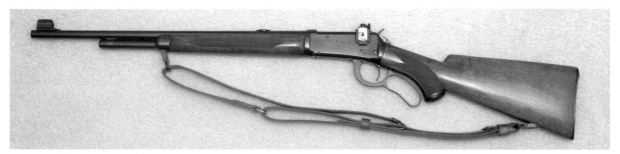

A fine example of a pre-WWII model 64 in the desirable "deluxe carbine" version. It has the later but correct Lyman 66A receiver sight and a deluxe Winchester rear sight filler. The standard version would be identical with the exception of the wood – standard models had uncheckered stocks and forends and uncapped pistol-grips. As with the rifle version they also did not have factory slings or swivel mounts. (Author's collection)

Illustration of the magazine tube retainer used on the Model 64. This was standard on all versions, regardless of barrel length, as was the length of the tube and the distance of the retainer to the forend. All versions held 4 + 1 rounds of ammunition regardless of the caliber. (Klein photo)

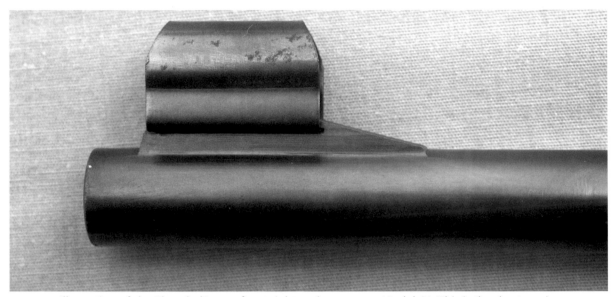

Illustration of the "hooded" type front sight and ramp on a Model 64. This is the short version used on the 20-inch barreled models. A longer version was used on the standard 24-inch or 26-inch barrels. (Klein photo)

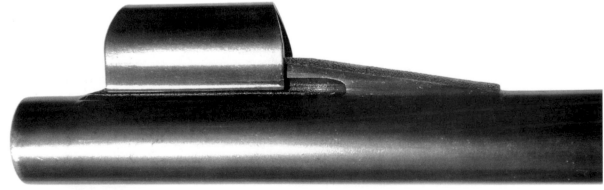

This is the noticeably longer standard ramp and hood front sight used on both the 24 inch or 26-inch barrels. (Klein photo)

STOCKS

Stocks on all variations are of the pistol-gripped type buttstock with a rifle type forend. The forend for all barrel lengths was the nominal standard rifle length of 9-3/8 inches that was fairly consistent on most Winchester models with barrel lengths of 20 inches or more. No shorter forends have been noted. There were, however, three differently contoured forends. Originally offered on the standard grade was the same slim, graceful, uncheckered, forend that is found on the Model 55, 94 and 92 rifles. Of course barrel inletting measurements on forends could vary slightly depending on barrel length and caliber (see Chapter 5). On the deluxe version was a slightly wider and nicely checkered forend with a designation of "semi-beavertail." Earlier (pre-war) versions of the deluxe may also exhibit a finer checkering pattern than the later varieties and the slim contour of the standard version. As mentioned in Chapter 5, there was a denser grade of walnut readily available in the earlier, pre-WWII period, and it was easier to provide a finer pattern on this denser wood. It is also likely that much of the available walnut at this time was used for military applications thus decreasing the supply allocated for domestic production. Very late in production we will also find specimens with a very wide, full-beavertail type forend, and at this time either the semi-beavertail or full-beavertail type may be found on both checkered and uncheckered specimens. The widest versions were originally only used on the checkered (deer rifle) guns and the 219 Zipper but later could be found interspersed on almost any examples.

Buttstocks were pistol-gripped and uncapped on the standard grade guns but were still made of a rather high quality walnut. Buttstocks on the deluxe models were pistol-gripped, capped and nicely checkered at the wrist part of the stock to match the forend. The wood used on the deluxe versions was of an even better grade of walnut than the standard models and was almost always quarter sawn. This gave the wood a nicer grain pattern from the receiver to the buttplate and due to the straighter grain flow was somewhat stronger at the wrist portion than were the normally cut stock blanks. Deluxe guns in very late post-war production may or may not have this feature and some standard grade guns in any era of production may

be seen with this feature. (Typical Winchester inconsistency.) Wood availability regarding quality and density was always an issue and therefore so was the final product. The stock measurements remained at the standard for Winchester rifles at a nominal 1-3/4 x 2-1/2 x 13 inches. As on the Model 55, the stocks were designed by Col. Townshend Whelan in concert with the N.R.A. and have his design trademark of a deeply fluted comb. Deluxe versions have beautifully inletted sling swivel mounts and even some standard grade guns have been authenticated with the same inletted mounts (though very infrequently – and when they are seen they also have the modified forend cap as on the deluxes).

A fine illustration of the three different Model 64 forend widths. (Klein photo)

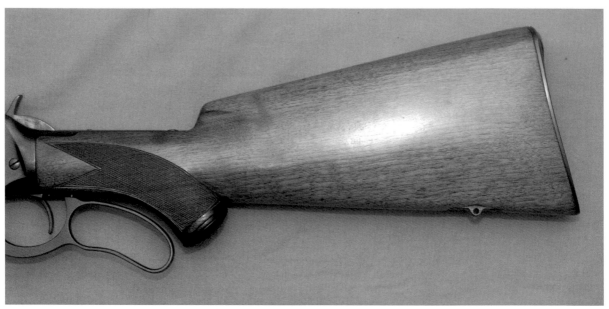

A "pre-war" Model 64 deluxe style buttstock. Note the fine quality of the checkering and the quarter-sawn wood graining. This earlier type checkering was standard at 20 lines per inch. (Klein photo)

A "pre-war" Model 64 deluxe style forend, finer checkering. (Klein photo)

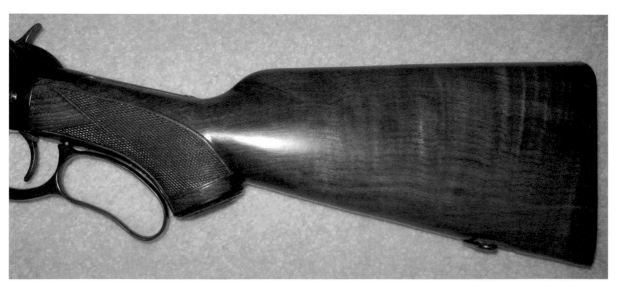

A "post-war" model 64 deluxe style buttstock. Note the coarser checkering pattern but the very fine and fancy wood graining. Later checkering standards were changed to 18 lines per inch. (Klein photo)

A "post-war" Model 64 deluxe style forend, coarse checkering. (Klein photo)

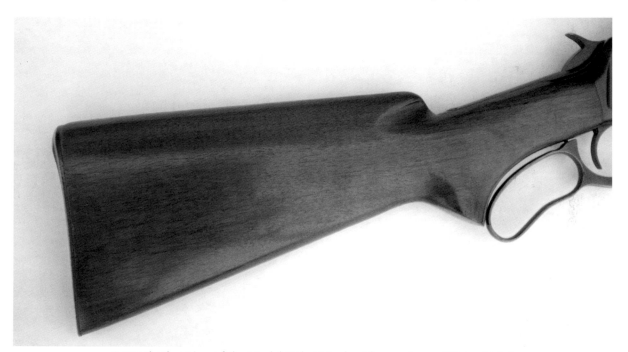

A standard version of the Model 64 buttstock with no gripcap. (Klein photo)

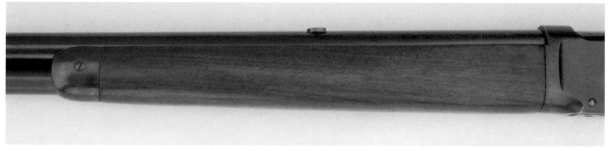

A standard version of the Model 64 forend. (Klein photo)

An illustration of the finely inletted rear swivel mount on a deluxe Model 64. (Klein photo)

BUTTPLATES

Buttplates on either version were the same unless a different buttstock was specially ordered. If so the buttplate would be matched to the buttstock style. Standard versions were usually steel, sometimes but very rarely phenolic or plastic, and they were bordered and checkered with a pointed rollover at the top similar to those found on the Model 70. Some early versions may be found with the Winchester logo centered between the mounting screws. No phenolic/plastic or hard rubber buttplates have been authenticated as original as of this writing but they have been very briefly referred to in the past in some historical writings.

GRIPCAPS

Unlike the Model 55, gripcaps were only fitted to the deluxe version stocks and were made of hard rubber and stylized with "Winchester Repeating Arms Co." lettering. They were fastened with a center screw that was usually but

This is the buttplate that is standard on the Model 64. It is common to the standard and the deluxe versions. Ostensibly, the plastic or phenolic version was the same design. With optional stocking, the appropriately matching buttplate would be installed. (Klein photo)

An illustration of the dimensional differences found on early and late Model 64 gripcaps. This difference is not entirely inclusive to all later specimens but will be found accompanied with the very wide style of forend and grip. Note the slight difference in the engraving style of the mounting screw. The mounting screws are seen with several different engraving styles, probably according to the whims of the engraver of the day. Additionally, the screws are often found devoid of any engraving whatsoever. (Klein photo)

not always lightly engraved on the exposed head (flower-type engraving). Gripcaps will be found in two sizes (otherwise identical) with the larger size being consistent with the later guns with the wider full-beavertail type forend and a matching, slightly wider wrist/grip area.

MARKINGS

All Model 64s had proofmarks on the receiver as well as on the barrel.

As previously mentioned, there are three Pre-64 variations and one Post-64. In this four variation grouping we may find five different barrel markings and four different tang markings. However, all four groups follow exactly the changes found on the Model 94, also having the as noted, "overlapping" of serial ranges.

BARREL MARKINGS

VARIATION I

Serials from approximately 1,087,000 to 1,250,000 have the Type 7 barrel markings substituting 64 for 94. (See Chapter 7, Type

7.) The right side barrel marking also follows the pattern of the Model 94 and the Model 55; however, the marking is sometimes slightly smaller than that used with the Type 6 Model 94 marking and sometimes has a period (.) after "Co." It appears that the period part of the roll die used for this marking had a propensity for breaking off during sustained use and then of course was missing from the marking until the damaged die was discovered. This is not to be considered a value-enhancing discovery as are the "error dated" barrels (see Chapter 7) and will also be noted on some versions of the Models 55 and 94.

VARIATION II

Serials from approximately 1,250,000 to 2,000,000 have the Type 8 barrel markings of the period Model 94s, substituting 64 for 94. (see Chapter 7, Type 8). When this marking is seen, the rear sight dovetail is almost always at the final five-inches-from-the-receiver location. In this marking change we will find other notable variables; the caliber designation for

30 WCF changes to 30-30 WIN. near serials of 1,600,000 and the model 22 type rear sight now is a less expensively to make stamping and has a noticeably "stubbier" point forward of the mounting dovetail than those used previously. The 32B elevator still dominates on the Model 64 while the 3C seems more common on the 94. Likely the elevator change is different between the models due to the Model 94's now only being available in the carbine version.

VARIATION III

Serials from approximately 1,900,000 to the conclusion of Model 64 production have the Type 9, 9A barrel markings of the Model 94, again only changed by substituting 64 for 94 (see Chapter 7, Type 9, 9A). The Type 9A marking is basically the same as the Type 9 but has

no dashes surrounding the "Trade Mark" or the "Made in U.S.A." The rear sight is still a stamping, and continues to have a stubbier front end near the dovetail-mounting portion. Now it will be noted to have prominent screw-type adjustments on the forward face of the sighting blade; it will almost exclusively have a 3C type elevator. For a clear illustration of sights and their evolution, see Chapters 7 and 11.

VARIATION IV

Serials in the 3,400,000 range (Model 64A) have the Type 10 barrel markings of the Model 94, now substituting 64A for 94. (See Chapter 7, type 10). Note: Types 10A or 10B markings have not been noted on this variation but with Winchester – who knows? Rear sights and elevators are identical to those used on the Model 94.

Typical Model 64 barrel marking. This is a "pre-war" type marking. Later markings follow exactly the pattern of those found on the Model 94s of the same era, substituting 64 or 64A for 94. (see Chapter 7 – Types G7, H8, I9 or 9a and 10 on the Model 64A). (Klein photo)

This is the barrel marking on a rare "deluxe" Model 64 in caliber 219 Zipper. Quite notable is the additional width of the forend and the coarseness of the checkering.

An example of the barrel marking on the very rare "deluxe" Model 64 in the caliber 25-35.

TANG MARKINGS

Interestingly, although there are five different barrel marking variations there are only three distinctly different tang markings.

VARIATION I

This variation has the same tang marking as those of the Model 94 in the serial range of 1,087,000 to 1,180,000. (See Chapter 7C - Type 6).

VARIATION II

This variation has the same tang marking as those of the Model 94 in the serial range of 1,150,000 to 1,350,000. (See Chapter 7C - Type 7).

VARIATION III & IV

These variations (beginning at serials near 1,350,000 and 3,400,000 respectively) have a blank tang with no lettering and no mounting holes for a tang-mounted rear sight. So as not to be confusing: the designations of Variation III and IV refer to the Pre-64 version and the Post-64 version although they are visually exactly the same. If encountered with a tang

Typical (blued) second model hammer used on the Models 55, 64 and 94 (94 after serials of about 700,000). (Klein photo)

Typical third model hammer used on the later versions of the models 64 and 94. The 3A version is used on the Model 64 and the 3B is used on the Model 64A, see chapter 4. (Klein photo)

sight, the drilling and tapping of the forward mounting hole for the sight was almost assuredly done outside the factory. (See Chapter 7C - Type 8).

HAMMERS

Hammer designs on the Model 64 also follow the introduction and change dates as those on the Model 94.

VARIATION I

Serials from approximately 1,087,000 to 1,385,000 will have the second design hammer (See Chapter 4).

VARIATION II

Serials from approximately 1,350,000 to the end of the Model 64 production in 1957 (near serials in the 2,200,000 range) will have the third design, 3a type hammer (see Chapter 4).

VARIATION III

Serials in the 3,400,000 range (64A) will have the third design, 3b type hammer (see Chapter 4).

SIGHTS

The front sight on all Model 64s is the same design as that of the corresponding era Model 94. A blade type sight assembly is mounted in a 3/8-inch dovetail in the aforementioned front sight ramp that is semi-permanently attached to the barrel – not integral. All Model 64s were supplied with a sight-protecting hood that was slipped into a groove machined in the ramp. The hood is often missing on out-of-the-box or otherwise used specimens.

The standard rear sight on the Model 64 was the Winchester 22H sporting or semi-buckhorn type with various configurations of the sight itself as well as the graduations on the elevator. They may have either a 3C or a 32B type elevator with the 3C dominating on the 20-inch versions and the 32B type dominating on the longer lengths. As with the Model 94, and as earlier mentioned in the Barrel Marking section – Variation II and III, the configuration and quality of the type 22 sight changes slightly with the era of manufacture. The el-

An illustration of the earlier type Lyman 56 receiver mounted sight. This sight and all receiver mounted sights were used to increase the sight radius and therefore potentially increase ease of sighting and therefore accuracy.

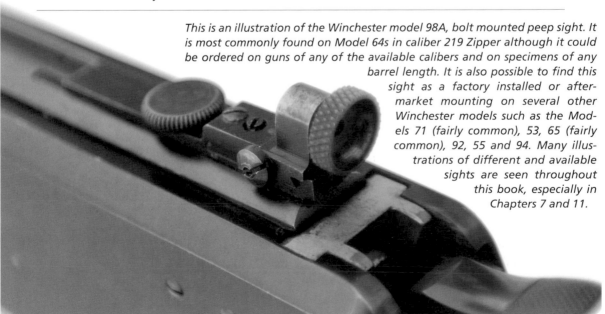

This is an illustration of the Winchester model 98A, bolt mounted peep sight. It is most commonly found on Model 64s in caliber 219 Zipper although it could be ordered on guns of any of the available calibers and on specimens of any barrel length. It is also possible to find this sight as a factory installed or after-market mounting on several other Winchester models such as the Models 71 (fairly common), 53, 65 (fairly common), 92, 55 and 94. Many illustrations of different and available sights are seen throughout this book, especially in Chapters 7 and 11.

An illustration of the later and updated version of the Lyman 56 receiver sight known as the Lyman 66A.

evator changes are according to the caliber and whether or not the gun was customer designated, and so ordered, to be sighted in for the use of "Super Speed" ammunition. Again, the elevators for the 219 Zipper were designed and calibrated to be unique to that caliber.

All factory-made and after-market sights were available as extra-cost options on the Model 64. Those other than mentioned above are very scarce and they are all but impossible to verify as original. If verifiable, and/or unusual, they may add a substantial premium to the value of the specimen.

PACKAGING

All Model 64 packaging follows that design of all Winchester models of the era (see Chapter 10).

PART IV:
MISCELLANY

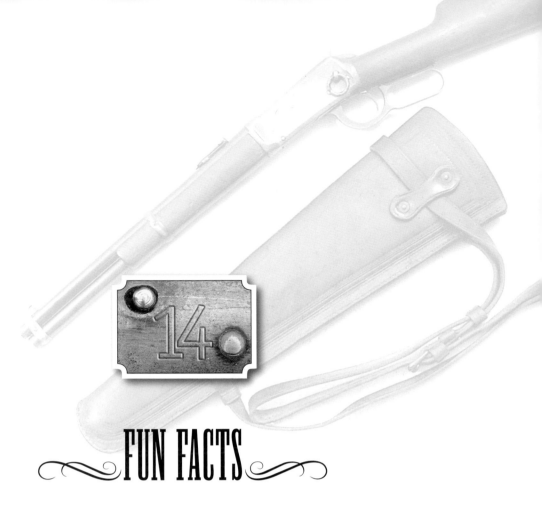

FUN FACTS

INTRODUCTION

This is a random compilation of Model 1894/94 and Model 55 and 64 facts, some garnered from factory letters on specific examples; some from other research including some gleaned in the early 1990s from BBHC employees researching the actual factory ledgers; some from hands-on observation; some from hearsay (only the most reliable and trusted hearsay) – but all are the best and most accurate snippets of information we currently have.

There is no particular order to this section – just a few interesting items to read about and ponder. They do, however, show undisputedly that serial numbers, particularly of the earlier guns, are not a basis for concluding when the gun was produced or shipped. Only the records that still exist can prove that. And do remember, all those early records were hand-entered with even more of the attendant possibilities of error and omission than data entry of today. And also remember – there are no reliable records for any Model 1894s with serial numbers above 353,999 except those observed and recorded from examples themselves. Rather extensive (up into the 1940s, '50s and '60s) dating

information that is considerably more reliable than previously published manufacturing/dating figures has recently become available from the BBHC museums "polishing room" records. Enjoy!

The first Model 1894 carbine was sent to the warehouse on November 1, 1894, and shipped on November 3, 1894. There is also a warehouse date of November 20, 1894, and a release date of November 21, 1894, listed for this gun, nicely illustrating the conflicting data entry problems mentioned in the beginning of this section. It is completely standard in configuration, the serial number is 471 and it is in caliber 38-55.

There are very few first model carbines known to exist (approximately seven or eight as of this writing). Two of these are serials 1296 and 1297. Number 1296 left the warehouse on December 26, 1894, to order number 4379 and number 1297 left the warehouse on February 1, 1895, to order number 7005. Neither had any further distribution information listed. They are together today in a private collection and are the only known consecutively serial numbered pair of first model 1894 carbines in existence. Pictures can be found further along in this section and also in Part I.

There are at least three sets of consecutively serial numbered pairs of first models in existence, with all three of those presently in the same collection. A fourth pair is known but they are not together at the present time and consist of the astonishing rarity of a

A serial number view of a phenomenal pair of consecutively numbered, standard, octagon barreled first models. Both are in caliber 38-55. Another, full-size picture of this pair can be found elsewhere in the book. (Klein photo)

Another consecutive pair of first models rifles, these with three digit serial numbers. Serial number 975 is a standard round barreled gun in caliber 38-55 and serial number 976 is a standard octagon barreled gun in 30 WCF. Example 976 letters as a 38-55 but has all the early markings and characteristics of the early barrel change situation discussed in Chapter 1, and another picture of the pair can be found elsewhere in the book. Round and octagon barreled consecutive guns – can you say rare? (Klein photo)

An illustration of the serial numbers of the ultra-rare consecutive pair of the first and second model rifles illustrated on pages 32-33. (Klein photo)

consecutive pair of first and second models.

The earliest known and existing Model 1894 carbine (by serial number) is number 46. It is also the only known Model 1894 carbine with a Model 1892 style staple and saddle ring assembly. It is caliber 38-55 and was sent to the warehouse on March 26, 1895, and shipped on September 24, 1895. Detailed pictures are shown in Chapter I.

Serial numbers 3, 5, and 8 are known to be in existence but have no, or incomplete, factory records.

Serial number 8 was a standard, caliber 38-55, octagonal barreled rifle. It was sent to the warehouse in November of 1895 – that is the extent of the records for it or any other guns prior to serial number 18.

There are no existing records of any kind for serial numbers 1 through 7 or 9 through 17.

Serial number 18 is the first fully recorded Model 1894 in the records; how-

ever, its existence is so far unknown as are serial numbers 19, 20 and 21. It was sent to the warehouse on January 12, 1896 (yes, 1896) and shipped on January 19, 1896.

Serial number 22 is still in existence and is the lowest existing serial numbered Model 1894 that has a complete record. It was assembled on the first day of the Model 1894's production – October 20, 1894. It is a standard 26-inch octagonal barreled rifle in caliber 38-55. It was shipped on October 27, 1894, to order number 251. This example has two good photos elsewhere in this book.

On the first day of Model 1894 production (according to existing records), only eight guns were completed. The serial numbers are, 21, 22, 26, 39, 57, 76, 78 and 81.

The first day of shipment for the Model 1894 was October 26, 1894. It was to order number 173 and consisted of 20 guns that were sent to the warehouse on October 22, 1894. Likely it consisted of two cases of 10 guns each but this is not a certainty – the records do not say. This original group of Model 1894s to leave the factory were serials 24, 36, 48, 49, 54, 55, 64, 70, 81, 85, 91, 98, 99, 100, 106, 107, 109, 110, 128, and 131. Of them, I know for certain that serial number 55 is still in existence. The rest? Who knows? Maybe you'll find one or maybe you know of one!

The first Model 1894 with the takedown feature by serial number and date was 134. The second and third numbers were 136 and 137.

The first Model 1894 with the takedown feature to leave the factory was serial number 136. It was also the first takedown completed. It was sent to the warehouse on November 1, 1894, and shipped on November 3, 1894.

Model 1894 takedown serial number 139 still exists and is the earliest known to exist takedown on record. It was the second or third takedown version assembled (number 137 and 139 were both assembled and sent to the warehouse on November 14,1894) but there is no way to determine which of these was actually completed first. Serial number 139 was the second Model 1894 takedown shipped – on November 17, 1894. A full-size illustration of number 139 is pictured elsewhere in this book.

The factory record on serial number 138 is illegible.

Model 1894 serial number 734 is a standard model takedown rifle in caliber 32-40. It was produced on February 11, 1895 and shipped on March 2, 1895. As of this writing, it is the earliest (by serial number) second model takedown known to exist. It may very well be the first second model takedown produced AND the first takedown in caliber 32-40. Number 764 is pictured elsewhere in this book.

This is one of my favorites: Model 1894 serial number 6242, verified as a first model. It was ordered in caliber 38-55 with a 24-inch (two inches shorter than standard) octagon barrel, no rear sight slot (but no sight options listed), a checkered and pistol-gripped shotgun style buttstock and a 1/2 length magazine tube. It also has one of the rarest of 1894 options, a casecolored receiver! It was sent to the warehouse on September 27, 1895, and shipped the same day.

The highest serial number claimed so far for a Model 1894 with a first model re-

ceiver is reputedly in the 7400 range. This has not been personally verified – 1st and 2nd models cannot be distinguished from the records; they must be visually identified. It is a deluxe, pistol-gripped and checkered 38-55 octagonal barreled rifle. It was sent to the warehouse on September 4, 1895 and shipped on September 5, 1895.

There were only 982 Model 1894s logged in as completed in the year 1894 – but not all of these were delivered in that year and Model 1894s were certainly not sequential in their completion.

The first Model 1894 produced with a casecolored receiver is serial number 564. It was an octagon barreled deluxe rifle with a checkered pistol-gripped stock. It was sent to the warehouse on November 28, 1894, and shipped on November 30, 1894.

Model 1894 serial number 838 was the first listed Model 1894 with full nickel plating. It was a checkered, pistol-gripped octagon barreled rifle in caliber 38-55. It was sent to the warehouse on January 15, 1895 and shipped on the same day.

The first Model 1894 in caliber 32-40 (by serial number) was serial number 545. It was delivered to the warehouse on March 26, 1895 and was a rifle of standard configuration but is listed with deluxe wood. It was shipped on April 1, 1895. Although unverified, this is likely to be the lowest serial numbered second model receiver.

The first Model 1894 in caliber 32-40 (by date) was 692. It was sent to the warehouse on December 14, 1894 and shipped on the same day. It is likely that this is the first second model receiver used (no 32-40 first models have been observed or documented as of this writing). This could also be the only 32-40 produced in the year 1894 (?).

Model 1894 serial number 15147 is interesting in the extreme. Sent to the warehouse on February 8, 1896, it is listed as a rifle, caliber 38-55 with an EXTRA HEAVY octagonal barrel in the unusual length of 28 inches – two inches longer than standard. It also has plain grained pistol-gripped and checkered wood, a Swiss buttplate and a cheekpiece. All these wood options on plain wood – incredible. Now the best! It has a casecolored receiver – one of the rarest options on a Model 1894. It was delivered to its new owner on February 10, 1896.

Model 1894 serial number 15266 is another very interesting entry. Sent to the warehouse on July 7,1896 it is listed as a deluxe, pistol-gripped, checkered model with an EXTRA HEAVY round barrel (round barrels are much rarer than octagon especially with a serial number this early and in a deluxe variant). It is in caliber 32-40 with a military windgage rear sight and a Beach front sight. It also has the unusual recorded entry of having a sling and swivels. Sights and slings are not often noted in factory records and this is one of only two known listings with an extra heavy barrel. It was delivered from the warehouse on July 9, 1896 – obviously a very special order.

The first Model 1894 "trapper" was an otherwise standard 15-inch barreled carbine, caliber 38-55, serial number 20124; it was sent to the warehouse on April 23, 1897 and shipped on April 30, 1897.

The first Model 1894, 38-55, deluxe (checkered, pistol-gripped by date and serial number) was serial number 62. It was sent to the warehouse on October 27, 1894 and shipped on the same day. It is likely the first "deluxe" Model 1894 produced and the only one delivered in 1894. Whether or not it had a first or second model receiver is unknown but with a serial number this low and in caliber 38-55 it is highly unlikely that it was a second model.

The earliest serial numbered short rifle is serial number 1248. It was a caliber 38-55 deluxe model with a non-specified style of checkering, a pistol-gripped shotgun style buttstock that was ordered one inch short of standard length and had a 22-inch round barrel (the short shotgun buttstock was also the first to be installed on the Model 1894). It also had a Winchester express rear sight. It was sent to the warehouse on October 15, 1894 and shipped on October 17, 1895.

Model 1894 "muskets" were produced experimentally and are noted in several factory documents and museum records. There were apparently different configurations as well as at least two bayonet options. One is known to be in a private collection but only sketchy production figures and configuration records are currently available. (See Chapter 2).

The first Model 1894 rifle produced in caliber 32 Special (by date) was serial number 107731 – it was sent to the warehouse on October 5, 1901 and shipped on October 16, 1901. Many Model 1894s in 32 Special will be found with lower serial numbers than this but were shipped at a later date, e.g., serial number 10675 is the lowest serial numbered 32 Special on record but was sent to the warehouse on August 23, 1902, and shipped on August 27, 1902. The caliber 32 Special was introduced in 1901.

The first 32 Special carbine (by date) is serial number 142899. It was sent to the warehouse on May 10,1902 and shipped on May 12, 1902.

The first 32 Special carbine (by serial number) is serial number 22967. It was sent to the warehouse on August 27, 1902 and shipped on August 29, 1902.

The first Model 1894 rifle in caliber 30 WCF by date is serial number 3314. It was sent to the warehouse on May 29, 1895, and shipped the same day. Whether or not it is has a first model receiver is unverified.

The first 30 WCF carbine (by date) is serial number 4787. It was sent to the warehouse on June 24, 1895, and shipped on July 2, 1895. Whether or not it has a first model receiver is unverified.

The first Model 1894 takedown model in caliber 30 WCF with a verified first model receiver is serial number 5056. It was sent to the warehouse on September 4, 1895, and shipped the same day. This may be the first 30 WCF takedown model with a first model receiver. It also may be the first and perhaps will remain as the only verified 30 WCF first model of any style.

The first Model 1894 rifle in caliber 25-35 (by date) is serial number 5014. It was sent to the warehouse on July 18, 1895 and shipped the same day.

The first Model 1894 rifle in caliber 25-35 (by serial number) is serial number 2347. It was a rifle, sent to the warehouse on July 23,1895 and shipped on September 23, 1895.

The first Model 1894 carbine in caliber 25-35 (by serial number and date) is serial number 6506. It was received in the warehouse on October 1, 1895 and shipped on October 3, 1895.

There are nine Model 1894s listed with a smooth-bored barrel. Seven are in caliber 38-55 and two are in caliber 32-40. Two (one of each caliber) are part of a multi-barreled set.

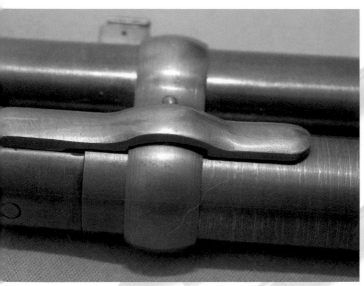

Takedown carbine ?? (Klein photo)

The first monogrammed Model 1894; serial number 4176. Monograms without other embellishments are VERY rare on any Winchester. (Klein photo)

There are persistent rumors of two 10-inch barreled Model 94s in a Midwestern bank vault; however, there are no listings of any carbines with barrel lengths shorter than 14 inches or rifles with barrel lengths shorter than 14 inches.

There are also persistent rumors of factory built Pre-64 Model 1894 takedown carbines.

The first deluxe factory engraved Model 1894 is serial number 1835. It has a second model receiver and is in caliber 38-55. It was sent to the warehouse on March 5, 1895 and shipped the same day. It is pictured elsewhere in this book.

The first factory inscribed (engraved initials) Model 1894 was serial number 4176. It is a deluxe first model and is inscribed with the initials "AJS." It was sent to the warehouse on April 8, 1895 and shipped on April 9, 1895.

There are several (87) recorded Model 1894s in 34 very unusual calibers. These were very early guns. Some were experimental, some were obviously recording errors, eg., 25-20, 25-55, 30US, 30 Gov, 38-40, 35-55, 44. As of this writing I have not seen any of these, nor have any been verified as still existing. Factory verified experimental specimens of all eras and especially any in private collections are rare but have been encountered.

Only four officially documented factory experimental calibers are listed: 7.63 Mauser, 7.65 Mauser, .38 Colt and .38 Colt Auto. These were all built in December of 1903.

There are 22 entries of Model 1894s with wood other than walnut, e.g., birds-eye maple, cherry, mahogany and redwood among others. Nine different wood types are listed.

There are no records of other-than-wood stocks. Some other models do have these listed.

There are 68 recorded serial numbers of receivers that were "broken up" by the factory. They were likely rejects or experimentals.

There are 2067 ledger entries for the Model 1894 that are completely blank.

There are 336 Model 1894 rifles and 19 carbines listed as factory engraved.

There are 200 Model 1894 rifles and three carbines listed as having matted barrels.

There is only one entry listing a factory installed Maxim silencer.

There are two Model 1894s listed as carbines with casecolored receivers.

There is only one listing for a Model 1894 with a matted receiver.

Military issued Model 94s? Several governmental and private guard agencies ordered them including the U.S. Government. U.S. acceptance markings can be found on Model 94s produced during WWI and even some as late as those with serial numbers indicating WWII production. Other agency markings both domestic and foreign are found in all serial ranges. (See Chapter 7).

There is in existence, from a VERY reliable source, that there is a 20-inch barreled Model 55 takedown with a full magazine and "extra finish" wood that is 100 percent factory original. Now the best part – it's in caliber 38-55.

From a trusted and reliable source: The lowest known serial number on a Model 55 so far is number 4. Serial number 3 has been rumored to exist with a pistol gripped stock – this is not verified and other particulars for this specimen are not available at present.

The Model 55 is the only Winchester model for which the takedown version is more commonly encountered (and had higher production numbers) than the solid frame version.

The Model 64 with the 20-inch barrel is more commonly encountered as a "Deluxe" than a standard version.

Pre-war Model 94 carbine with serial number 1,257,531 was factory produced with a SRC buttstock. It also had the typical "W" beneath the serial number and was in caliber 38-55. It was assembled some time in 1940. Caliber 38-55 is quite rare in this era but not unheard of – all others verified so far have been noted with the typical pre-war buttstocks and buttplates.

 The last Model 94 produced prior to WWII is in the 1,310,000 serial range.

Model 94 serial number 1,343,643 was factory produced with a Model 64 barrel.

The first Model 94 produced after WWII is in the 1,350,000 serial range.

Model 94s have been verified with "prewar" serrated (Model 55 style) buttplates as late as serials denoting 1946 manufacture.

There is on record a Model 64 serial number 2,493,465 – it was made in 1962! There is no explanation regarding this specimen.

The last "Pre-64" Winchester Model 94 is still thought to be serial number 2,600,298.

The highest seen-and-verified serial number on a "Pre-64" Model 94 is currently 2,599,632. I'm still looking for a number higher than that or especially any 2.6 million numbered specimen. Recently studied "polishing room" records indicate the last (highest numbered) 1963 model to be number 2,599,694 and the lowest verified 1964 version to be found so far is number 2,703,262.

The serial number of the last Model 94 produced (2006) is not known at this time. All records from USRAC were turned over to the ATFE upon the closing of the factory and they "ain't talking." A strongly held belief is that the number is in the 7.0 to 7.1 million range.

Rumor has it that several of the models illustrated in the final Winchester Catalog (2006), were "teaser" models meant to excite the public and hopefully create a further demand. Reputedly, they were never produced beyond the "wish list" or perhaps the experimental stage.

Despite the illustrations in the 2006 catalog, there were no substantiated "new style" takedown models other than experimentals and none are known to have left the factory.

The 1987-88 Deluxe model is the only Model 94 to have a factory inscribed "DELUXE" designation. It is found on the right side of the barrel.

Some guns delivered in 1986 have the earlier 1983 type receivers. These are parts guns made up during the bankruptcy period.

There was a "Post-64" contracted version of the Model 94 marketed by the Sears

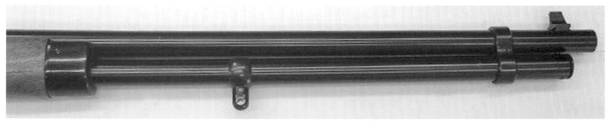

The front end of the Sears Model 100/Model 54. Note the different forend cap vs. barrel band and the magazine tube/barrel arrangement. The buttstock is the same as the Model 94 Winchester but the buttplate is plastic and has a Sears Roebuck & Co. logo. (Author photo)

The barrel marking for the Model 94 that was contracted from Winchester and marketed as the Sears Ted Williams Model 100. The Model 54 had the same inscription except it said "Model 54" in place of the "Ted Williams Model 100." Note that except for the caliber marking, there is a complete lack of any reference to Winchester. (Author photo)

Roebuck Company. It was denoted the "Ted Williams Model 100" or the "Sears Model 54." It had a rather crudely manufactured ranger-style front barrel band and front sight arrangement, a slightly shorter-than-barrel-length magazine tube, a slightly modified forend arrangement with a cap instead of a carbine-type forend band and no Winchester markings of any kind other than 30-30 Win. as the caliber – this is the only caliber known to be offered. Any logos were differently designed and even the proof-marks were contract specific. These specimens had their own S&R Co. serial range (usually prefixed with a "V"). Production numbers and accurate dates of manufacture are unknown.

Commemoratives and all manner of special orders for Model 94s, beginning with the Wyoming Jubilee issue in 1964, account for about 2 million additional units of production not serial numbered into the Model 1894/94 sequence. This also includes some Model 55s, the original BigBore models, the 9410 (a 410 shotgun variation of the Model 94) and a few examples in the early days of the angle eject introduction of both BigBore and standard models (See Chapter 1 – about 19000 AEs were specially serialized). It would not be surprising to find that

over 10 million Model 94s were produced.

The company of O.F.Mossberg & Sons Inc., has introduced a Model 94 look-alike denoted the Model 464. It is presently available in 30-30 caliber; it has two stocking variants, is pistol-gripped with checkering and straight gripped uncheckered. It is totally different from the Model 94 mechanically, and it has gotten some excellent reviews.

Sadly, and as stated elsewhere, no company, world-wide, has been willing to take on the continuation of the Winchester Model 94. So far!

There was a patent pending unloading device for the Model 94 that did not require the operation of the action to unload the magazine. It was ugly and ungainly and is rarely seen. It was NOT a factory item.

For early carbines with the post-style front sight, (pre ramp and hood), there was a replacement front barrel band developed. It had a third "opening" or loop that surrounded and protected the front sight – it was a replacement rather rather than an addition. I have seen one example but never one that was factory installed. The item does appear to be factory made however.

There is a rumor from a well-regarded source of a Model 94 20-inch carbine in caliber .219 zipper.

 Some very late specimens found near the end of production in 2006 are seen with NO markings other than the caliber, serial number and proofmark. These have been seen in the 6.8 million serial range.

 The last recorded 14" carbine was serial number 1,090,560.

 The last recorded number for a Model 55 in its own serial range is 12002. It is dated 3/1928.

 The last recorded 16" pre-64 carbine was serial number 1,330,740 – it's dated 4/1942.

 The last recorded Model 94 rifle was serial number 1,090,649. It is dated 6/1933.

 There are examples of barrels with double-era markings – no explanation.

 There were "gunsmith installed" plugs for the saddle ring hole. They are scarce but quite often seen.

 There has finally been discovered, a pair of pre-64 Model 94s in the 2,600,000 range. These are *authenticated!* They consist of a consecutive pair, numbers 2,600,010 and 2,600,011 and are still new and in their original packaging. They are deluxe stocked models and were special ordered by a very "high end" collector. They were completed on February 7, 1963. Note: these may be the highest serial numbers known to exist in the pre-64 configuration, but they are NOT necessarily the last pre-64s manufactured. New discoveries are never-ending!

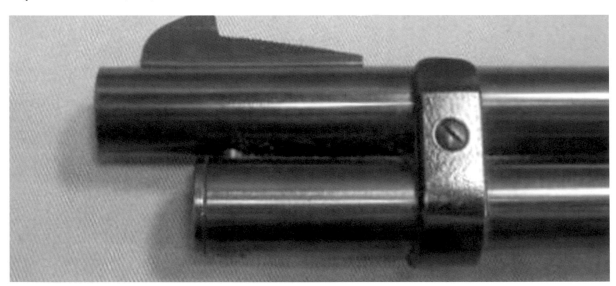

Front sight and barrel band detail of Sears 54/100 models. (Author photo)

Forend and forend cap detail of Sears 54/100 models. (Author photo)

EPILOGUE

What can be said about an invention so well received and so revered that it enjoyed an astonishing and unbroken production run of well over 100 years and an estimated 10,000,000 copies?

The Model 1894/94 and its true siblings, the Model 55 and the Model 64, thoughtfully modified and modernized throughout its history but essentially unchanged since the its introduction in October of 1894, continued inexorably onward – through wars, through depressions, through politics and through almost everything the world could muster – onward until that fateful day in March of 2006 when its parent company, which by then had evolved through many owners and many company name changes into "The Winchester Repeating Arms Company" (USRAC), failed financially and was finally forced to close its doors.

I could wax politically here on management strategies vs. labor costs vs. worker production vs. material costs vs. profits vs. etc, etc., but I won't. We all know. . . .

The bottom line is always the bottom line.

Will there be a return? Indications are sadly to the contrary. Only one company (Norinco-China) was willing to try to manufacture a true replacement. Although many replicas and even veritable exact copies of other Winchester models are being produced throughout the world, some in contract with the Winchester parent company and others on their own – and most with great success – only Norinco had the foresight and the confidence to take on the manufacture of a worthy replica of the Winchester icon, the Model 94. Although it was a formidable attempt, it has so far failed (now Norinco is no longer allowed by Federal mandate to export arms to the U.S.) and all known prototypes have been destroyed.

In the previous epilogue to this book I confidently said, "Can it sustain? How can it not? There's the venerable Model 70 and the magnificent flagship the Model 21, and then of course there's the Model 94 – the superb Model 94 – "America's Deer Rifle" – it's Winchester's logo – it must sustain."

But that was then and this is now. I was mistaken.

Sad.

APPENDIX

(No Model.)

2 Sheets—Sheet 1.

J. M. BROWNING.
MAGAZINE GUN.

No. 524,702.

Patented Aug. 21, 1894.

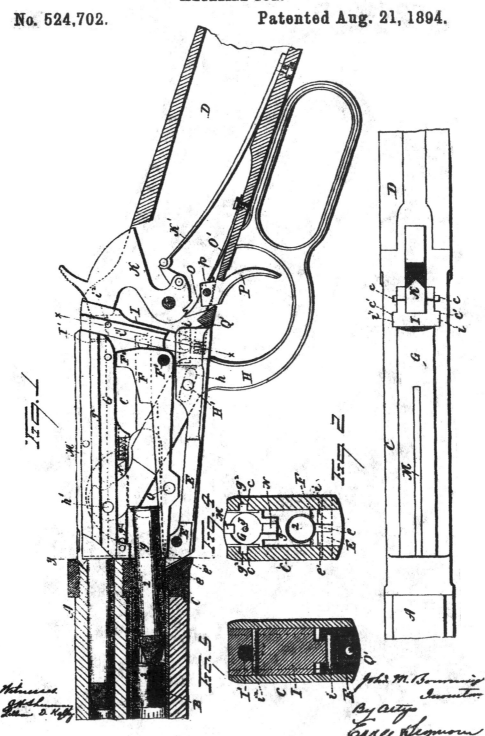

J. M. BROWNING.
MAGAZINE GUN.

No. 524,702.

Patented Aug. 21, 1894.

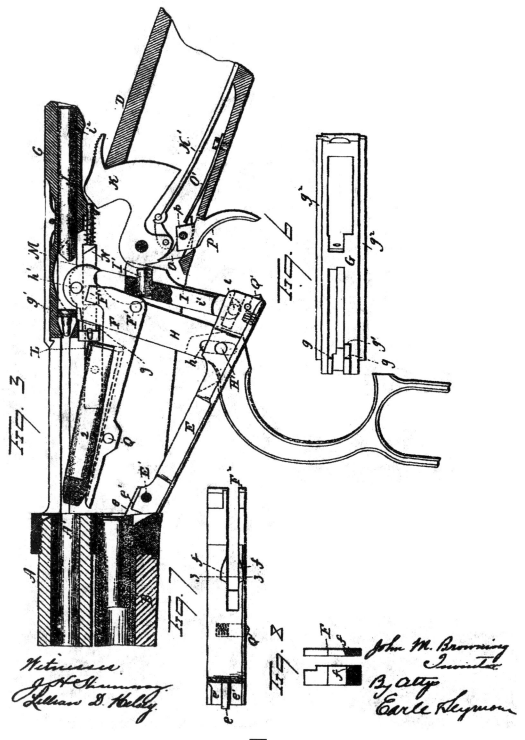

UNITED STATES PATENT OFFICE.

JOHN M. BROWNING, OF OGDEN, UTAH TERRITORY, ASSIGNOR TO THE WINCHESTER REPEATING ARMS COMPANY, OF NEW HAVEN, CONNECTICUT.

MAGAZINE-GUN.

SPECIFICATION forming part of Letters Patent No. 524,702, dated August 21, 1894.

Application filed January 19, 1894. Serial No. 497,416. (No model.)

To all whom it may concern:

Be it known that I, JOHN M. BROWNING, of Ogden, in the county of Weber and Territory of Utah, have invented a new Improvement
5 in Magazine-Firearms; and I do hereby declare the following, when taken in connection with accompanying drawings and the letters and figures of reference marked thereon, to be a full, clear, and exact description of the
10 same, and which said drawings constitute part of this specification, and represent, in—

Figure 1, a broken view partly in section and partly in inside elevation of a magazine fire-arm constructed in accordance with my
15 invention, and shown in its closed position; Fig. 2, a plan view of the arm; Fig. 3, a view corresponding to Fig. 1, but showing the gun in its open position; Fig. 4, a view in transverse section on the line *y—y* of Fig. 1, look-
20 ing rearward; Fig. 5, a view in transverse section on the line *x—x* of Fig. 1, looking forward; Fig. 6, a detached reverse plan view of the sliding breech-block; Fig. 7, a detached plan view of the carrier; Fig. 8, a view thereof
25 in transverse section on the line *z—z* of the preceding figure.

My invention relates to an improvement in magazine fire-arms, the object being to produce a simple, compact, safe and reliable gun,
30 in which the number of parts and the liability to derangement are reduced, which is constructed with particular reference to avoiding the choking of the gun by the incorrect presentation of a cartridge, or the failure of
35 a cartridge to be properly handled by the breech mechanism, and which is designed to adapt the gun to take a longer cartridge than has heretofore been available for use in a similar gun having a receiver of the same
40 length.

With these ends in view, my invention consists in a magazine fire-arm having certain details of construction, as will be hereinafter described and pointed out in the claims.

45 My improvements are applied to a gun having a barrel A, magazine B, receiver C, and stock D, all of approved construction, and not needing special description or illustration.

In carrying out my invention, I employ an
50 operating-plate E, hung at its forward or muzzle end on a horizontal pin E', and mov-

ing up and down in a vertical plane on the said pin as a center. The extreme forward end of this plate is constructed with a lug or nose *e*, which rises, when the rear end of the 55 plate is depressed, into the path taken by the cartridges 2, as they emerge from the magazine into the receiver, whereby the said lug or nose forms a magazine cut-off operating to prevent more than one cartridge from enter- 60 ing the receiver at a time. The said nose or lug rises into the path of the cartridges at the beginning of the opening movement of the gun, and is not retired or moved out of the said path until the gun is again closed. It 65 insures the easy operation of the gun, as it prevents the head of the incoming cartridge from resting upon or impinging against the forward end of the carrier F, and thus causing the same to work with difficulty. It also 70 prevents the choking of the gun where the cartridges differ slightly in length, in which case, but for the said nose or lug, a short cartridge on the carrier might allow the next cartridge in the magazine to secure a partial entrance 75 into the receiver, and by fouling the action of the carrier, choke the gun. By the use of this lug or nose, I secure an effective magazine cut-off without complicating the gun by special independently organized devices for that pur- 80 pose. The forward end of the operating plate E is also constructed with two lifting faces *e' e'*, corresponding to each other, and respectively located below and on opposite sides of the lug or nose *e* forming the magazine cut- 85 off. The extreme forward end of the carrier F, rests upon the said lifting faces *e' e'* when the gun is closed, as shown in Fig. 1 of the drawings, the said end of the carrier being slotted or cut away to clear the magazine cut- 90 off lug *e*. At the beginning of the opening movement of the gun, the said lifting faces *e' e'* lift the carrier slightly, and hence the head of the cartridge, whereby the said head is brought into range with a projection *g*, 95 formed upon the under face of the forward end of the sliding breech-block G, whereby the breech-block is caused to positively engage with the cartridge, and draw the same back into the receiver upon the carrier F, 100 which is constructed as shown by Figs. 7 and 8 of the drawings, with a depression or pocket

f, located below the level of its floor, and provided to let the head of the cartridge drop down, after the cartridge has been fully drawn into the receiver and cleared from the magazine, and disengage from the projection g so as to permit the sliding breech-block to complete its rearward movement. I thus provide for positively locating each cartridge in right position upon the carrier by means of the breech-block, so that no matter how rapidly the gun may be fired, it cannot choke, by reason of the carrier being elevated to present the cartridge to the gun-barrel A before the cartridge is in right position upon it. I conceive it to be necessary to thus provide for insuring the right location of the cartridges upon the carrier by means of the breech-block, in a gun wherein the cartridge is not, when the first opening motion of the gun begins, located entirely on the carrier.

With the rear end of the operating plate E, I pivotally connect the finger or operating lever H, by means of a pin H′, which extends into an elongated slot h formed in the lever, the upper end of which is connected by a pin h' with the forward end of the sliding breech-block G, which is moved back and forth by the action of the said lever. This finger-lever has the incidental function of guarding the trigger, and is sometimes called the trigger-guard, but I have chosen to describe it in connection with its larger function. The said lever is also called the operating-lever. I also connect with the rear end of the operating plate E and at a point in rear of the connection therewith of the finger-lever H, a locking-block I, the lower end of which is pivotally connected with the rear end of the plate by means of a pin i. This locking block moves up and down in the receiver at an angle slightly inclined rearward from the vertical, being constructed upon its opposite edges with guides i' i', which take into corresponding grooves c c formed in the opposite walls of the receiver, as shown in Fig. 2. In its elevated position the upper end of this locking-block stands directly back of the rear end of the breech-block, the same being then in its closed position. On the other hand when the sliding-block is depressed by the opening of the gun, its upper end retires below the path of the breech-block, as shown in Fig. 3, and permits the rearward or opening movement thereof. The upper end of this locking block is furnished with a short striking-piece I′, limited in endwise movement by means of a pin i^2, as clearly shown in Fig. 1 of the drawings. This striking-piece is arranged so that when the block is in its elevated or closed position, it transmits the blow or impact of the hammer K upon its rear end to the firing-pin J, which engages with its forward end.

A locking-block constructed and arranged as described, provides simple and effective means for locking the breech-block in its closed position, and by reason of its location,

enables a longer cartridge to be used than has heretofore been possible in a gun constructed with a receiver of the same length.

The carrier F is pivotally hung upon a horizontal pin F′ mounted in the receiver and passing through its rear end, and is swung or lifted into its elevated position, in which it is shown by Fig. 3 of the drawings, by the engagement of a shoulder g' depending from the lower face of the sliding breech-block, with an upwardly projecting operating lug F², formed at the rear end of the carrier. The upward motion of the carrier is checked by two corresponding guides L, of which one is shown in Fig. 3 of the drawings, these guides being set into grooves provided for them in the opposite walls of the receiver, and being located so that they arrest the upward movement of the carrier when it has brought the cartridge carried by it into right presentation in front of the chamber A′ in the gun-barrel A. The sliding breech-block G, is furnished with an extractor M set into its upper face, and with an ejector N depending from its lower face, the said extractor and ejector being of ordinary construction and operation. The breech-block itself is constructed with two corresponding longitudinal ribs g^2 g^2, (Fig. 4) which enter suitable grooves c' c' formed to receive them in the opposite walls of the receiver in the ordinary manner. The hammer K is furnished with a hammer-spring K′, and co-operates with a sear O having a sear-spring and trigger O′. A trigger P mounted on the same center p with the sear O, operates the same to release the hammer. As herein shown, the operating-link E and the carrier F, are furnished with friction pins Q, Q′ of ordinary construction and operation, but these may be dispensed with, or otherwise located as desired.

Having now described in detail the construction of my improved gun, I will proceed to briefly set forth the mode of its operation. Assuming that the gun is closed, as shown in Fig. 1 of the drawings, and that the magazine-spring has partly introduced the cartridge 2 into the receiver and upon the carrier, we will suppose that the finger or operating lever is thrown down and forward; this will operate to depress the rear end of the operating-plate E, and therefore to draw down the locking-block I, so as to permit the sliding breech-block to be moved rearward. At the same time the rear end of the plate E, is being depressed, its forward end and hence the nose e and the lifting-faces e' e' are being elevated, the latter then operating to slightly lift the forward end of the carrier, and hence the cartridge; and the former rising into the path of the cartridge so as to be in position to act as a magazine cut-off the instant the cartridge has passed entirely into the receiver. The lifting of the forward end of the carrier and hence the cartridge by the lifting faces e' e', brings the cartridge into position to be positively engaged by the projection g of the breech-block G, and positively drawn into the receiver in case the magazine-spring does not act quickly enough or powerfully enough to push the cartridge unaided into the receiver; then just before the finger-lever reaches its extreme forward position, as shown in Fig. 3, the shoulder or projection g' of the breech-block engages with the operating lug F^2 of the carrier, and swings the same on its pivot so as to cause its forward end to be lifted, and present the point of the cartridge in right position before the cartridge chamber A', to be forced thereinto by the breech-block as the same moves forward, which it will immediately begin to do when the closing movement of the finger-lever is begun. Then after the breech-block has moved forward into its closed position and the cartridge has been introduced into place in the cartridge-chamber A', the locking-block moves into place back of the breech-block, and the operating-plate assumes its closed position, in which its nose e is depressed below the path of the cartridges, and in which its lifting faces e' e' permit the forward end of the carrier to take its lowest position.

It will be seen from the foregoing that my improved gun is composed of comparatively few parts, compactly arranged, and is not liable to derangement, and that it may be operated with great rapidity without danger of choking.

It is obvious that in carrying out my invention some changes from the construction herein shown and described may be made, and I would have it understood that I do not limit myself to such construction, but hold myself at liberty to make such changes and alterations therein as fairly fall within the spirit and scope of my invention.

Having fully described my invention, what I claim as new, and desire to secure by Letters Patent, is—

1. In a magazine fire-arm, the combination with the barrel, magazine and receiver thereof, of an operating-plate pivotally hung at its forward end, a downwardly movable finger or operating lever and an upwardly movable locking-block connected with the rear end of the said plate, and a sliding breech-block connected with the upper end of the finger or operating lever and actuated thereby, substantially as set forth.

2. In a magazine fire-arm, the combination with the barrel, magazine and receiver thereof, of an operating plate pivotally hung at its forward end, a downwardly movable finger or operating lever pivotally connected with the rear end of the operating-plate and forming a guard for the trigger, an upwardly movable locking-block pivotally connected with the rear end of the said plate at a point in rear of the pivotal connection of the said finger or operating lever, and arranged to move up and down in the receiver, and a sliding breech-block connected with the upper end of the finger-lever and actuated thereby, substantially as set forth.

3. In a magazine fire-arm, the combination with the barrel, magazine and receiver thereof, of a plate pivotally hung at its forward end and constructed thereat with a nose or lug forming a magazine cut-off, and rising into the path in which the cartridges emerge from the magazine when the rear end of the plate is depressed, a sliding breech-block, and a finger or operating lever pivotally connected with the rear end of the said plate, and connected at its upper end with the breech-block which it actuates, and forming a guard for the trigger substantially as described.

4. In a magazine fire-arm, the combination with the magazine and carrier thereof, of a plate hung at its forward end and constructed thereat with two lifting faces upon which the forward end of the carrier rests when the same is in its lowest position, and whereby the carrier and the cartridge upon it are slightly lifted when the rear end of the plate is depressed, substantially as set forth.

5. In a magazine fire-arm, the combination with the barrel, magazine and receiver thereof, of an operating-plate pivotally hung at its forward end and constructed thereat with a nose or lug forming a magazine cut-off, and with a lifting face, a carrier located within the receiver, and resting at its forward end when in its lowest position upon the said lifting face, a sliding breech-block, a finger or operating lever pivotally connected with the rear end of the operating plate, connected at its upper end with the breech-block which it actuates, and forming a guard for the trigger and means for locking the breech-block in its closed position, substantially as described.

6. In a magazine fire-arm, the combination with a sliding breech-block and an operating-plate pivotally hung at its forward end, of a carrier resting at its forward end, when in its lowest position, upon the said plate which lifts the said end of the carrier when the plate is operated in the opening movement of the gun, the said breech-block being constructed upon its lower face to engage the head of the cartridge when the carrier is lifted, as described, and the said carrier being constructed to permit the cartridge to drop away from the breech-block after the cartridge has been fully entered into the receiver of the arm, substantially as set forth.

7. In a magazine fire-arm, the combination with the barrel, magazine and receiver thereof, of a plate pivotally hung at its forward end, a downwardly movable finger or operating lever pivotally connected with the rear end of the plate and operating the same, and forming a guard for the trigger, an upwardly movable locking-block connected with the rear end of the said plate, a sliding breech-block connected with the upper end of the finger or operating lever, and actuated thereby, and a carrier located within the receiver and arranged to have an initial lifting move-

ment imparted to it by the plate, substantially as described.

3. In a magazine fire-arm, the combination with the barrel, magazine and receiver thereof, of a plate pivotally hung at its forward end, a finger or operating lever pivotally connected with the rear end of the plate, forming a guard for the trigger, a sliding breechblock connected with the upper end of the finger or operating lever and actuated thereby, a carrier located within the receiver, and a locking block connected with the rear end of the operating plate, arranged to play up and down in the receiver and provided with a striking piece which, in the closed position of the breech-block, is aligned with the firing-pin carried thereby, substantially as described.

In testimony whereof I have signed this specification in the presence of two subscribing witnesses.

JOHN M. BROWNING.

Witnesses:
  FRED C. EARLE,
  GEO. D. SEYMOUR.

Winchester Repeating Rifle, Model 1894.

Made For .25-35 And .30 Winchester, .32 W. S., .32-40 And .38-55 Cartridges.

Sporting Rifle, Model 1894, .32-40 And .38-55.

Twenty-six Inch Round Barrel, Full Magazine, Plain Trigger, Weight about 7¾ pounds, Magazine Capacity 8, ...$18.00
Twenty-six Inch Octagon Barrel, Full Magazine, Plain Trigger, Weight about 8 pounds, Magazine Capacity 8, ... 19.50

Sporting Rifle, Model 1894, .25-35, .30 Winchester Smokeless And .32 Winchester Special.

Twenty-six Inch Round Nickel Steel Barrel, Full Magazine, Plain Trigger, Weight about 8 pounds, Magazine Capacity 8, ...$23.00
Twenty-six Inch Octagon Nickel Steel Barrel, Full Magazine, Plain Trigger, Weight about 8 pounds, Magazine Capacity 8, ... 24.50

Fancy Sporting Rifle, Model 1894, .32-40 And .38-55.

Twenty-six Inch Octagon Barrel, Full Magazine, Plain Trigger, Fancy Walnut Pistol Grip Stock and Forearm Checked, Weight
about 8¼ pounds, Magazine Capacity 8, ...$37.50
Twenty-six Inch Round Barrel, same style of finish as above, Weight about 8 pounds, ... 36.00

Fancy Sporting Rifle, Model 1894, .25-35, .30 Winchester Smokeless And .32 Winchester Special.

Twenty-six Inch Octagon Barrel, same style of finish as above, Weight about 8¼ pounds, ...$42.50
Twenty-six Inch Round Barrel, same style of finish as above, Weight about 8¼ pounds, ... 41.00

When ordering, specify whether the gun should be sighted for Black or Smokeless powder cartridges.

42

Winchester Repeating Rifle, Model 1894.

Made For .25-35 And .30 Winchester, .32 W. S., .32-40 And .38-55 Cartridges.

Sporting Rifle, Model 1894 "Take Down," .32-40 And .38-55.

Twenty-six Inch Octagon Barrel, Half Magazine, Plain Trigger, Pistol Grip Stock and Forearm of Plain Walnut Checked, Weight
about 8 pounds, Magazine Capacity 4, ...$31.50
Twenty-six Inch Round Barrel, Half Magazine, Plain Trigger, Pistol Grip Stock and Forearm of Plain Walnut Checked, Weight about
8 pounds, Magazine Capacity 4, ... 30.00

Sporting Rifle, Model 1894 "Take Down," .25-35, .30 Winchester Smokeless, And .32 Winchester Special.

Twenty-six Inch Octagon Nickel Steel Barrel, Half Magazine, Plain Trigger, Pistol Grip Stock and Forearm of Plain Walnut Checked,
Weight about 8 pounds, Magazine Capacity 4, ...$34.50
Twenty-six Inch Round Nickel Steel Barrel, Half Magazine, Plain Trigger, Pistol Grip Stock and Forearm of Plain Walnut Checked,
Weight about 8 pounds, Magazine Capacity 4, ... 33.00

43

Carbine, Model 1894, .32-40 And .38-55.

Twenty Inch Round Barrel, Full Magazine, Plain Trigger, Weight about 6¼ pounds, Magazine Capacity 6, ...$17.50

Carbine, Model 1894, .25-35, .30 Winchester Smokeless, And .32 Winchester Special.

Twenty Inch Round Nickel Steel Barrel, Full Magazine, Plain Trigger, Weight about 6¼ pounds, Magazine Capacity 6, ... $21.00

When ordering, specify whether the gun should be sighted for Black or Smokeless powder cartridges.
All of the above can be furnished with Half Magazines or Shotgun Butt Stocks, with either metal or rubber butt plate, at same price.
For Extras, see page 96.

Available variations, options and calibers of the Model 1894, taken from the 1916 salesmen's catalog.

Winchester Repeating Rifle.

Component Parts, Model 1894.

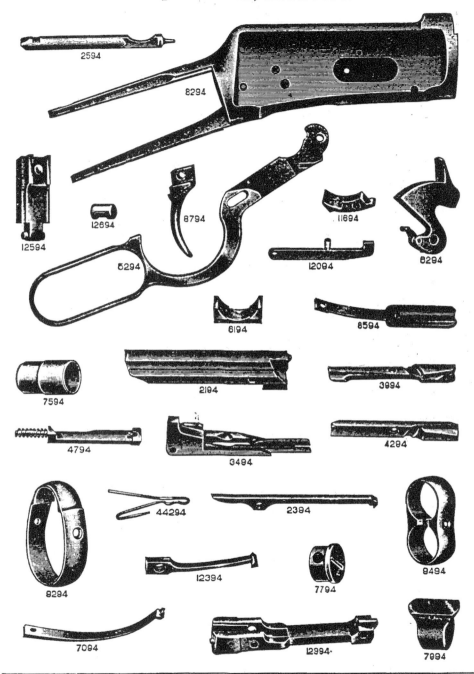

When ordering parts, *always give their name and number*, *also caliber* of rifle for which they are wanted. If possible, also give **number** of the rifle.

Parts breakdown and price list from a 1916 sales catalog.

Winchester Repeating Rifle.

Price List Of Component Parts, Model 1894.

194	Barrel, Round................	$6.50
294	Barrel, Round, Extra Light....	7.00
394	Barrel, Round, Nickel Steel....	10.00
494	Barrel, Round, Nickel Steel, Extra Light..............	12.00
594	Barrel, Octagon.............	8.00
694	Barrel, Octagon, Extra Light..	8.50
794	Barrel, Octagon, Nickel Steel..	11.50
894	Barrel, Octagon, Nickel Steel, Extra Light..............	13.50
994	Barrel, Half Octagon.........	8.50
1094	Barrel, Half Octagon, Extra Light.................	9.00
1194	Barrel, Half Octagon, Nickel Steel...............	12.00
1294	Barrel, Half Octagon, Nickel Steel, Extra Light........	14.00
1394	Barrel, Carbine.............	5.50
1494	Barrel, Carbine, Nickel Steel..	10.00
2294	Breech Bolt............	$1.75
2394	Extractor..............	.25
2494	Extractor Pin............	.05
2594	Firing Pin..............	.50
2694	Firing Pin Stop Pin.........	.05
2194	*Breech Bolt complete.........*	2.60
3094	Butt Stock..............	1.80
3194	Butt Plate..............	.80
3294	Butt Plate Screws (2), each	.05
2994	*Butt Stock complete..........*	2.70
3494	Carrier..............	.75
3894	Carrier Screws (2), each......	.05
12394	Carrier Spring.............	.25
12494	Carrier Spring Screw.........	.05
3994	Cartridge Guide, Right Hand .	.30
4294	Cartridge Guide, Left Hand...	.30
4694	Cartridge Guide Screws (2), each	.05
4894	Ejector.................	.30
5094	Ejector Spring............	.05
26794	Ejector Stop Pin........	.05
4794	*Ejector complete..............*	.40
5294	Finger Lever.............	1.65
5694	Finger Lever Pin...........	.05
5794	Finger Lever Pin Stop Screw..	.05
26894	Finger Lever Link Screw......	.05
5894	Forearm.................	.60
5994	Forearm Tip.............	.85
6094	Forearm Tip Screws (2), each	.05

6194	Forearm Tip Tenon..........	$0.15
9494	Front Band, Carbine.........	.40
9594	Front Band Screw, Carbine....	.05
6494	Hammer Stirrup........	$0.10
6594	Hammer Stirrup Pin.....	.05
6294	*Hammer complete...........*	.75
13094	Link....................	1.00
5394	Friction Stud...........	.10
5494	Friction Stud Spring.....	.05
5594	Friction Stud Stop Pin...	.05
12994	*Link complete...............*	1.20
21294	Link Pin................	.05
21394	Link Pin Stop Screw........	.05
12894	Locking Bolt...........	.50
12694	Firing Pin Striker.......	.05
12794	Firing Pin Striker Stop Pin	.05
12594	*Locking Bolt complete........*	.60
7094	Main Spring............	.30
7194	Main Spring Screw.......	.05
7294	Main Spring Strain Screw....	.05
7494	Magazine Tube.........	1.80
7594	Magazine Follower......	.05
7694	Magazine Spring.......	.10
7794	Magazine Plug........	.10
7894	Magazine Plug Screw....	.05
7994	Magazine Ring.........	.30
8094	Magazine Ring Pin......	.05
7394	*Magazine complete...........*	2.45
51194	Peep Sight Plug Screw........	.05
8294	Receiver with Lower Tang	7.95
8394	Lower Tang............	1.45
8494	Hammer Screw.........	.05
8194	*Receiver complete.............*	8.00
9294	Rear Band, Carbine..........	.35
9394	Rear Band Screw, Carbine....	.05
8594	Spring Cover..............	.35
8694	Spring Cover Screw..........	.05
11694	Sear....................	.20
11794	Sear Pin................	.05
44294	Sear and Safety Catch Spring	.10
44694	Sear and Safety Catch Spring Screw..................	.05
12094	Safety Catch.............	.15
12294	Safety Catch Pin............	.05
8794	Trigger.................	.20
9194	Upper Tang Screw...........	.05

Price List of Component Parts, Model 1894, "Take Down."

39494	Extension Adjusting Screw....	$0.05
39594	Magazine Tube..............	1.80
39694	Magazine Lever.............	.60
39794	Magazine Lever Screw........	.05
39894	Magazine Lever Plunger......	.05

39994	Magazine Lever Plunger Spring	$0.05
40094	Magazine Plug.............	.30
40194	Magazine Plug Screw........	.05
40294	Magazine Follower Stop Ring .	.05

When ordering parts, **always give their name and number, also caliber** of rifle for which they are wanted. If possible, also give **number** of the rifle.

Parts breakdown and price list from a 1916 sales catalog.

MODELS 94 AND 55 LEVER ACTION REPEATING RIFLES

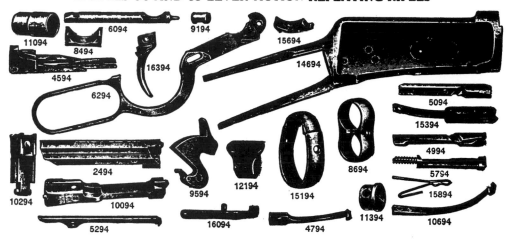

It is absolutely necessary that the numbers shown at the left of each item be specified when ordering.

In ordering Barrels give length, caliber, round or octagon, solid frame, or take down, rifle or carbine.

194	Barrel, round, full magazine, Solid-frame........	$ 9.00
294	*Barrel, round, full magazine, Take-down..........	9.00
394	Barrel, round, ¾ magazine, Solid-frame..........	9.00
494	*Barrel, round, ¾ magazine, Take-down..........	9.00
594	Barrel, round, ⅔ magazine, Solid-frame..........	9.00
694	*Barrel, round, ⅔ magazine, Take-down..........	9.00
794	Barrel, round, ½ magazine, Solid-frame..........	9.00
894	*Barrel, round, ½ magazine, Take-down..........	9.00
994	Barrel, octagon, full magazine, Solid-frame......	12.00
1094	*Barrel, octagon, full magazine, Take-down......	12.00
1194	Barrel, octagon, ¾ magazine, Solid-frame......	12.00
1294	*Barrel, octagon, ¾ magazine, Take-down......	12.00
1394	Barrel, octagon, ⅔ magazine, Solid-frame......	12.00
1494	*Barrel, octagon, ⅔ magazine, Take-down......	12.00
1594	Barrel, octagon, ½ magazine, Solid-frame......	12.00
1694	*Barrel, octagon, ½ magazine, Take-down......	12.00
1794	Barrel, carbine, full magazine..................	9.00
1894	Barrel, carbine, ¾ magazine....................	9.00
1994	Barrel, carbine, ⅔ magazine....................	9.00
2094	Barrel, carbine, ½ magazine....................	9.00
2094A	*Interchangeable Round Barrels Complete Take Down	20.00
2094B	*Interchangeable Octagon Barrels Complete Take Down	23.00
2155	*Barrel, 30 W.C.F., light weight, round, ½ magazine, Take-down model 55	12.00
2255	*Barrel, 25/35, light weight, round, ½ magazine, Take-down model 55	12.00
2355	*Barrel, 32 W.S., light weight, round, ½ magazine, Take-down model 55	12.00
2355½	*Interchangeable Barrels Light Weight ½ Mag Take Down Model 55 Round Barrel	20.00
2494	Breech bolt with extractor and pin..............	3.30
2594	Breech bolt complete, comprising bolt with extractor and pin, firing pin, firing pin stop pin, ejector, ejector spring, and ejector stop pin	4.60
2694	Butt stock, rifle	4.00
2794	Butt stock complete, rifle	5.25
2894	Butt stock, carbine	3.50
2994	Butt stock complete, carbine	4.55
3094	Butt stock, shot butt, for metal butt plate....	4.00
3194	Butt stock complete, shot butt, metal butt plate	5.05
3294	Butt stock, shot butt for rubber butt plate......	4.00
3394	Butt stock complete, shot butt, rubber butt plate	4.80
	Stock complete comprises: stock with butt plate and (2) butt plate screws.	
3494	Butt stock, rifle, pistol grip..................	8.00
3594	Butt stock, complete, rifle, pistol grip..........	9.25
3694	Butt stock, shot butt, for metal butt plate, pistol grip	8.00
3794	Butt stock complete, shot butt, metal butt plate, pistol grip	9.05
3894	Butt stock, shot butt, for rubber butt plate, pistol grip	8.00
3994	Butt stock complete, shot butt, rubber butt plate, pistol grip	8.80
	Stock complete comprises: stock with butt plate and (2) butt plate screws, and pistol grip cap and screw.	

4094	Butt plate, rifle	$ 1.05
4194	Butt plate, carbine	.85
4294	Butt plate, shot butt, metal (give length)......	.85
4394	Butt plate, shot butt, rubber (give length)....	.60
4494	Butt plate screws (2) each	.10
4594	Carrier	1.40
4694	Carrier screw (2) each	.10
4794	Carrier spring	.35
4894	Carrier spring screw	.10
4994	Cartridge guide, right hand	.55
5094	Cartridge guide, left hand	.50
5194	Cartridge guide screws (2) each)	.10
5294	Extractor	.40
5394	Extractor pin	.10
5494	*Extension, Take-down	2.25
5594	Extension adjusting screw, Take-down (3) each	.10
5694	Ejector	.65
5794	Ejector complete comprising ejector with spring and pin	.85
5894	Ejector spring	.10
5994	Ejector stop pin	.10
6094	Firing pin	.35
6194	Firing pin stop pin	.10
6294	Finger lever	2.00
6394	Finger lever, pistol grip	2.25
6494	Finger lever pin	.10
6594	Finger lever pin stop screw	.10
6694	Finger lever link screw	.10

In ordering Forearms give length.

6794	Forearm, octagon, Solid-frame	1.40
6894	Forearm, octagon, Take-down	1.40
6994	Forearm, round, Solid-frame	1.40
7094	Forearm, round, Take-down	1.40
7194	Forearm, carbine, full magazine.............	1.40
7294	Forearm, carbine, ½ magazine	1.40
7355	Forearm, light weight, ½ magazine, Take-down, model 55	1.40
7494	Forearm tip, octagon, full magazine, Take-down	1.45
7594	Forearm tip, octagon, full magazine, Solid-frame	1.45
7694	Forearm tip, round, full magazine, Solid-frame	1.45
7794	Forearm tip, round, full magazine, Take down	1.45
7894	Forearm tip, octagon, ½ magazine, Take-down	1.45
7994	Forearm tip, octagon, ½ magazine, Solid-frame	1.45
8094	Forearm tip, round ½ magazine, Solid-frame	1.45
8194	Forearm tip, round, ½ magazine, Take-down	1.45
8255	Forearm tip, light weight, ½ magazine, model 55, Take-down	1.45
8394	Forearm tip screws (2) each	.10
8494	Forearm tip tenon	.40
8555	Forearm tip tenon model 55	.40
8694	Front band, carbine	.65
8794	Front band screw, carbine	.10
8894	Friction stud	.15
8994	Friction stud spring	.10
9094	Friction stud stop pin	.10

In replacing parts marked (*) when desired for Take-Down guns it is necessary to send gun to the Factory.
(Continued on Next Page)

Parts breakdown and price list from a 1931 sales catalog.

(Continued From Preceding Page)

No.	Part	Price
9194	Firing pin striker	$ .15
9294	Firing pin striker stop pin	.10
9394	Hammer stirrup	.25
9494	Hammer stirrup pin	.10
9594	Hammer complete with stirrup and pin	1.25
9694	Hammer screw	.10
9794	Link	1.75
9894	Link pin	.10
9994	Link stop screw	.10
10094	Link complete, comprising link with friction stud, stud spring, and stud stop pin	2.10
10194	Locking bolt	.95
10294	Locking bolt complete, comprising locking bolt with striker and striker stop pin	1.20
10394	Lower tang	1.55
10494	Lower tang, pistol grip	1.85
10594	Lower tang complete, comprising tang with hammer complete, mainspring, mainspring screw, mainspring strain screw, trigger, sear, sear pin, sear and safety catch spring, sear and safety catch spring screw, safety catch, safety catch pin and hammer screw	5.15
10694	Mainspring	.50
10794	Mainspring, pistol grip	.60
10894	Mainspring screw	.10
10994	Mainspring strain screw	.10
11094	Magazine follower	.10
11194	Magazine follower stop ring, Take-down	.10
11294	Magazine spring, (give length of magazine tube)	.15
11394	Magazine plug, full magazine (No. 4) rifle and carbine, Solid-frame	.25
11494	Magazine plug, ½ magazine (No. 5) rifle and carbine, Solid-frame	.25
11594	Magazine plug, ½ magazine (No. 6) carbine	.25
11694	Magazine plug, full magazine (No. 11) rifle, Take-down	.40
11794	Magazine plug, ½ magazine (No. 12) rifle, Take-down	.40
11855	Magazine plug, ½ magazine (No. 12) rifle, model 55 Take-down	.40
11994	Magazine plug screw (B) Solid-frame	.10
12094	Magazine plug screw (C) Take-down	.10
12194	Magazine ring, Solid-frame	.65
12294	Magazine ring, Take-down	.65
12394	Magazine ring pin, Solid-frame	.10
12494	Magazine tube, full magazine, rifle, Solid-frame	1.10
12594	Magazine tube, full magazine, rifle, Take-down	1.65
12694	Magazine tube, ¾ magazine, rifle, Solid-frame	1.10
12794	Magazine tube, ¾ magazine, rifle, Take-down	1.65
12894	Magazine tube, ⅔ magazine, rifle, Solid-frame	1.10
12994	Magazine tube, ⅔ magazine, rifle, Take-down	1.65
13094	Magazine tube, ½ magazine, rifle, Solid-frame	1.10
13194	Magazine tube, ½ magazine, rifle, Take-down	1.65
13255	Magazine tube, ½ magazine, rifle, model 55 Take-down	1.65
13394	Magazine tube, full magazine, carbine	1.10
13494	Magazine tube, ¾ magazine, carbine	1.10
13594	Magazine tube, ⅔ magazine, carbine	1.10
13694	Magazine tube, ½ magazine, carbine	1.10
13794	Magazine tube complete, rifle, Solid-frame, comprising magazine tube with mag. follower, mag. spring, mag. plug, mag. plug screw, mag. ring, and mag. ring pin	2.45
13894	Magazine tube complete, carbine, comprising magazine tube with mag. follower, mag. plug, mag. plug screw, and spring	1.70
13994	Magazine tube complete, rifle, Take-down	4.05
14055	Magazine tube complete, rifle, model 55, ½ magazine, Take-down	4.05
	Magazine tube complete, comprises, magazine tube with mag. follower, mag. spring, mag. plug, mag. plug screw, mag. lever, mag. lever screw, mag. lever plunger, mag. and lever plunger spring.	
14194	Magazine lever, Take-down	$ .70
14294	Magazine lever screw, Take-down	.10
14394	Magazine lever plunger, Take-down	.10
14494	Magazine lever plunger spring, Take-down	.10
14594	Peep sight plug screw	.10
14694	Receiver, rifle, with lower tang and hammer screw, Solid-frame	10.15
14794	*Receiver, rifle, with lower tang and hammer screw, Take-down	10.15
14894	Receiver, carbine, with lower tang and hammer screw and carbine sling ring	10.15
14994	Receiver, rifle, complete with action, Solid-frame	28.15
15094	*Receiver, rifle, complete with action, Take-down	28.15
	Receiver, rifle, complete with action, comprises: Receiver with lower tang complete, breech bolt complete, right and left hand cartridge guides, cartridge guide screws (2), spring cover and screw, link complete, finger lever, link pin, link pin stop screw, carrier spring and screw, locking bolt complete, finger lever pin stop screw, carrier, carrier screw (2), and peep sight plug screw.	
15194	Rear band, carbine	.65
15294	Rear band screw	.10
15394	Spring cover	.70
15494	Spring cover screw	.10
15594	Sling ring hole plug screw	.10
15694	Sear	.40
15794	Sear pin	.10
15894	Sear and safety catch spring	.15
15994	Sear and safety catch spring screw	.10
16094	Safety catch	.25
16194	Safety catch, pistol grip	.25
16294	Safety catch pin	.10
16394	Trigger	.45
16494	Upper tang screw	.10
16594	Upper tang screw, pistol grip	.10
16694	Upper tang screw, peep sight	.10
16794	Upper tang screw, peep sight, pistol grip	.10

MODELS 94 AND 55

No.	Part	Price
	Parts necessary to change from plain to double set trigger	8.00
16894	Front trigger	.80
16994	Front trigger pin	.10
17094	Front trigger spring	.10
17194	Hammer complete, comprising hammer with fly, fly pin, stirrup and pin	1.95
17294	Hammer screw	.10
17394	Hammer fly	.30
17494	Hammer fly pin	.10
17594	Hammer stirrup	.35
17694	Hammer stirrup pin	.10
17794	Lower tang	1.75
17894	Lower tang, pistol grip	2.00
17994	Mainspring	.60
18094	Mainspring, pistol grip	.50
18194	Mainspring screw	.10
18294	Mainspring strain screw	.10
18394	Rear trigger	1.10
18494	Rear trigger pin	.10
18594	Rear trigger spring	.10
18694	Rear trigger stop pin	.10
18794	Sear	.60
18894	Sear spring	.10
18994	Sear spring screw	.10
19094	Trigger guide pin	.10
19194	Trigger adjusting screw	.10

In replacing parts marked thus (*) when desired for Take-down Guns it is necessary to send gun to the Factory.

INSTRUCTIONS

When ordering parts always give their name and number and caliber of rifle for which they are wanted. State also whether solid-frame or take-down. Also give, if possible, number of rifle and state whether barrel is round, octagon or carbine.

Shipping—When shipping to us for repair work box the arm lightly but securely, mark plainly "Repair Division, Winchester Repeating Arms Co., New Haven, Conn.," put your own name and address in one corner, prepay transportation charges and write us when shipment is made. If you fail to case gun properly the express company will charge you double first class rates.

In fitting new interchangeable barrels to any of our take-down rifles or shotguns it is necessary for us to have the entire gun, together with the extra barrel, if there is one, at the factory.

On guns sent to the factory for repairs, it is found necessary due to increased costs, to levy a service charge of $3.50 on models 94 and 55 rifles. This "service" covers receiving, inspecting, recording, testing, including shooting, cleaning, greasing, packing and shipping.

IMPORTANT

Prices quoted do not include carrying charges. A small amount to cover postage should be added.

Our minimum charge on any shipment will be 25c.

Shipments to those who do not have an account with us will be sent C. O. D. unless funds to cover accompany order.

Parts breakdown and price list from a 1931 sales catalog.

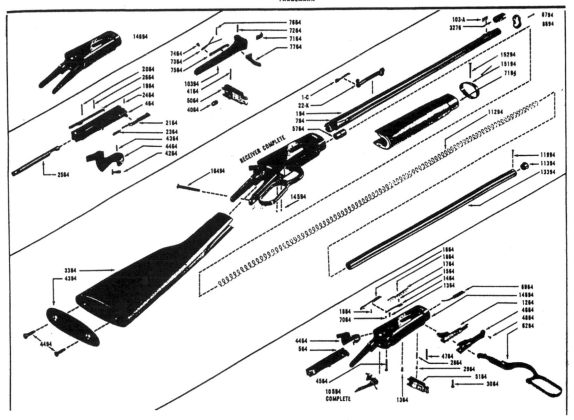

MODEL 94 Lever Action Carbine

It is absolutely necessary that the numbers shown at the left of each gun part be specified when ordering.

In ordering any Pistol Grip part be sure to specify if serial number is higher than 1084891.

194	†Barrel, Carbine, full magazine, .30-30 with ramp, Solid-frame, 20".....................$21.75	
794	†Barrel, Carbine, full magazine, .32 cal., 20" with ramp	21.75
464	†Breech bolt with extractor pin	9.40
564	†Breech bolt complete, comprising: bolt with extractor and pin, firing pin, firing pin stop pin, ejector, ejector spring and ejector stop pin	13.10
3394	Butt stock complete	11.95
	Stock complete comprises: stock with butt plate and (2) butt plate screws.	
4394	Butt plate	1.50
4494	Butt plate screws (2) each	.25
1264	Carrier	3.85
1364	Carrier screw (2) each	.25
1464	Carrier spring	.90
1564	Carrier spring screw	.25
1664	Cartridge guide, right hand	1.95
1764	Cartridge guide, left hand	1.75
1864	Cartridge guide screws (2) each	.25
1964	Extractor	1.35
2064	Extractor pin	.25
2164	Ejector	2.05
2264	Ejector complete comprising: ejector with spring and pin	2.50
2364	Ejector spring	.25
2464	Ejector stop pin	.25
2564	Firing pin	1.50
4064	Firing pin striker	.70
4164	Firing pin striker stop pin	.25
2664	Firing pin stop pin	.25

6294	Finger lever	7.15
2864	Finger lever pin	.25
2964	Finger lever pin stop screw	.25
3064	Finger lever link screw	.25
7194	Forearm, carbine, full magazine	4.15
8694	Front band, carbine	1.60
8794	Front band screw, carbine	.25
3764	Friction stud	.70
3864	Friction stud spring	.25
3964	Friction stud stop pin	.25
4264	Hammer stirrup	.90
4364	Hammer stirrup pin	.25
4464	Hammer complete with stirrup and pin	3.95
4564	Hammer screw	.25
4664	Link	5.15
4764	Link pin	.25
4864	Link pin stop screw	.25
4964	Link complete, comprising: link with friction stud, stud spring, and stud stop pin	5.60
5064	†Locking bolt	3.05
5164	†Locking bolt complete, comprising: locking bolt with firing pin striker and striker stop pin	3.65
10394	Lower tang	5.40
10594	Lower tang complete, comprising: tang with hammer complete, mainspring, mainspring screw, mainspring strain screw, trigger, sear, sear pin, sear and safety catch spring, sear and safety catch spring screw, safety catch, safety catch pin and hammer screw	17.55
10694	Mainspring	1.80

5564	Mainspring screw	.25
5664	Mainspring strain screw	.25
5764	Magazine follower	.25
11294	Magazine spring	.45
11394	Magazine plug	.95
11994	Magazine plug screw (B) Solid-frame	.25
13394	Magazine tube	3.20
13894	Magazine tube complete, comprising: magazine tube with mag. follower, mag. plug, mag. plug screw and spring	4.95
14594	Peep sight plug screw	.25
14694	**Receiver, with lower tang and hammer screw, Solid-frame	26.70
15194	Rear band, carbine	1.85
15294	Rear band screw	.25
6964	Spring cover	2.20
7064	Spring cover screw	.25
7164	Sear	1.35
7264	Sear pin	.25
7364	Sear and safety catch spring	.70
7464	Sear and safety catch spring screw ..	.25
7564	Safety catch	1.10
7664	Safety catch pin	.25
7764	Trigger	1.95
16494	Upper tang screw	.25

SIGHT AND SIGHT COVERS

A-3276	Front Sight Cover for Model 94 Carbine with Ramp	.75
103A	Front Sight .260 high carbine, 1st Style	1.65
103B	Front Sight, 2nd Style	1.65
22K	Rear Sight with 3-C elevator, carbine	2.20

Refinishing	Complete	Metal Only	Wood Only
Standard Rifle	$29.30	$17.55	$11.75

Service Charge $6.85 Net

The service charge is made to defray the expense of unpacking, incoming and final inspection, proof testing, function firing and repacking for shipment.

**Sold for factory installation only — return complete firearm.

*Sold only to gunsmiths who have executed an agreement with us — otherwise for factory installation only.

†Not sold to consumers. Installation must be made by a gunsmith. Orders from dealers and distributors will be accepted on the understanding that the parts will be fitted by a gunsmith.

A Pre-64 illustrated parts breakdown from the 1960 sales catalog.

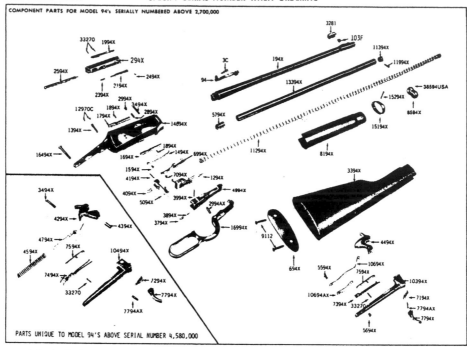

It is absolutely necessary that the numbers shown at the left of each gun part be specified when ordering.
The unique parts for the New Model 94 — 44 Magnum Lever Action Carbine and the Model 64A — Lever Action Rifle are in separate lists following this main listing.

†194X	Barrel, Carbine, Full Magazine, 30-30, Solid-Frame, 20"
†794X	Barrel, Carbine, Full Magazine, 32 Cal, Solid-Frame, 20"
†10194X	Barrel, Carbine, 30-30 Cal. 16" — "Trapper"
†10994X	Barrel, Carbine, 32 Win. Spec. 16" "Wrangler"
†294X	Breech Bolt with Extractor and Pins
†894X	Breech Bolt Complete, comprising: Bolt with Extractor and Pins, Firing Pin, Ejector, Ejector Spring and Ejector Stop Pin
3394X	Butt Stock Complete

1294X	Carrier
1394X	Carrier Screw
1494X	Carrier Spring
1594X	Carrier Spring Screw
1694X	Cartridge Guide, Right Hand
1794X	Cartridge Guide, Left Hand
1894X	Cartridge Guide Screws (2 Required)
1994X	Extractor
33270	Extractor Pins (2 Required)
2194X	Ejector

4094X	Firing Pin Striker
4194X	Firing Pin Striker Stop Pin
8194X	Forearm, Carbine, Full Magazine
8594X	Front Band — Requires #38594USA
8994X	Front Band — "Trapper" — Requires #38594USA

A Post-64 illustrated parts breakdown including the parts for the post serial 4,850,000 coil type mainspring change from a factory component parts catalog.

WINCHESTER®

NEW MODEL 94XTR TOP EJECT — .375 WINCHESTER "BIG BORE" — LEVER ACTION CARBINE

COMPONENT PARTS   **SPECIFY SERIAL NUMBER WHEN ORDERING**

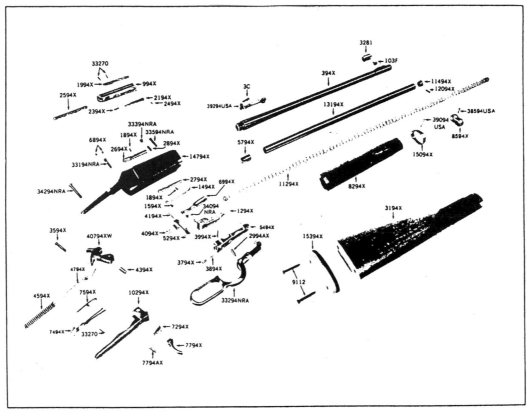

It is absolutely necessary that the numbers shown at the left of each gun part be specified when ordering.

†394X	Barrel, Carbine, (.375 Win.) 20" Round	2194X	Ejector
†994X	Breech Bolt with Extractor and Pins	2294X	Ejector Complete, comprising: Ejector with Spring and Pin
†1094X	Breech Bolt Complete, comprising Bolt with Extractor and Pins, Firing Pin, Ejector, Ejector Spring and Ejector Stop Pin	2394X	Ejector Spring
		2494X	Ejector Stop Pin
		1994X	Extractor
		33270	Extractor Pins (2 Required)
		33294NRA	Finger Lever
		2994AX	Finger Lever Link Pin
*15394X	Butt Pad	33594NRA	Finger Lever/Link Screw
9112	Butt Pad Screws (2 Required)	2894X	Finger Lever Pin
3194X	Butt Stock Complete, comprising: Butt Pad and (2) Butt Pad Screws	33394NRA	Finger Lever Pin Stop Screw
		2594X	Firing Pin
		4094X	Firing Pin Striker
1294X	Carrier	4194X	Firing Pin Striker Stop Pin
33194NRA	Carrier Screw	8294X	Forearm
1494X	Carrier Spring	3794X	Friction Stud (Hollow Type)
1594X	Carrier Spring Screw	6194X	Friction Stud (Shank Type)
2694X	Cartridge Guide, L.H.	3894X	Friction Stud Spring (Hollow Type)
2794X	Cartridge Guide, R.H.		
1894X	Cartridge Guide Screws (2 Required)	6094X	Friction Stud Spring (Shank Type)

3994X	Friction Stud Stop Pin (Hollow Type)
6394X	Friction Stud Spring Pin (Shank Type)
8594X	Front Band (Requires #38594USA)
18794X	Front Band Screw (Tapered)
38594USA	Front Band Screw (Non Tapered)
40794XW	Hammer
4394X	Hammer Bushing
3594X	Hammer Screw
4594X	Hammer Spring
4794X	Hammer Spring Guide Rod
5494X	Link Complete, comprising: Link w/Friction Stud, Stud Spring and Stud Stop Pin
†5294X	Locking Bolt
†5394X	Locking Bolt Complete, comprising: Locking Bolt with Firing Pin Striker and Pin
10294X	Lower Tang
10894X	Lower Tang Complete, comprising: Lower Tang with Hammer, Hammer Bushing, Ham-

mer Spring, Hammer Spring Guide Rod, Sear, Trigger, Trigger Pin, Trigger Stop, Trigger Stop Pin and Trigger Stop Spring

5794X	Magazine Follower
11494X	Magazine Plug
12094X	Magazine Plug Screw
11294X	Magazine Spring
13194X	Magazine Tube
13294X	Magazine Tube Complete, comprising: Magazine Tube with

Magazine Follower, Magazine Plug, Magazine Plug Screw and Magazine Spring

15094X	Rear Band
39094USA	Rear Band Screw
**14794X	Receiver
7294X	Sear
6894X	Sight Plug Screw (2 Required)
6994X	Spring Cover
34094NRA	Spring Cover Screw
7794X	Trigger
7794AX	Trigger Pin

7594X	Trigger Stop
33270	Trigger Stop Pin
7494X	Trigger Stop Spring
34294NRA	Upper Tang Screw

SIGHTS AND SIGHT COVERS

103F	Front Sight, .360 High
3281	Front Sight Cover
39294USA	Rear Sight Assembly
94A	Rear Sight Binding Screw (2 Required)
94B	Rear Sight Blade
3C	Rear Sight Elevator

Refinishing   **Price on Application**

An illustrated parts breakdown for the top eject Big Bore model from a factory component parts catalog.

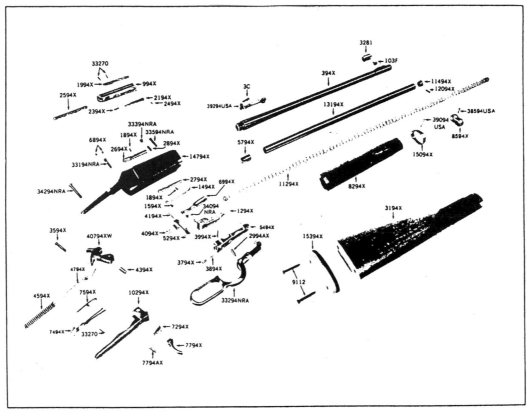

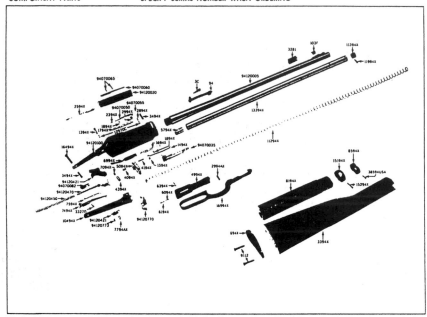

It is absolutely necessary that the numbers shown at the left of each gun part be specified when ordering. The unique parts for the New Model 94 "XTR" Angle Eject (30-30 Win.), (7-30 Waters), (307 Win.), (356 Win.) and (3375 Win.) Firearms are in separate list following this main listing.

†94120005	Barrel, Carbine (30-30 Win.) 20" — "Standard"	94070230	Butt Stock Complete — "Big Bore", comprising: Stock with Butt Pad and (2) Butt Pad Screws	94070050	Ejector
†94160005	Barrel, Carbine (30-30 Win.) 16" — "Trapper"	■ 15394X	Butt Pad — "Big Bore"	94070051	Ejector Complete, comprising: Ejector with Spring and Ejector Stop Pin
†94300005	Barrel, Carbine (30-30 Win.) 20" — "Ranger"	■ 694X	Butt Plate — "Standard", "Trapper" & "Wrangler II"	2394X	Ejector Spring
†94380005	Barrel, Carbine (38-55 Win.) 16" — "Wrangler II"	9112	Butt Plate/Pad Screws (2 Required)	94070055	Ejector Stop Pin
†94070205	Barrel, Carbine (307 Win.) 20" — "Big Bore"	94070035	Carrier	94070060	Extractor
†94070210	Barrel, Carbine (356 Win.) 20" — "Big Bore"	1394X	Carrier Screw	94070065	Extractor Retaining Screw (2 Required)
†94070215	Barrel, Carbine (375 Win.) 20" — "Big Bore"	1494X	Carrier Spring	1894X	Finger Lever
94120020	Breech Bolt	1594X	Carrier Spring Screw	11094X	Finger Lever (Large Bow) "Wrangler II"
†94120025	Breech Bolt Complete, comprising: Bolt with Extractor and Screws, Firing Pin, Ejector, Ejector Spring and Ejector Stop Pin	1794X	Cartridge Guide, L.H. — "Standard", "Ranger" and "Trapper"	2994AXX	Finger Lever Link Pin
		2694X	Cartridge Guide, L.H. — "Big Bore" (375 Win.) and "Wrangler II"	3494X	Finger Lever Link Screw
94300030	Butt Stock Complete — "Ranger", comprising: Stock with Butt Plate and (2) Butt Plate Screws	94070040	Cartridge Guide, L.H. — "Big Bore" (307 Win.) and (356 Win.)	2894X	Finger Lever Pin
		1894X	Cartridge Guide, R.H. — "Standard", "Ranger" and "Trapper"	2994X	Finger Lever Pin Stop Screw
3394X	Butt Stock Complete — "Standard", "Trapper" and "Wrangler II"	2794X	Cartridge Guide, R.H. — "Big Bore" (375 Win.) and "Wrangler II"	2594X	Firing Pin
		94070045	Cartridge Guide, R.H. — "Big Bore" (307 Win.) and (356 Win.)	4094X	Firing Pin Striker
		1894X	Cartridge Guide Screw (2 Required)	4194X	Firing Pin Striker Stop Pin
				94300030	Forearm — "Ranger"
				8194X	Forearm — "Standard", "Trapper", "Wrangler II"
6094X	Friction Stud Spring		Stop Pin, Trigger Stop Spring and Trigger Spring	94070270	Forearm — "Big Bore"
6394X	Friction Stud Stop Pin	5794X	Magazine Follower	6194X	Friction Stud
8594X	Front Band — "Standard" & "Ranger"	11394X	Magazine Plug — Standard "Ranger", "Trapper" and "Wrangler II"		& 356 Win.)
8994X	Front Band — "Trapper" & "Wrangler II"			**94070301	Receiver — "Big Bore" (375 Win.)
94070275	Front Band — "Big Bore"	94070291	Magazine Plug — "Big Bore"	13968	Saddle Ring Assembly — "Trapper" & "Wrangler II"
38594USA	Front Band Screw	11994X	Magazine Plug Screw — "Standard", "Ranger", "Trapper" and "Wrangler II"	17594X	Saddle Ring Plug Screw — "Trapper" & "Wrangler II"
**94120421	Hammer and Sear	94070292	Magazine Plug Screw — "Big Bore"	**94120421	Sear and Hammer
4394X	Hammer Bushing	11294X	Magazine Spring — "Big Bore", "Standard" and "Ranger"	94	Sight Assembly, Rear — "Standard", "Trapper" and "Wrangler II"
3494X	Hammer Screw — "Standard", "Ranger", "Trapper" and "Wrangler II"	47694LAW	Magazine Spring — "Trapper" & "Wrangler II"	4002	Sight Assembly, Rear, Lyman 16A — "Big Bore"
94070284	Hammer Screw — "Big Bore"	13394X	Magazine Tube — "Standard"	32G	Sight, Rear — "Ranger"
94120450	Hammer Spring	94300200	Magazine Tube — "Ranger"	94A	Sight Binding Screw, Rear (2 Required)
94120470	Hammer Spring Guide Rod	14194X	Magazine Tube — "Trapper" & "Wrangler II"	94B	Sight Blade, Rear
94070082	Hammer Spur Assembly	94070293	Magazine Tube — "Big Bore"	3281	Sight Cover, Front
4994X	Link Complete — "Standard", "Big Bore" (375 Win.), "Ranger", "Trapper" and "Wrangler II" comprising: Link with Friction Stud, Friction Stud Spring and Friction Stud Stop Pin	13894X	Magazine Tube Complete — Standard, Comprising Magazine Tube with Magazine Follower, Magazine Plug, Magazine Plug Screw and Magazine Spring	3C	Sight Elevator, Rear — "Standard", "Trapper" and "Wrangler II"
				5C	Sight Elevator, Rear — "Ranger"
				103E	Sight, Front — (.310 High) "Big Bore"
94070285	Link Complete — "Big Bore" (307 Win. & 356 Win.)	94300201	Magazine Tube Complete — "Ranger"	103F	Sight, Front — (.360 High) "Standard"
†5094X	Locking Bolt — "Standard", "Ranger", "Trapper" and "Wrangler II"	14294X	Magazine Tube Complete — "Trapper" and "Wrangler II"	94300140	Sight, Front — (.575 High) "Ranger"
†94070090	Locking Bolt — "Big Bore"	94070294	Magazine Tube Complete — "Big Bore"	48294LAW	Sight, Front — "Trapper" & "Wrangler II"
†5194X	Locking Bolt Complete — "Standard", "Ranger", "Trapper" and "Wrangler II", comprising: Locking Bolt with Firing Pin Striker and Firing Pin Striker Pin	Fig. 14	Quick Detachable Swivel (2 Required) "Big Bore"	12970C	Sight Plug Screw, Telescope (4 Required)
		15194X	Rear Band — "Standard", "Ranger", "Trapper" and "Wrangler II"	8994X	Spring Cover
†94070091	Locking Bolt Complete — "Big Bore"	94070295	Rear Band — "Big Bore"	7094X	Spring Cover Screw
1049X	Lower Tang	15294X	Rear Band Screw	27717	Stock Swivel Stud — "Big Bore"
**94121040	Lower Tang Complete, comprising: Lower Tang with Hammer, Hammer Bushing, Hammer Spring, Hammer Spring Guide Rod, Sear, Trigger w/Hammer Block Asm., Trigger Pin, Trigger Stop, Trigger	**94120100	Receiver — "Standard" and "Ranger"	94070140	Swivel Clamp Assembly, Front — "Big Bore"
		**94160100	Receiver — "Trapper"	94120770	Trigger with Hammer Block Assembly
		**94380100	Receiver — "Wrangler II"	7794AX	Trigger/Sear Pin
		**94070300	Receiver — "Big Bore" (307 Win.	94120773	Trigger Spring
				7594X	Trigger Stop
				33270	Trigger Stop Pin
				7494X	Trigger Stop Spring
				16494X	Upper Tang Screw

An illustrated parts breakdown for the angle eject model including the Big Bore model from a factory component parts catalog.

TURPENTINE-OIL
FLOOR WAX
172 LBS.
FIRST OF THE SEASON. NOV. 16-1933
SHOT BY O.S. WALLACE.
WRIGHT PHOTO
SAN BENITO-TEXAS

This is the original owner–scoundrel of the beautiful outfit pictured and described on page 59. The rifle and scabbard are clearly seen. Apparently he was a rather popular character. Here's to Mr. O. S. Wallace, a true "Winchester Model 94 Man"!

BIBLIOGRAPHY/RESOURCES

Gogan, Art and Hill, Rick. "Hybrid Winchesters."
The Winchester Collector, Vol. 12. Spring 1989.

Madis, George. The Winchester Book.
Brownsboro: Art & Reference House, 1979.

Pirkle, Arthur. Winchester Lever Action Repeating Firearms, Vol. 3.
Tustin, California: North Cape Publications, 1998.

West, Bill. Winchester for Over a Century, Vols. II through V.
Glendora, California: West Arms Library, 1965-75.

West, Bill. Winchester Handbook, Vols. I and II.
Glendora, California: West Arms Library, 1981.

Wilson, R. L. Winchester Engraving, 1st Edition.
North Hollywood, California: Beinfeld Publishing, 1975.

The Buffalo Bill Historical Center: David Kennedy (Curator),
Bert Hartman (Volunteer), Connie Miller and Jessica Bennett of the
Records and Research Department, B.B.H.C., Cody, Wyoming